Globalex Workshop on Linked Lexicography 2020

Marseille, France
11 – 16 May 2020

Editors:

Ilan Kernerman   Jorge Gracia
Simon Krek   Sina Ahmadi
John P. McCrae   Besim Kabashi

ISBN: 978-1-7138-1261-6

LREC 2020 Workshop
Language Resources and Evaluation Conference
11–16 May 2020

Globalex Workshop on Linked Lexicography

PROCEEDINGS

Editors:

Ilan Kernerman, Simon Krek, John P. McCrae,

Jorge Gracia, Sina Ahmadi and Besim Kabashi

Proceedings of the LREC 2020
Globalex Workshop on Linked Lexicography

Edited by: Ilan Kernerman, Simon Krek, John P. McCrae, Jorge Gracia, Sina Ahmadi and Besim Kabashi

For more information:
European Language Resources Association (ELRA)
9 rue des Cordelières
75013, Paris
France
http://www.elra.info
Email: lrec@elda.org

Introduction to the Proceedings of Globalex 2020 Workshop on Linked Lexicography

Ilan Kernerman[1], Simon Krek[2], John P. McCrae[3],
Jorge Gracia[4], Sina Ahmadi[3] and Besim Kabashi[5]

[1] K Dictionaries, Israel
[2] Jožef Stefan Institute, Slovenia
[3] SFI Insight Research Centre for Data Analytics, Data Science Institute, National University of Ireland Galway, Ireland
[4] Aragon Institute of Engineering Research (I3A), University of Zaragoza, Spain
[5] Friedrich-Alexander University of Erlangen-Nuremberg and Ludwig-Maximilian University of Munich, Germany

ilan@kdictionaries.com, simon.krek@ijs.si, john@mccr.ae, jogracia@unizar.es,
sina.ahmadi@insight-centre.org, besim.kabashi@fau.de

Abstract

The 3rd GLOBALEX Workshop at LREC 2020 has the focus of linking data from different lexicographic resources, highlighting aspects related to the automated linking of content from dictionaries and other lexical sources, with the aim of linguistic data enrichment and reinforcement. The main track of the workshop includes general research papers and is supplemented by two specific tracks, on linking monolingual data and linking bilingual and multilingual data, respectively, each combined with a shared task. The monolingual linking task was conducted as part of the ELEXIS project and the results were evaluated against novel dictionary linking data covering 15 languages developed in this project. The bilingual and multilingual linking was conducted as part of the third edition of the Translation Inference Across Dictionaries (TIAD) shared task and covered three languages matched against language pairs of K Dictionaries. These workshop proceedings include a total of 19 papers, abstracts and system descriptions, in addition to the introduction, reporting on new methodologies and techniques applied to enhance the linking of different types of lexicographic resources.

Keywords: linked lexicography, monolingual, bilingual, multilingual

1 Preface

The third Globalex workshop in conjunction with the LREC conference series[1] has become one of the numerous casualties of the COVID-19 epidemic, since LREC 2020 including all satellite workshops had to be cancelled, but its substance may live on in these proceedings.

The workshop topic of linked lexicography is embodied in these pages in the form of its 19 would-be presentations, including full papers, extended abstracts and system descriptions by scholars from across Europe and elsewhere. The focus is on linking data from different lexicographic resources, highlighting automated processes, in the aim of linguistic data enrichment and enhancement.

Linking lexicographic data sets to each other and with other lexical resources, and the interoperability of lexicography with linguistic linked data (LLD) methodologies in particular and semantic web technologies in general, have increasingly been gaining attention in recent years, becoming a subject for research projects by and collaboration between the academia and industry, including support of

---

[1] `https://globalex2020.globalex.link//`

the public sector. Most notably, the W3C community group on Ontology-Lexica[2] was established following the release of the lemon model, which constituted the first de-facto standard for representing ontology-lexica, with the mission to "develop models for the representation of lexica (and machine readable dictionaries) relative to ontologies" [17]. The ensuing OntoLex-lemon model [19] has served since 2016 as the leading option for converting lexicographic data into LLD, and was updated and finetuned through the Lexicog module released in 2019[3]. This trend has been complemented since 2015 by relevant literature (e.g. [10, 14, 4]), conference papers (e.g. [7, 1, 5, 12, 6]) and mainly EU-funded projects (LDL4HELTA, ELEXIS, Prêt-à-LLOD), and continues to be pursued and advanced as further attested in this volume.

The main track of the workshop included general research papers on linked lexicography and related topics, described in section 2. This was complemented by two in-focus tracks with corresponding shared tasks, on linking monolingual lexicographic resources, in conjunction with ELEXIS, described in section 3, and on linking bilingual and multilingual lexicographic resources, in conjunction with TIAD shared task (TIAD 2020), described in section 4. In section 5 we report on our conclusions.

Globalex 2020 was endorsed by Globalex[4], the Global Alliance for Lexicography, following up on the first Globalex Workshop on Lexicographic Resources and Human Language Technology at LREC 2016[5] and the second Globalex Workshop on Lexicography and Wordnets at LREC 2018[6], with the support of ELEXIS and TIAD.

2   Linking Lexicography

This general track of the workshop includes three papers and three abstracts directly related to the workshop's main theme of linked lexicography as well as three papers and two abstracts on other lexicographic topics.

The first paper, **Modelling frequency and attestations for OntoLex-Lemon**, by Christian Chiarcos, Maxim Ionov, Jesse de Does, Katrien Depuydt, Anas Fahad Khan, Sander Stolk, Thierry Declerck and John Philip McCrae, describes the new FrAC extension of the OntoLex model for corpus-related information. The Ontolex-Lemon W3C community has been shaping up since 2012 and released the state-of-the-art Lexicog module for lexicography in 2019. FrAC aims to make new grounds dealing with "supplementary information drawn from corpora such as frequency information, links to attestations in corpora, and collocation data ... that not only covers the requirements of digital lexicography, but also accommodates essential data structures for lexical information in natural language processing". The paper also illustrates use-cases that implement the model on diverse resources serving different purposes.

The next paper, **SynSemClass linked lexicon: Mapping synonymy between languages**, by Zdenka Uresova, Eva Fucikova, Eva Hajicova and Jan Hajic, presents a cross-lingual study of verb synonymy through verb classes, valency information and semantic roles and "reports on an extended version of a synonym verb class lexicon ... [which] stores cross-lingual semantically similar verb senses in synonym classes extracted from a richly annotated parallel corpus", making use of valency relations and linking them to semantic roles and external lexicons. The aims include comparing "semantic roles and their syntactic properties and features across languages within and across synonym groups, [offering] gold standard data for automatic NLP experiments with such synonyms" and, most notably, building "an

---

[2]https://www.w3.org/community/ontolex/
[3]https://www.w3.org/2019/09/lexicog/
[4]https://globalex.link/
[5]https://globalex2016.globalex.link/
[6]https://globalex2018.globalex.link/

event type ontology that can be referenced and used as a human-readable and human-understandable "database" for all types of events, processes and states". In addition to describing its content, the authors present a preliminary design of a linked data-compatible format of their lexicon.

The third paper, **Representing etymology in the LiLa knowledge base of linguistic resources for Latin**, by Francesco Mambrini and Marco Passarott, describes "the process of inclusion of etymological information in a knowledge base of interoperable Latin linguistic resources", applying Linked Open Data principles based on the Ontolex-Lemon ontology and the lemonEty extension. The authors present their motivation, methodology and modelling strategies as well as possible applications and further developments.

The papers are followed by three abstracts. The first, **An automatically generated Danish Renaissance Dictionary**, by Mette-Marie Møller Svendsen, Nicolai Hartvig Sørensen and Thomas Troelsgård, describes "[b]uilding a period dictionary by reducing and merging relevant existing dictionary resources". The main goal of this project is "to present a series of Danish hymn books from the Lutheran Reformation" including digitizing and making searchable texts and music as well as access to partially digitized dictionaries that are relevant to this period, including an integrated dictionary function to look up words in the text and present sense keywords extended from the dictionary entries as well links to full dictionary entries."

The second abstract, **Linking the Open Dutch Wordnet with Dutch lexicographic resources**, by Thierry Declerck, describes ongoing work on linking wordnet resources from the Open Multilingual Wordnet initiative to morphological ones, with the aim of mutual enrichment. At the first stage, Romance language resources were mapped onto the OntoLex-Lemon model, with interlinking carried out "automatically ... by selecting the identical lemmas encoded on both sides, based on string matching [followed by m]anual correction for linking homographs to their ... Wordnet entries"; as a result, morphological variants were added to the lexical data, realizing the Wordnet concepts, with the added value of formulating lexical restrictions. The experiment continued with interlinking Wordnets to richer resources (beyond solely morphology) in the form of a comprehensive dictionary of Dutch, which turned out to be more complex and required metadata comparisons.

The third abstract, **Widening the discussion on 'false friends' in multilingual dictionaries and linked lexicographic resources**, by Hugo Gonçalo Oliveira and Ana Luís, discusses potential problems of false friends in the multilingual alignment of existing wordnets, with a specific use case providing examples of erroneous alignments between English and Portuguese synsets. The authors suggest to "exploit lists of false friends from the literature for cleaning multilingual wordnets, ... remove false friends from linked synsets, or even to remove the connections between those synsets,... [and that] an RDF property could perhaps be used for explicitly linking pairs of lexical items, in different languages ...".

The second part of this general track section includes three papers relating to specific languages and two abstracts on domain-specific lexicography/terminology. The first paper, **Pinchah Kristang: A dictionary of Kristang**, by Luís Morgado da Costa, describes "the development and current state of ... an online dictionary for Kristang[,] a critically endangered language of the Portuguese-Eurasian communities residing mainly in Malacca and Singapore". This dictionary constitutes a central tool to the revitalization of the language, collating "information from multiple sources, including existing dictionaries and wordlists, ongoing language documentation work, and new words that emerge regularly from relexification efforts by the community", and is powered by the Princeton and Open Kristang wordnets.

The next two papers concern Scandinavian languages from the opposite "privileged" extreme of the scale. **Building sense representations in Danish by combining word embeddings with lexical resources**, by Ida Rørmann Olsen, Bolette Pedersen and Asad Sayeed, concerns a project for identification of suitable sense representation for NLP in Danish. The authors "investigate sense inventories that correlate with human interpretations of word meaning and ambiguity as typically described in dictionaries and wordnets and that are well reflected distributionally as expressed in word embeddings ... study a number of highly ambiguous Danish nouns and examine the effectiveness of sense representations constructed by combining vectors from a distributional model with the information from a wordnet. We establish representations based on centroids obtained from wordnet synests and example sentences as well as representations established via a clustering approach [and] tested in a word sense disambiguation task[, concluding] that the more information extracted from the wordnet entries ... the more successful the sense representation vector".

Then, **Towards a Swedish Roget-style thesaurus for NLP**, by Niklas Zechner and Lars Borin, examines whether and how a digitized Swedish thesaurus originally published in 1930 can serve multiple NLP applications, concluding that "to be useful in our NLP systems, polysemous lexical items need to be disambiguated, and a large amount of modern vocabulary must be added in the proper places". The authors describe "experiments aiming at automating these two tasks, at least in part, where we use the structure of an existing Swedish semantic lexicon" both for disambiguating ambiguous thesaurus entries and adding new entries.

The abstract, **Design and development of an adaptive web application for OLIVATERM**, by Mercedes Roldán Vendrell, describes the project dedicated to designing "the first systematic multilingual terminological dictionary in the scientific and socio-economic area of the olive grove and olive oils", and the work that continues on the development of "a multichannel technological solution [to enable] greater and more efficient transfer to the business sector" combined with a responsive website and an interactive web-based application offering dynamic transfer of relevant information to and from users.

In the last abstract concluding this section, **Building a domain-specific bilingual lexicon resource with Sketch Engine and Lexonomy: Taking ownership of the issues**, Zaida Bartolomé-Díaz and Francesca Frontini question the value of modern methods to accelerate and standardize the elaboration of specialized bilingual dictionaries, "offering not only a relation of terms, but also a representation of a conceptual field" in contrast to "the viability of their use by a lambda user and the previous knowledge" needed for such efficient use, and the possible problems that might occur. The authors propose methodological solutions based on a small corpus consisting of 82 documents extracted from the web, using a list of selected terms, aimed to create automatically a dictionary extract of about 25 terms.

3   Linking monolingual lexicographic resources

3.1   Task Description

The Monolingual Word Sense Alignment (MWSA) task was concerned with the linking of two dictionaries in a single language at the sense level. For example, multiple senses of a word such as for "chair", the sense with definition "a seat for one person, with a support for the back" would be linked to another sense in another dictionary "a movable single seat with a back", while the sense for "the officer who presides at the meetings of an organization" would be linked to "the presiding officer of an assembly". The dataset used for this evaluation was the one prepared by [2] which covers 15 languages and includes alignments between 17 dictionaries. This resource lists all the sense links between the two dictionaries classified with one of the following relationships:

Language	Metric	Baseline	ACDH	RACAI	UNIOR NLP
English	Accuracy	0.752	0.763	**0.798**	0.759
	Precision	0.000	0.619	**0.746**	0.586
	Recall	0.000	0.782	0.353	**0.692**
	F-Measure	0.000	**0.691**	0.480	0.634
Basque	Accuracy	**0.789**	0.407	-	-
	Precision	0.211	**0.223**	-	-
	Recall	0.050	**0.738**	-	-
	F-Measure	0.081	**0.342**	-	-
Bulgarian	Accuracy	**0.728**	0.395	-	-
	Precision	0.250	**0.331**	-	-
	Recall	0.011	**0.842**	-	-
	F-Measure	0.020	**0.475**	-	-
Danish	Accuracy	**0.817**	0.522	-	-
	Precision	**0.300**	0.253	-	-
	Recall	0.023	**0.756**	-	-
	F-Measure	0.043	**0.379**	-	-
Dutch	Accuracy	0.936	0.940	**0.944**	0.931
	Precision	0.000	0.636	**0.846**	0.455
	Recall	0.000	**0.241**	0.190	0.086
	F-Measure	0.000	**0.350**	0.310	0.145
Estonian	Accuracy	0.482	**0.565**	-	-
	Precision	0.545	**0.707**	-	-
	Recall	0.093	**0.806**	-	-
	F-Measure	0.159	**0.754**	-	-
German	Accuracy	0.7777	**0.798**	-	-
	Precision	0.000	**0.738**	-	-
	Recall	0.000	**0.608**	-	-
	F-Measure	0.000	**0.667**	-	-
Hungarian	Accuracy	**0.940**	-	-	-
	Precision	**0.053**	-	-	-
	Recall	**0.012**	-	-	-
	F-Measure	**0.020**	-	-	-
Irish	Accuracy	**0.583**	0.549	-	-
	Precision	**0.680**	0.631	-	-
	Recall	0.185	**0.891**	-	-
	F-Measure	0.291	**0.739**	-	-
Italian	Accuracy	0.693	0.537	0.761	**0.766**
	Precision	0.000	0.418	**0.760**	0.729
	Recall	0.000	0.719	0.333	**0.754**
	F-Measure	0.000	0.529	0.463	**0.741**
Portuguese	Accuracy	**0.921**	0.870	-	0.933
	Precision	0.083	0.311	-	**0.541**
	Recall	0.024	0.762	-	**0.786**
	F-Measure	0.037	0.441	-	**0.641**
Russian	Accuracy	**0.754**	0.606	-	-
	Precision	**0.438**	0.372	-	-
	Recall	0.179	**0.821**	-	-
	F-Measure	0.255	**0.512**	-	-
Serbian	Accuracy	0.853	**0.599**	-	-
	Precision	0.000	**0.190**	-	-
	Recall	0.000	**0.464**	-	-
	F-Measure	0.000	**0.269**	-	-
Slovene	Accuracy	**0.834**	0.442	-	-
	Precision	0.100	**0.173**	-	-
	Recall	0.009	**0.587**	-	-
	F-Measure	0.017	**0.268**	-	-
Spanish	Accuracy	0.678	-	0.786	**0.829**
	Precision	0.255	-	0.667	**0.742**
	Recall	0.127	-	0.655	**0.891**
	F-Measure	0.170	-	0.661	**0.810**
Average	Accuracy	0.769	0.615	0.822	**0.844**
	Precision	0.194	0.431	**0.755**	0.611
	Recall	0.048	**0.694**	0.383	0.642
	F-Measure	0.074	0.494	0.478	**0.594**

Table 1: Results of the evaluation of the MWSA task by team and language

Exact The sense are the same, for example the definitions are simply paraphrases

Broader The sense in the first dictionary completely covers the meaning of the sense in the second dictionary and is applicable to further meanings

Narrower The sense in the first dictionary is entirely covered by the sense of the second dictionary, which is applicable to further meanings

Related There are cases when the senses may be equal but the definitions in both dictionaries differ in key aspects

None There is no match for this sense

The evaluation of the shared task therefore used multiple metrics to evaluate the results of the system. Firstly, *accuracy* measured the total number of links for which the correct class of relationship was predicted. Secondly, we provided *recall, precision* and *F-Measure* scores based on a 2-class classification problem, where the 'exact', 'broader', 'narrower' and 'related' links were merged into a single positive class. This was motivated by the fact that many applications do not care about the specific type of link and that detecting the presence of the link was harder task from predicting the type of the link. We provided this analysis for each of the languages and scored the systems overall based on a macro-average of the accuracy, precision, recall and F-Measure.

3.2 Participants

The task was organized using CodaLab[7] and three external teams[8] participated, although not all teams participated for all languages. The baseline model was quite simple: for each sense pair the Jaccard similarity of the gloss was calculated, then the Hungarian Algorithm [15] was used to find the most likely unique assignment between these senses. The baseline only predicted the 'exact' class (and 'none') so it was expected that the results would be quite poor. The other approaches taken by participants were as follows:

RACAI The RACAI system viewed this task as a case of word-sense disambiguation, from this multiple features were extracted including scores based on the Lesk algorithm [16] as well as features from BERT [8] and other features, which were combined using a random forest [13].

ACDH A variety of features were combined in this approach including simple similarity methods such as used in the baseline as well as similarities coming from ELMo [22] and BERT. These were also combined using a supervised learning framework, and different settings were used for each language.

UNIOR NLP This approach used BERT as well as Siamese LSTMs [21] improved with lexico-semantic information related to the lemma's part-of-speech category.

The overall results are presented in Table 1, and we can see that the overall strongest result in accuracy and F-Measure was obtained by the UNIOR NLP team. However, all systems can be said to have performed best on some of the tasks (even the baseline) and given that all systems used BERT, more research is needed into the best way to fine-tune BERT for this task.

---

[7] https://competitions.codalab.org/competitions/22163

[8] A fourth team participated, but withdrew after submitting results

4 Linking bilingual and multilingual lexicographic resources

In this section we give an overview of the goals and results of the 3rd edition of the Translation Inference Across Dictionaries (TIAD) initiative, co-located with Globalex 2020.

4.1 Task description

The shared task for Translation Inference Across Dictionaries was aimed at exploring methods and techniques for automatically generating new bilingual (and multilingual) dictionaries from existing ones. The main aim of TIAD is to support a coherent experiment framework that enables reliable validation of results and solid comparison of the processes used. This initiative also aims to enhance further research on the topic of inferring translations across languages, and continues the first and second TIAD workshops, which took place on June 18, 2017 in Galway (Ireland) and in Leipzig (Germany) on May 20, 2019, respectively, co-located with the 1st and 2nd editions of the Language Data and Knowledge (LDK) conference.

The experimental setup for this year's evaluation campaign has been the same as in the 2nd TIAD edition [11] with minor differences such as the inclusion of a validation data set (a sample of 5% of the test data set) and the curation of the test data (see later). The participating systems were asked to generate new translations automatically among three languages - English, French, Portuguese - based on known translations contained in the Apertium RDF graph[9]. As these languages (EN, FR, PT) are not directly connected in this graph, no translations can be obtained directly among them there. Based on the available RDF data, the participants had to apply their methodologies to derive translations, mediated by any other language in the graph, between the pairs EN/FR, FR/PT and PT/EN. See the TIAD 2020 website[10] for more technical details on the experimental setup and results.

The evaluation of the results was carried out by the organisers against manually compiled pairs of K Dictionaries (KD), extracted from its Global Series (https://lexicala.com/).

4.2 Results

Nine systems participated in the shared task, coming from four different teams. The participant teams submitted a system description paper including: a description of their system or systems, the way data was processed, the applied algorithms, the obtained results, as well as the conclusions and ideas for future improvements. The system papers were reviewed by the organising committee to confirm that all these aspects were well covered.

This is the list of the participating teams along with a short description of their contributions:

CUD. A *multi-strategy* system was deveoped by Centro Univesritario de la Defensa (CUD), Spain, which combines several strategies to analyse the Apertium RDF graph, taking advantage of characteristics such as translation using multiple paths, synonyms and similarities between lexical entries from different lexicons and cardinality of possible translations through the graph. Several combinations of such strategies were presented to the shared task, showing that the combination of all of them produces better results than without joining all the strategies.

---

[9]http://linguistic.linkeddata.es/apertium/
[10]https://tiad2020.unizar.es

NUIG. This is the contribution of National University of Ireland Galway (NUIG) to TIAD. The proposed system combines unsupervised NLP and Graph Metrics for Translation Inference. This system includes graph-based metrics calculated using novel algorithms, with an unsupervised document embedding tool called ONETA and an unsupervised multi-way neural machine translation method. The results improve the system that the authors presented in the last TIAD edition [18] and produces the highest precision among all systems in the task while preserving a reasonable recall.

ACoLi. The Applied Computational Linguistics (ACoLi), Goethe University Frankfurt, Germany, contributed with a method based on symbolic methods and the propagation of concepts over a graph of interconnected dictionaries, which evolves the system presented by the authors in the previous TIAD edition [9]. Given a mapping from source language words to lexical concepts (e.g., synsets) as a seed, they use bilingual dictionaries to extrapolate a mapping of pivot and target language words to these lexical concepts. Translation inference is then performed by looking up the lexical concept(s) of a source language word and returning the target language word(s) for which these lexical concepts have the respective highest score. They participated with two instantiations of such a system: one using WordNet synsets as concepts, and one using lexical entries (translations) as concepts.

UNIZAR. University of Zaragoza (UNIZAR), Spain, contributed with two different systems to the shared task. On the one hand `Cycles-OTIC`, a hybrid technique based on graph exploration that combines a method that explores the density of cycles in the translations graph [24] with the translations obtained by the One Time Inverse Consultation (OTIC) method [23], which obtained better coverage than OTIC alone but slightly reduced precision. On the other hand, *Cross-lingual embeddings*, based on the distribution of embeddings across languages [3], were used to build cross-lingual word embeddings trained with monolingual corpora and mapped afterwards through an intermediate language.

We have run two baselines to be compared with the participating systems:

Baseline 1 - Word2Vec. The method uses Word2Vec [20] to transform the graph into a vector space. A graph edge is interpreted as a sentence and the nodes are word forms with their POS tag. Word2Vec iterates multiple times over the graph and learns multilingual embeddings (without additional data). For a given input word, we calculated a distance based on the cosine similarity of a word to every other word with the target-POS tag in the target language. In our evaluation, we applied an arbitrary threshold of 0.5 to the confidence degree. Note that in the TIAD 2020 edition the Word2Vec baseline, although based on the same principles of TIAD 2019, has been re-implemented and re-trained and lead to different results than in the previous TIAD edition.

Baseline 2 - OTIC. The idea of the One Time Inverse Consultation (OTIC) method [23] is to explore, for a given word, the possible candidate translations that can be obtained through intermediate translations in the pivot language. Then, a score is assigned to each candidate translation based on the degree of overlap between the pivot translations shared by both the source and target words. In our evaluation, we have applied the OTIC method using Spanish as pivot language, and using an arbitrary threshold of 0.5.

The results can be seen in Table 2 and demonstrate that most of the systems show good precision (all of them over 0.6 but the Word2Vec baseline) but a lesser recall (none of them reached 0.5). The OTIC baseline continues being a simple but hard to beat baseline. Overall the results have been better that the ones obtained in TIAD 2019 [11], with F-measure results in the range [0.25, 0.56], compared with the range [0.11, 0.37] in 2019. One of the main reasons, in addition the particular systems improvements, is that the golden standard data have been curated with respect to the previous version in two aspects:

by removing duplicated entries caused by the presence of non-breaking spaces in Apertium, and by removing some entries that were not in the intersection between Apertium and KD data; thus leading to an increased recall.

System	Precision	Recall	F-measure	Coverage
BASELINE(OTIC)	0.7	0.47	0.56	0.7
Cycles-OTIC	0.64	0.47	0.54	0.76
NUIG	0.77	0.35	0.49	0.54
Multi-StrategyI+II+III+IV	0.61	0.33	0.43	0.63
Multi-StrategyI+II+III	0.62	0.33	0.43	0.63
CL-embeddings	0.62	0.32	0.42	0.59
Multi-StrategyI+II	0.65	0.3	0.4	0.59
ACOLIbaseline	0.6	0.28	0.38	0.48
BASELINE(Word2Vec)	0.3	0.37	0.33	0.68
Multi-StrategyI	0.63	0.22	0.32	0.44
ACOLIwordnet	0.61	0.16	0.25	0.28

Table 2: TIAD 2020 averaged system results, ordered by F-measure in descending order.

5 Conclusion

While this workshop has not been able to physically take place this year, these proceedings show that the work in the area of digital lexicography is still very much alive. In particular, with the introduction of the two shared tasks, we have made a closer connection between lexicographers and computer scientists, allowing state-of-the-art methods in natural language processing including deep learning to be applied to solve challenges in lexicography. Moreover, we continue to see the value in semantic web technologies for the representation of lexicographic resources and are encouraged to see more work supporting this and the use of linked data methodologies in lexicography in line with the workshop's theme of *linked lexicography*.

References

[1] Frank Abromeit, Christian Chiarcos, Christian Fäth, and Maxim Ionov. Linking the Tower of Babel: modelling a massive set of etymological dictionaries as RDF. In *Proceedings of the 5th Workshop on Linked Data in Linguistics (LDL-2016): Managing, Building and Using Linked Language Resources*, pages 11–19, 2016.

[2] Sina Ahmadi, John P. McCrae, Sanni Nimb, Thomas Troelsgård, Sussi Olsen, Bolette S. Pedersen, Thierry Declerck, Tanja Wissik, Monica Monachini, Andrea Bellandi, Fahad Khan, Irene Pisani, Simon Krek, Veronika Lipp, Tamás Váradi, László Simon, András Győrffy, Carole Tiberius, Tanneke Schoonheim, Yifat Ben Moshe, Maya Rudich, Raya Abu Ahmad, Dorielle Lonke, Kira Kovalenko, Margit Langemets, Jelena Kallas, Oksana Dereza, Theodorus Fransen, David Cillessen, David Lindemann, Mikel Alonso, Ana Salgado, José Luis Sancho, Rafael-J. Ure na Ruiz, Kiril Simov, Petya Osenova, Zara Kancheva, Ivaylo Radev, Ranka Stanković, Cvetana Krstev, Biljana Lazić, Aleksandra Marković, Andrej Perdih, and Dejan Gabrovšek. A Multilingual Evaluation Dataset for Monolingual Word Sense Alignment. In *Proceedings of the 12th Language Resource and Evaluation Conference (LREC 2020)*, 2020.

[3] Mikel Artetxe, Gorka Labaka, and Eneko Agirre. A robust self-learning method for fully unsupervised cross-lingual mappings of word embeddings. In *Proceedings of the 56th Annual Meeting of the Association for Computational Linguistics (Volume 1: Long Papers)*, pages 789–798, 2018.

[4] Julia Bosque-Gil, Jorge Gracia, and Asunción Gómez-Pérez. Linked data in lexicography. *Kernerman Dictionary News*, (24):19–24, 2016.

[5] Julia Bosque-Gil, Jorge Gracia, and Elena Montiel-Ponsoda. Towards a Module for Lexicography in OntoLex. In *LDK Workshops*, pages 74–84, 2017.

[6] Julia Bosque-Gil, Dorielle Lonke, Jorge Gracia, and Ilan Kernerman. Validating the OntoLex-lemon Lexicography Module with K Dictionaries' Multilingual Data. In *Electronic lexicography in the 21st century. Proceedings of the eLex 2019 conference*, pages 726–746, 2019.

[7] Thierry Declerck, Eveline Wandl-Vogt, and Karlheinz Mörth. Towards a Pan-European lexicography by means of linked (open) data. *Proceedings of eLex*, pages 342–355, 2015.

[8] Jacob Devlin, Ming-Wei Chang, Kenton Lee, and Kristina Toutanova. BERT: Pre-training of deep bidirectional transformers for language understanding. *arXiv preprint arXiv:1810.04805*, 2018.

[9] Kathrin Donandt and Christian Chiarcos. Translation inference through multi-lingual word embedding similarity. In *Proceedings of TIAD-2019 Shared Task – Translation Inference Across Dictionaries, at 2nd Language Data and Knowledge (LDK) conference*. CEUR-WS, May 2019.

[10] Jorge Gracia. Multilingual dictionaries and the Web of Data. *Kernerman Dictionary News*, (23):1–4, 2015.

[11] Jorge Gracia, Besim Kabashi, Ilan Kernerman, Marta Lanau-Coronas, and Dorielle Lonke. Results of the Translation Inference Across Dictionaries 2019 Shared Task. In Jorge Gracia, Besim Kabashi, and Ilan Kernerman, editors, *Proceedings of TIAD-2019 Shared Task – Translation Inference Across Dictionaries co-located with the 2nd Language, Data and Knowledge Conference (LDK 2019)*, pages 1–12, Leipzig (Germany), 2019. CEUR Press.

[12] Jorge Gracia, Ilan Kernerman, and Julia Bosque-Gil. Toward linked data-native dictionaries. In *Electronic Lexicography in the 21st Century: Lexicography from Scratch. Proceedings of the eLex 2017 conference*, pages 19–21, 2017.

[13] Tin Kam Ho. Random decision forests. In *Proceedings of the 3rd international conference on document analysis and recognition*, volume 1, pages 278–282. IEEE, 1995.

[14] Bettina Klimek and Martin Brümmer. Enhancing lexicography with semantic language databases. *Kernerman Dictionary News*, (23):5–10, 2015.

[15] Harold W Kuhn. The Hungarian method for the assignment problem. *Naval research logistics quarterly*, 2(1-2):83–97, 1955.

[16] Michael Lesk. Automatic sense disambiguation using machine readable dictionaries: How to tell a pine cone from an ice cream cone. In *Proceedings of the 5th annual international conference on Systems documentation*, pages 24–26, 1986.

[17] John McCrae, Guadalupe Aguado de Cea, Paul Buitelaar, Philipp Cimiano, Thierry Declerck, Asunción Gómez-Pérez, Jorge Gracia, Laura Hollink, Elena Montiel-Ponsoda, Dennis Spohr, and Tobias Wunner. Interchanging lexical resources on the Semantic Web. *Language Resources and Evaluation*, 46(6):701–709, 2012.

[18] John P. McCrae. TIAD shared task 2019: Orthonormal explicit topic analysis for translation inference across dictionaries. In *Proceedings of TIAD-2019 Shared Task – Translation Inference Across Dictionaries, at 2nd Language Data and Knowledge (LDK) conference*. CEUR-WS, May 2019.

[19] John P. McCrae, Julia Bosque-Gil, Jorge Gracia, Paul Buitelaar, and Philipp Cimiano. The OntoLex-Lemon Model: development and applications. In *Proceedings of eLex 2017*, pages 587–597, 2017.

[20] Tomas Mikolov, Kai Chen, Greg Corrado, and Jeffrey Dean. Efficient Estimation of Word Representations in Vector Space. In *Proceedings of the International Conference on Learning Representations (ICLR)*, 2013.

[21] Jonas Mueller and Aditya Thyagarajan. Siamese recurrent architectures for learning sentence similarity. In *thirtieth AAAI conference on Artificial Intelligence*, 2016.

[22] Matthew E Peters, Mark Neumann, Mohit Iyyer, Matt Gardner, Christopher Clark, Kenton Lee, and Luke Zettlemoyer. Deep contextualized word representations. *arXiv preprint arXiv:1802.05365*, 2018.

[23] Kumiko Tanaka and Kyoji Umemura. Construction of a Bilingual Dictionary Intermediated by a Third Language. In *COLING*, pages 297–303, 1994.

[24] Marta Villegas, Maite Melero, Núria Bel, Jorge Gracia, and Núria Bel. Leveraging RDF Graphs for Crossing Multiple Bilingual Dictionaries. In *Proceedings of trhe 10th Language Resources and Evaluation Conference (LREC'16) Portorož (Slovenia)*, pages 868–876, Paris, France, may 2016. European Language Resources Association (ELRA).

Organizers

Ilan Kernerman, K Dictionaries
Simon Krek, Globalex, Jožef Stefan Institute

Track 1 Organizers

John McCrae, National University of Ireland Galway
Sina Ahmadi, National University of Ireland Galway

Track 2 Organizers

Jorge Gracia, University of Zaragoza
Besim Kabashi, Friedrich-Alexander University of Erlangen-Nuremberg and Ludwig-Maximilian
University of Munich

Program Committee

Anna Braasch. University of Copenhagen, Denmark
Sara Carvalho. University of Aveiro, Portugal
Philip Cimiano. University of Bielefeld, Germany
Rute Costa, Universidade Nova de Lisboa, Portugal
Thierry Fontenelle. European Investment Bank, Luxembourg
Radovan Garabik. Ľ. Štúr Institute of Linguistics, Slovakia
Jorge Gracia, University of Zaragoza, Spain
Dagmar Gromann. University of Vienna, Austria
Ales Horak. Masaryk University, Czech Republic
Besim Kabashi. Friedrich-Alexander-Universität Erlangen-Nürnberg, Germany
Ilan Kernerman. K Dictionaries, Israel
Iztok Kosem. Jožef Stefan Institute, Slovenia
Simon Krek. Jožef Stefan Institute, Slovenia
Nikola Ljubešić. Jožef Stefan Institute, Slovenia
Dorielle Lonke. K Dictionaries, Israel
Patricia Martín Chozas. Madrid Polytechnic University, Spain
John Philip McCrae. National University of Ireland Galway, Ireland
Krzysztof Nowak. Institute of Polish Language, Poland
Maciej Piaceski. Wroclaw University of Science and Technology, Poland
Carole Tiberius. Instituut voor Nederlandse Lexicologie, Netherlands
Lars Trap-Jensen. Society for Danish Language and Literature, Denmark
Marieke van Erp. KNAW Humanities Cluster, Netherlands

Table of Contents

Conference Program

GlobalLex Presentations

Main Track

Modelling Frequency and Attestations for OntoLex-Lemon
Christian Chiarcos, Maxim Ionov, Jesse de Does, Katrien Depuydt, Anas Fahad Khan, Sander Stolk, Thierry Declerck and John Philip McCrae

SynSemClass Linked Lexicon: Mapping Synonymy between Languages
Zdenka Uresova, Eva Fucikova, Eva Hajicova and Jan Hajic

Representing Etymology in the LiLa Knowledge Base of Linguistic Resources for Latin
Francesco Mambrini and Marco Passarotti

An automatically generated Danish Renaissance Dictionary
Mette-Marie Møller Svendsen, Nicolai Hartvig Sørensen and Thomas Troelsgård

Towards an Extension of the Linking of the Open Dutch WordNet with Dutch Lexicographic Resources
Thierry Declerck

Widening the Discussion on "False Friends" in Multilingual Wordnets
Hugo Gonçalo Oliveira and Ana Luís

Pinchah Kristang: A Dictionary of Kristang
Luís Morgado da Costa

Building Sense Representations in Danish by Combining Word Embeddings with Lexical Resources
Ida Rørmann Olsen, Bolette Pedersen and Asad Sayeed

Towards a Swedish Roget-Style Thesaurus for NLP
Niklas Zechner and Lars Borin

Design and development of an adaptive web application for OLIVATERM
Mercedes Roldán Vendrell

Proceedings of the Globalex Workshop on Linked Lexicography, pages 1–9
Language Resources and Evaluation Conference (LREC 2020), Marseille, 11–16 May 2020
© European Language Resources Association (ELRA), licensed under CC-BY-NC

Modelling Frequency and Attestations for OntoLex-Lemon

**Christian Chiarcos[1], Maxim Ionov[1], Jesse de Does[2], Katrien Depuydt[2],
Anas Fahad Khan[3], Sander Stolk[4], Thierry Declerck[5], John P. McCrae[6]**

[1]Goethe-Universität Frankfurt am Main
[2]Instituut voor de Nederlandse Taal, Leiden, the Netherlands
[3]Istituto di Linguistica Computazionale "A. Zampolli" (ILC-CNR) Pisa, Italy
[4]Leiden University, Leiden, the Netherlands
[5]DFKI GmbH, Multilinguality and Language Technology
[6]Data Science Institute, National University of Ireland Galway
[1]{chiarcos,ionov}@informatik.uni-frankfurt.de, [2]{dedoes,depuydt}@ivdnt.org
[3]fahad.khan@ilc.cnr.it, [4]s.s.stolk@hum.leidenuniv.nl, [5]declerck@dfki.de, [6]john@mccr.ae

Abstract

The OntoLex vocabulary enjoys increasing popularity as a means of publishing lexical resources with RDF and as Linked Data. The recent publication of a new OntoLex module for lexicography, *lexicog*, reflects its increasing importance for digital lexicography. However, not all aspects of digital lexicography have been covered to the same extent. In particular, supplementary information drawn from corpora such as frequency information, links to attestations, and collocation data were considered to be beyond the scope of *lexicog*. Therefore, the OntoLex community has put forward the proposal for a novel module for frequency, attestation and corpus information (FrAC), that not only covers the requirements of digital lexicography, but also accommodates essential data structures for lexical information in natural language processing. This paper introduces the current state of the OntoLex-FrAC vocabulary, describes its structure, some selected use cases, elementary concepts and fundamental definitions, with a focus on frequency and attestations.

Keywords: lexical resources, community standards, linguistic linked (open) data, OntoLex

1. Background

The primary community standard for publishing lexical resources as linked data is the OntoLex-Lemon vocabulary, which is based on the *lemon* model (McCrae et al., 2012), that has been designed as a model for complementing ontologies with lexical information in the Monnet project.[1] With its further development in the context of the W3C OntoLex Community Group, its scope was broadened and it developed towards the primary RDF vocabulary for lexical information. In 2016, the OntoLex vocabulary was published as a W3C Report[2] (Cimiano et al., 2016).

The model's primary element is the lexical entry (see Fig. 1), which represents a single lexeme with a single part-of-speech (when appropriate) and a set of grammatical properties. This entry is composed of a number of forms as well as a number of senses which enumerate its various meanings. The meanings of these senses can be defined formally by reference to an ontology or informally by a lexical concept, which defines a concept in a cross-lingual manner. This paper describes the on-going development of a novel OntoLex module for frequency, attestation and corpus information (OntoLex-FrAC). FrAC extends OntoLex and its recently published *lexicog* vocabulary[3] with the capability to represent important supplementary information used in digital lexicography (collocations, distributional similarity, attestations, frequency information). As this information is equally relevant for both digital lexicography and for applications in fields such as natural language processing, the W3C OntoLex Community decided to treat such information within a separate module and to remove the corresponding concepts from the lexicography module.

Important motivations to extend OntoLex core and lexicography modules are the Elexis project (Krek et al., 2019),[4] where strategies, tools and standards for extracting, structuring and linking lexicographic resources are developed for their inclusion in Linked Open Data and the Semantic Web, as well as the Prêt-à-LLOD project (Declerck et al., 2020)[5] on making linguistic linked open data ready-to-use for knowledge services across sectors.

The goal of the module is to complement the OntoLex-Lemon core elements with a vocabulary layer to represent lexicographical and semantic information derived from or defined with reference to corpora and external resources in a way that (1) generalizes over use cases from digital lexicography, natural language processing, artificial intelli-

---

[1]A European Union Funded project in multilingual ontologies that ran from 2010-2013.

[2]https://www.w3.org/2016/05/ontolex/

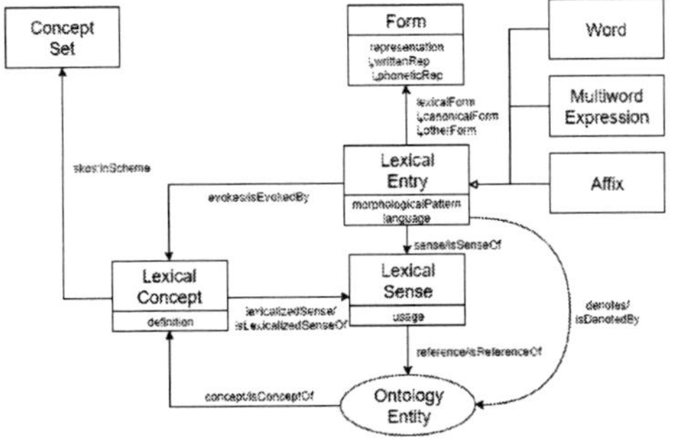

Figure 1: OntoLex-Lemon core model

[3]https://www.w3.org/2019/09/lexicog/
[4]See also https://elex.is/.
[5]See also http://www.pret-a-llod.eu.

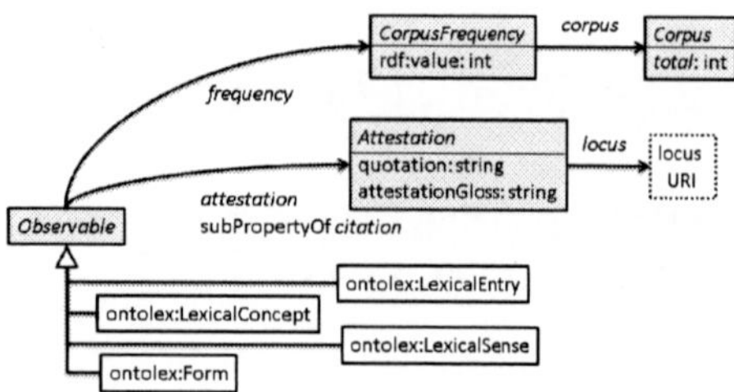

Figure 2: OntoLex-FrAC module structure

gence, computational philology and corpus linguistics, that (2) facilitates exchange, storage and re-usability of such data along with lexical information, and that (3) minimizes information loss.

The scope of the model is three-fold:

1. Extending the OntoLex-lexicog model with corpus information to support existing challenges in corpus-driven lexicography.
2. Modelling existing lexical and distributional-semantic resources (corpus-based dictionaries, collocation dictionaries, embeddings) as linked data, to allow their conjoint publication and inter-operation by Semantic Web standards.
3. Providing a conceptual / abstract model of relevant concepts in distributional semantics that facilitates building linked data-based applications that consume and combine both lexical and distributional information.

Based on this, the following parts of the module can be distinguished: (1) Frequency, (2) attestations, and (3) corpus-derived information.

This paper provides an account for frequency and attestations, for which a consensus model has already been reached. Corpus information beyond that includes various information about lexically relevant concepts that can be created on grounds of corpora. This includes, for example, distributional similarity scores, collocation vectors or embeddings.

The overall structure is presented in Figure 2, which reflects the current state of modelling. Extensions for embeddings, collocations and similarity are still under development.

For OntoLex, we assume that frequency, attestation and corpus information can be provided about *every* linguistic content element in the core model and the OntoLex modules. This includes `ontolex:Form` (token frequency, etc.), `ontolex:LexicalEntry` (frequency of disambiguated lemmas), `ontolex:LexicalSense` (sense frequency), `ontolex:LexicalConcept` (e.g., synset frequency), `lexicog:Entry` (if used for representing homonyms: frequency of non-disambiguated lemmas), etc. Formally, we define the domain of FrAC properties by the concept `frac:Observable` that we introduce as a generalization over these concepts:[6] Everything for which we provide frequency, attestation or corpus information must be observable in a corpus or another linguistic data source.

---

[6]It is to be expected that other, subsequent OntoLex modules

2. Frequency

Frequency information is a crucial component in human language technology. Corpus-based lexicography originates with the Brown corpus (Kučera and Francis, 1967) and, subsequently, the analysis of frequency distributions of word forms, lemmas and other linguistic elements has become a standard technique in lexicography and philology, and given rise to the field of corpus linguistics. Information on frequency is used in computational lexicography and is essential for NLP and corpus linguistics. The FrAC module includes terminology to capture such information, both absolute and relative frequency, in order to facilitate sharing and utilising this valued information.

2.1. Model

For modelling, we focus on absolute frequencies, as relative frequencies can be derived if absolute frequencies and totals are known.

In order to avoid confusion with `lexinfo:Frequency` (which provides lexicographic assessments such as *commonly used*, *infrequently used*, etc.), this is defined with reference to a particular dataset, a corpus.

CorpusFrequency (Class) provides the absolute number of attestations (rdf:value) of a particular frac:Observable in a particular language resource (frac:corpus).

  SubClassOf: rdf:value exactly 1 xsd:int, frac:corpus exactly 1

frequency (ObjectProperty) assigns a particular frac:Observable a frac:CorpusFrequency.

  Domain frac:CorpusFrequency

  Range frac:Observable

Corpus frequency is always defined relative to a corpus. We do not provide a formal definition of what a corpus is (it can be any kind or collection of linguistic data at any scale, structured or unstructured), except that we expect it to define a total of elements contained (`frac:total`). In many practical applications, it is necessary to provide relative counts, and in this way, these can be easily derived from the absolute (element) frequency provided by the `CorpusFrequency` class and the total defined by the underlying corpus.

Corpus (Class) represents any type of linguistic data or collection thereof, in structured or unstructured format. At the lexical level, a corpus consists of individual elements (tokens, 'words'), and data providers should provide the total number of elements. It should also provide provenance information, e.g., the tokenization strategy, preprocessing steps, etc.

  SubClassOf: frac:total exactly 1 xsd:int

corpus (Property) assigns a corpus to a particular frac:CorpusFrequency.

---

may require a similar generalization, and then, it would be advisable to create a class `ontolex:LexicalElement` (or the like) in the core model and use that one, instead.

Domain: frac:CorpusFrequency

Range: frac:Corpus

total (Property) assigns a corpus the total number of elements that it contains. In the context of OntoLex, these are instantiations of lexemes, only, i.e., tokens ('words').

Domain: frac:Corpus

Range: integer (long)

Note that we expect a corpus to apply a specific tokenization strategy to define a total of elements. If different tokenization strategies of the same dataset occur, these result in different `frac:Corpus` elements.

2.2. Illustrative Example

The Electronic Penn Sumerian Dictionary (ePSD)[7] is an effort to provide an exhaustive dictionary of Sumerian, an isolate language of the ancient Near East, written between the 3rd and 1st millennium BCE being the oldest known written language. The Pennsylvania Sumerian Dictionary Project is carried out at the University of Pennsylvania Museum of Anthropology and Archaeology and funded by the National Endowment for the Humanities and private contributions. Its electronic edition has been developed in a corpus-based fashion, with information such as shown in Fig. 3: It provides frequency information per time period ("3000", "2500", "2000" etc.), orthographic variants ("[1]", "[2]", "[3]"), individual inflected forms (window "ePSD Forms"), and individual word senses ("1. (to be) strong" etc.), and it provides absolute and relative counts.

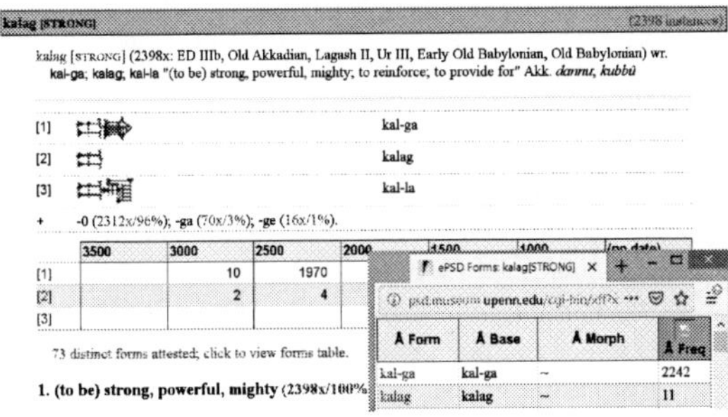

Figure 3: Electronic Penn Sumerian Dictionary (ePSD), sample entry *kalag*

Within the ePSD, frequency information is assigned to *any* element in the dictionary (at least forms, entries, senses), and separately for a large number of subcorpora (defined by time periods and regions/cultures).

An example in Listing 1 illustrates word and form frequencies for the Sumerian word *kalag* (n.) "(to be) strong" and the frequencies of the underlying corpus.

2.3. Shorthands for Data Modelling

The model sketched above is relatively verbose: It requires full provenance information to be provided with every frequency count. It is necessary to provide the link to the underlying corpus *for every frequency assessment* because the

---

[7]http://psd.museum.upenn.edu/

Listing 1: Word and form frequencies in ePSD

```
# word frequency, over all form variants
epsd:kalag_strong_v a ontolex:LexicalEntry;
   frac:frequency [
      a frac:CorpusFrequency;
      rdf:value "2398"^^xsd:int;
      frac:corpus
         <http://oracc.museum.upenn.edu/epsd2/pager>
] .

# form frequency for individual orthographical variants
epsd:kalag_strong_v a ontolex:canonicalForm [
   ontolex:writtenRep "kal-ga"@sux-Latn;
   frac:frequency [
      a frac:CorpusFrequency;
      rdf:value "2312"^^xsd:int;
      frac:corpus
         <http://oracc.museum.upenn.edu/epsd2/pager>
   ]
   ] .

epsd:kalag_strong_v a ontolex:otherForm [
   ontolex:writtenRep "kalag"@sux-Latn;
   frac:frequency [
      a frac:CorpusFrequency;
      rdf:value "70"^^xsd:int;
      frac:corpus
         <http://oracc.museum.upenn.edu/epsd2/pager>
   ]
   ] .
```

same element may receive different counts over different corpora. For querying and retrieval, having this information explicitly given is a very good means to ease access and processing. From the perspective of data modelling, however, it is highly redundant and should be avoided.

As corpus-derived information requires provenance and other metadata, the FrAC module uses reification (class-based modelling) for concepts such as frequency or embeddings. In a dataset, this information will be recurring, and for redundancy reduction, we recommend to provide resource-specific subclasses of concepts that provide metadata by means of `owl:Restrictions` that provide the value for the respective properties. This is illustrated in Listing 2 for the relevant FrAC classes.

For data modelling and sharing, we thus define a corpus- or collection-specific subclass of `frac:CorpusFrequency` with an invariant link to the underlying corpus (and additional provenance information, if required). For specifying absolute frequencies, we thus refer to this *constrained* frequency type.

This leads to more compact data and is more robust against information loss (i.e., if an RDF dump is incomplete, we either lose frequency metadata completely or we maintain its provenance, but it will not be incomplete).

Listing 2: Reifying provenance information for ePSD

```
:EPSDFrequency rdfs:subClassOf frac:CorpusFrequency .

:EPSDFrequency rdfs:subClassOf [
   a owl:Restriction ;
   owl:onProperty frac:corpus ;
   owl:hasValue
      <http://oracc.museum.upenn.edu/epsd2/pager>
] .

# frequency assessment
epsd:kalag_strong_v frac:frequency [
   a :EPSDFrequency;
   rdf:value "2398"^^xsd:int
] .
```

`frac:CorpusFrequency` can be extended with additional filter conditions to define sub-corpora. For example, we can restrict the subcorpus to a particular time period, e.g., the Neo-Sumerian Ur III period:

```
# ePSD frequency for the Ur-III period (aat:300019910)
:EPSDFrequency_UrIII
   rdfs:subClassOf :EPSDFrequency;
   rdfs:subClassOf [
      a owl:Restriction ;
      owl:onProperty dct:temporal ;
      owl:hasValue aat:300019910
   ] .

# frequency assessment for sub-corpus
epsd:kalag_strong_v frac:frequency [
   a :EPSDFrequency_UrIII;
   rdf:value "1916"^^xsd:int
] .
```

3. Attestations

According to Kilgarriff (1997):

> "the scientific study of language should not include word senses as objects in its ontology. Where 'word senses' have a role to play in a scientific vocabulary, they are to be construed as abstractions over clusters of word usages ... the basic units are occurrences of the word in context (operationalised as corpus citations)."

While dispensing with word senses is not an option for modelling dictionaries and lexica, one should take into account that it is by analysing corpus material that lexicographers, using their expert knowledge, can provide a careful description of the meanings of each word in the dictionary, together with the corpus evidence in the form of dictionary citations. Both the current OntoLex core model and the lexicography module lack a way to include this evidence. The main objective of modelling attestations for OntoLex is to do justice to the character of 'scholarly' lexicographical work by allowing us to "put the corpus into the dictionary".

3.1. Model

There are at least two different ways of linking lexical information with corpus evidence, each of which arises from a different tradition, in the first case that of scholarly lexicography and in the second case that of computational linguistics. These are:

- The use of references to corpora by a lexicographer to furnish evidence with reference to examples for the existence of a given lexical phenomena at a certain time period;
- Linking a computational lexicon with the corpora from which the lexical information is derived.

The attestation part of the FrAC module is intended to model both of these approaches in a unified way. It is important to have a flexible vocabulary to characterize the properties of attestations in dictionaries, allowing us to take account of, for instance, the presence of a context snippet and aspects of a cited attestation which relate to its being a scholarly hypothesis. Khan and Boschetti's *lemonBib* model for lexicographical citations (Khan and Boschetti,

2018) tackles some important issues relevant to the characterization of evidence in lexicography and proposes solutions based on the FRBR[8](Saur, 1998), CiTO and FaBIO ontologies (Peroni and Shotton, 2012). In particular (Khan and Boschetti, 2018) mention:

- The distinction between citations in general and citations which provide evidence (attestation)
- Enabling the marking of text readings as conjectural

In fact we can identify at least five axes of classification:

1. Attestation (Citation provides evidence for the word sense) versus other types of citation in a lexical entry.
2. Degree of certainty with regard to the source text (e.g., given a reconstructed text how sure can we be that the word was present in the original?)
3. Degree of certainty of the interpretation (e.g., is this really an instance of the relevant word sense?)
4. Is any textual context for the cited usage of the word given in the form of a quotation?
5. Is the occurrence (or multiple occurrences) of the headword in the context/snippet explicitly marked?

The attestation part of the module tries to provide the necessary vocabulary for the representation of this data.

- There always is an instance of an object for any type of citation. It is always linked to the `frac:Observable` with the `citation` object property. Several vocabularies for modelling citation information have been introduced, FrAC is thus underspecified with respect to the exact definition but relies on using such vocabularies. One candidate vocabulary is the previously mentioned CITO ontology which provides fine-grained information, e.g., the type of citation (cites as evidence, agrees with, etc.) can be reflected in the value of `cito:hasCitationCharacterization` property and by subclasses of `Citation`.
- (Un)certainty of source text reading and/or lexicographic interpretation can be modeled by two distinct boolean data properties associated with the `Citation` object.
- Presence of context is simply reflected by a non-empty value for the `quotation` data property.
- The `locus` object property can optionally be used to mark the place in the snippet in which the headword occurs (this is useful for computational applications use of dictionary quotations in e.g.). For expressing the locus, external vocabularies such as NIF or WebAnnotation can be used.

3.1.1. Classes and Concepts

Attestations constitute a special form of citation that provide evidence for the existence of a certain lexical phenomena; they can elucidate meaning or illustrate various linguistic features.

In scholarly dictionaries, attestations are a representative selection from the occurrences of a headword in a textual

---

[8] `http://purl.org/vocab/frbr/core#`

corpus. These citations often consist of quotation accompanied by a reference to the source. The quoted text usually contains the occurrence of the headword.

frac:Attestation class represents an exact or normalized quotation or excerpt from a source document that illustrates a particular form, sense, lexeme or features such as spelling variation, morphology, syntax, collocation, register.

A **Citation** is "a conceptual directional link from a citing entity to a cited entity, created by a human performative act of making a citation, typically instantiated by the inclusion of a bibliographic reference in the reference list of the citing entity, or by the inclusion within the citing entity of a link, in the form of an HTTP Uniform Resource Locator (URL), to a resource on the World Wide Web".

This definition is taken from CITO (Peroni and Shotton, 2012). The FrAC module does not prescribe a specific vocabulary for the citation object. If the CITO vocabulary is used, FrAC Citations can be defined as the subclass of CITO citations having `frac:Observable` as citing entity and attestations would correspond to citations with the `cito:hasCitationCharacterization` value `citesAsEvidence`.

In many applications, it is desirable to specify the location of the occurrence of a headword in the quoted text of an attestation, for example, by means of character offsets. Different conventions for referencing strings by character offsets do exist, representative solutions are string URIs as provided by RCF5147 (for plain text) and NIF (all mime-types),[9] and the selector mechanism of WebAnnotation.[10] As different vocabularies can be used to establish locus objects, the FrAC vocabulary is underspecified with respect to the exact nature of the locus object. Accordingly, the `locus` property that links an attestation with its source takes any URI as object.

3.1.2. Properties

frac:quotation (range: xs:String) This contains the text content of the dictionary quotation.

frac:attestationGloss (domain: frac:Attestation, range: xs:String) This contains the text content of an attestation as represented within a dictionary. This may be different from a direct quotation because the target expression may be omitted or normalized.

frac:citation (domain: frac:Observable) Associates a citation to the frac:Observable citing it.

frac:attestation (domain: frac:Observable, range: frac:Attestation) Associates an attestation to the frac:Observable. This is a subproperty of frac:citation using it as evidence.

frac:locus (domain: frac:Attestation) points to the location at which the relevant word(s) can be found.

3.1.3. Relation with other Vocabularies

When the dictionary citations refer to an accessible corpus, we could consider the link between corpus and lexicon as a (e.g. word sense) annotation of the corpus. Different vocabularies for this purpose exist.

Figure 4: The entry for ἀνώμαλος

The NLP Interchange Format NIF, for example, provides vocabulary to point to a more precise location of the relevant word(s) within the quotation:

nif:beginIndex (range: xs:Int) Initial character offset of the word to which the lexicographical interpretation is attached

nif:endIndex (range: xs:Int) Final character offset of the word to which the lexicographical interpretation is attached

Similarly, the Web Annotation Framework can be used for modelling loci (listing 6). In particular, Web Annotation provides a vocabulary to formalize loci by means of offsets as in NIF, but also by other means, e.g., XPath.

4. Use Cases

4.1. The Liddell-Scott-Jones Ancient Greek Lexicon

Our first use-case shows the application of the FrAC module to the modelling and publication of legacy lexical resources as linked data. In our particular case we will be working with the Liddell-Scott-Jones Ancient Greek Lexicon (LSJ) a scholarly dictionary in Ancient Greek-English originally published in the 19th century by Henry George Liddell and Robert Scott and then revised in 1940 by Henry Stuart Jones. The LSJ is still regarded as an authoritative lexicographic resource in Ancient Greek scholarship and is currently in print in its ninth edition (Liddell et al., 1996). In 2007 the Perseus project published a digital edition of the work which was made available on their website both in HTML and as a TEI source[11], which we take as a starting point of our work[12]. As may be imagined, the LSJ is an extremely rich resource and one that is particularly valuable with respect to its sense based attestations which it takes from the surviving corpus of Ancient Greek literature. We will look at one entry from that work and then show how the attestations may be modelled using the classes and properties which have been provisionally developed as part of the FrAC module. The entry in question is that for the word ἀνώμαλος 'uneven, irregular', from which the English word *anomalous* derives, see Fig. 4.

We will focus on the first sense of the word (the sense preceded by a bold capital letter 'A') which has 9 attestations, for some of which links are given. We will look at the TEI-XML source for the first three of these, see Fig. 5. The `<cit>` element is described as containing "a quotation

---

[9]https://tools.ietf.org/html/rfc5147, http://persistence.uni-leipzig.org/nlp2rdf/

[10]https://www.w3.org/TR/annotation-model/

[11]Text Encoding Initiative, https://tei-c.org/

[12]http://www.perseus.tufts.edu/hopper/text.jsp?doc=Perseus:text:1999.04.0057

```
▼<cit>
   <quote lang="greek">χώρα</quote>
  ▼<bibl n="Perseus:abo:tlg,0059,034:625d" default="NO" valid="yes">
     <author>Pl.</author>
     <title>Lg.</title>
     <biblScope>625d</biblScope>
  </bibl>
 </cit>
 ;
▼<cit>
   <quote lang="greek">φύσις</quote>
  ▼<bibl n="Perseus:abo:tlg,0059,031:58a" default="NO" valid="yes">
     <author>Id.</author>
     <title>Ti.</title>
     <biblScope>58a</biblScope>
  </bibl>
 </cit>
 ;
▼<cit>
   <quote lang="greek">τὸ ἀ. τῆς ναυμαχίας</quote>
  ▼<bibl n="Perseus:abo:tlg,0003,001:7:71" default="NO" valid="yes">
     <author>Th.</author>
     <biblScope>7.71</biblScope>
  </bibl>
 </cit>
```

Figure 5: The TEI encoding for ἀνώμαλος

from some other document, together with a bibliographic reference to its source". Additionally, in dictionaries it "may contain an example text with at least one occurrence of the word form, used in the sense being described, or a translation of the headword, or an example"; this obviously fits the citation in the third attestation. Note that in each case the quotation itself is contained within a `<quote>` element and the bibliographic reference in the `<bibl>` element. In cases where there isn't a quotation, as in, for example, the fourth, fifth and sixth attestations in the entry, the `<bibl>` element has been used by itself. In fact there is no single mechanism for representing attestations in TEI since, depending on the particular feature content in a dictionary, and the practice of the project regarding bibliographic information, a number of different mechanisms can be used including: `<cit>`, `<bibl>`, `<ref>` as well as pointer attributes like `@source`.[13]

In the FrAC module, however, our proposal is to define a generic mechanism to model the fact that a given lexical phenomenon, i.e., a given word sense, form, subcategorisation and valency information, etc., described in a lexical resource is attested to by a text, and to distinguish this from other kinds of citations. Returning to the example given above, looking at the first sense we see the following:

- Instances of attestations for words both with and without associated quotations;
- Instances of attestations where the quotation contains the headword and others where it does not;
- An instance of an attestation where the text referred to is conjectural (it has been reconstructed and may or may not be accurate), marked by the Latin *cj.*;
- A citation (marked as 'cf.', an abbreviation for the Latin *confere* 'compare') which may not be an attestation of the sense in question.

In the following we will make some remarks on the OntoLex-FrAC encoding of the example in RDF; the whole example is available on the Github repository. Listing below presents the entry with frequency information which lists its frequency in a corpus, which in this case is composed of Strabo's *Geography*:

```
:lsjEntry_ent_n10947 a ontolex:LexicalEntry;
   frac:frequency [
      a frac:CorpusFrequency;
      rdf:value "18"^^xsd:int
      frac:corpus
      <http://www.perseus.tufts.edu/hopper/text?
      doc=Perseus:text:1999.01.0197>] .
```

The first sense here is associated with 9 frac:Attestation resources:

```
:sense_n10947_0 a ontolex:LexicalSense ;
   frac:attestation :att_n10947_0_bib0,
      :att_n10947_0_bib1,
      :att_n10947_0_bib2,
      :att_n10947_0_bib3,
      :att_n10947_0_bib5,
      :att_n10947_0_bib6,
      :att_n10947_0_bib7,
      :att_n10947_0_bib8,
      :att_n10947_0_bib9 ;
ontolex:isSenseOf :lsjEntry_ent_n10947 .
```

The first attestation is encoded in RDF as follows:

```
:att_n10947_0_bib0 a frac:Attestation ;
   cito:hasCitedEntity :n10947_0_bib0 ;
   att:hasBiblScope "625d" ;
   att:attestationGloss
      "uneven, irregular "χωρα" Pl.Lg.625d".
```

Here we can see the use of a new datatype properties which complement the newly proposed FrAC properties. The first `hasBiblScope` is directly inspired by the corresponding TEI element `<biblScope>` which is defined as giving the "scope of a bibliographic reference". The listing also demonstrates the use of the FrAC property `attestationGloss` which gives the exact written text accompanying an attestation (this is important in the case of legacy and retrodigitized resources). We also use the property `hasCitedEntity` from the CITO vocabulary[14] (Peroni and Shotton, 2012) to link the attestation to a bibliographic record `:n10947_0_bib0` (the latter is described using the FRBR vocabulary). The second attestation is represented as follows in RDF with FrAC:

```
:att_n10947_0_bib2 a frac:Attestation ;
   cito:hasCitedEntity :n10947_0_bib2 ;
   att:hasBiblScope "7.71" ;
   frac:quotation "το α. τηςναυμαχιας" ;
   att:attestationGloss "'το α. τηςναυμαχιας'..." ;
   rdfs:seeAlso :cit_n10947_0_1, :cit_n10947_0_2;
   :conjectural 'True' .
```

Note the use of the `quotation` property here (since the quotation in the attestation gloss includes the word itself), as well as the use of `conjectural` here. We also use the rdfs property `seeAlso` to encode the two citations `cit_n10947_0_1` and `cit_n10947_0_2`.

4.2. Attestations in DiaMaNT

DiaMaNT (*Diachroon seMAntisch lexicon van de Nederlandse Taal*), is a diachronic semantic computational lexicon of Dutch, currently under development at the *Instituut voor de Nederlandse Taal* (Dutch Language Institute). This lexicon is the third component of the lexicographical infrastructure for historical Dutch, which is being developed at the Institute. The core of the infrastructure is formed by the four scholarly historical dictionaries of Dutch: the *Woordenboek der Nederlandsche Taal (WNT)* (Dictionary

---

[13]Personal Communication, Jack Bowers.

[14]https://sparontologies.github.io/cito/current/cito.html

of the Dutch Language), the *Middelnederlandsch Woordenboek (MNW)* (Dictionary of Middle Dutch), the *Vroegmiddelnederlands Woordenboek (VMNW)* (Early Middle Dutch Dictionary) and the *Oudnederlands Woordenboek (ONW)* (Dictionary of Old Dutch). The four dictionaries cover a language period from ca. 500 – 1976.

The first component of this infrastructure is the historical dictionary portal. The portal gives online access to the dictionaries so that a user can look up the meaning of a word. The second component is the morphosyntactic lexicon GiGaNT, containing information on possible variation in spelling and form of historical Dutch language, by means of which searching in historical texts was made easier. The third component is the DiaMaNT lexicon. It forms a layer on top of GiGaNT. It aims to resolve the issue of historical semantic variation. The main purpose of this lexicon is to enhance text accessibility and to foster research in the development of concepts, by interrelating attested word forms and semantic units (concepts), and tracing semantic variation through time. Core of the DiaMaNT lexicon is on the one hand the senses of the dictionaries and on the other hand the attestations. The latter give information as to the time period a certain sense occurred in. A first Linked Open Data version (Depuydt and de Does, 2018) has been elaborated and published in the Dutch CLARIAH infrastructure. The DiaMaNT lexicon is also available at `http://diamant.ivdnt.org/diamant-ui/`. For an example of the use of the attestations, see Fig. 6.

An excerpt of the lexicon using the FrAC module to model attestations is presented in Listing 3.

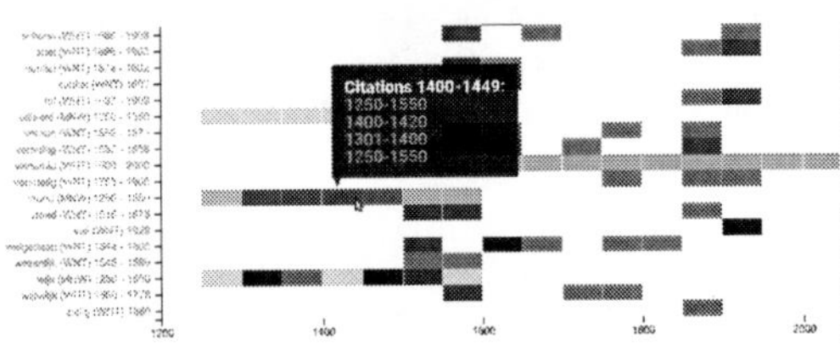

Figure 6: Application: chronology of synonyms; the DiaMaNT lexicon.

4.3. Attestations in the DOE Web Corpus

The Dictionary of Old English Web Corpus (DOEC) has been compiled for the Dictionary of Old English at the University of Toronto and consists of "at least one copy of every surviving Old English text" (diPaolo Healey et al., 2009), amounting to over 3 million written words.

Originally available as a set of TEI-XML files, the DOEC is currently accessible online as a Web corpus.

In this paper, we will illustrate modelling an attestation in DOEC of a lexical sense described in the Thesaurus of Old English (Roberts et al., 2000). The thesaurus provides an onomasiological ordering of the lexis that was available to speakers of Old English. This ordering allows users to traverse a hierarchy of meanings, described in present-day English, to Old English lexical items that express that meaning. This information has recently been transformed to Linguistic Linked Data (Stolk, 2019). This new form of the

Listing 3: Representation of attestations in the DiaMaNT lexicon

```
diamant:entry_WNT_M030758 a ontolex:LexicalEntry ;
  ontolex:sense diamant:sense_WNT_M030758_bet_207 .

diamant:sense_WNT_M030758_bet_207 a ontolex:LexicalSense;
  rdfs:label "V.-" ;
  frac:attestation diamant:attestation_2108540 ;
  skos:definition "Iemand een kat (of de kat)
                   aan het been jagen .... iemand
                   in moeilijkheden brengen." .

diamant:attestation_2108540 a frac:Attestation ;
  cito:hasCitedEntity diamant:cited_document_WNT_332819 ;
  cito:hasCitingEntity diamant:sense_WNT_M030758_bet_207;
  frac:locus diamant:locus_2108540 ;
  frac:quotation "... dat men licht yemant de cat
                  aen het been kan werpen," .

diamant:locus_2108540 a diamant:Occurrence ;
  nif:beginIndex 107 ;
  nif:endIndex 110 .

diamant:cited_document_WNT_332819
  frbr:Manifestation ;
  frbr:embodimentOf diamant:expression_WNT_332819 ;
  diamant:witnessYearFrom 1621 ;
  diamant:witnessYearTo 1621 .

diamant:expression_WNT_332819 a frbr:Expression ;
  dcterms:creator "N. V. REIGERSB." ;
  dcterms:title "Brieven van Nicolaes
                 van Reigersberch aan Hugo de Groot" ;
  frbr:embodiment diamant:quotation_WNT_332819 .
```

lexicographic work offers identifiers (or IRIs) for its concepts of meaning, its lexical entries, and its lexical senses. Thus, the single recorded sense of the entry *gēardagum* in TOE has its own IRI and is categorized under the concept named "Formerly, long ago".[15] Listing 5 shows an RDF sample of the entry, its sense, and the concept that expresses its meaning.

The lexical sense of *gēardagum* in TOE is attested in a number of Old English texts, including the poem *Beowulf*. In fact, its first occurrence is in the second line of the single surviving copy of the poem. Listing 4 shows that very occurrence, in bold, as it is presented in the DOEC.

The URL that provides access to the information above, is the following: `https://tapor.library.utoronto.ca/doecorpus/cgi-bin/oec-idx?type=bigger&byte=982592&q1=geardagum` . This Web address includes information on the type of visualization (i.e., 'type=bigger'), the location of the current corpus reference (i.e., 'byte=982592') and the query string to highlight using a bold font (i.e., 'geardagum'). The type of visualization, as can be seen in the snippet, includes a small context surrounding the currently selected token in the corpus. The three lines are preceded by sentence numbering in *Beowulf* (i.e., 0001, 0002, and 0003 respectively) and the line number on which the given sentence starts in the manuscript (i.e., 1, 1, and 4 respectively).

Rather than duplicating all the information from DOEC on

---

[15]Information on this lexical sense in the linguistic linked data form of A Thesaurus of Old English has been made available on the digital platform Evoke: `http://evoke.ullet.net/app/#/view?source=toe&iri=http://oldenglishthesaurus.arts.gla.ac.uk/sense/%23id%3D21808`.

Listing 4: Snippet from DOEC on *geardagum* in the first lines of the Old English poem *Beowulf*

```
[0001 (1)] Hwæt.
[0002 (1)] We Gardena in geardagum, þeodcyninga, þrym gefrunon, hu ða æþelingas ellen fremedon.
[0003 (4)] Oft Scyld Scefing <sceaþena> þreatum, monegum mægþum, meodosetla ofteah, egsode eorlas.
```

Listing 5: RDF sample of TOE as linguistic linked data

```
@base <http://oldenglishthesaurus.arts.gla.ac.uk/> .

<entry/#id=21808> a ontolex:LexicalEntry ;
    rdfs:label "gēardagum"@ang ;
    ontolex:canonicalForm [
        ontolex:writtenRep "gēardagum"@ang
    ] ;
    ontolex:sense <sense/#id=21808> .

<sense/#id=21808> a ontolex:LexicalSense ;
    ontolex:isLexicalizedSenseOf <category/#id=9880> .

<category/#id=9880> a ontolex:LexicalConcept ;
    skos:prefLabel "Formerly, long ago"@eng .
```

Listing 6: RDF representing the attestation in DOEC of the lexical sense of *gēardagum* from TOE

```
@base <http://oldenglishthesaurus.arts.gla.ac.uk/> .

ex:attestation412 a oa:Annotation ;
    oa:motivation oa:identifying ;
    oa:hasBody <sense/#id=21808> ;
    oa:hasTarget [
        # the source corpus is DOEC
        oa:hasSource
            <https://tapor.library.utoronto.ca/doecorpus/> ;
        # for selecting the entire sentence in DOEC
        oa:hasSelector [
            a oa:TextPositionSelector ;
            oa:start 982592 ;
            oa:end 982708 ;
        ] ;
        # for selecting the exact token in DOEC
        oa:hasSelector [
            a oa:TextPositionSelector ;
            oa:start 982607 ;
            oa:end 982616 ; ] ; ] .
```

the context of the particular attestation of *gēardagum* in the thesaurus, it would be more valuable to link that information to the relevant lexical sense in the thesaurus instead. Doing so will enable users from either resource to benefit from the complementary information provided by the other resource. Moreover, an additional advantage is that no licensing rights are violated in this manner: links between the two sources would simply refer to them without redistributing their content. Those who have the right to access the material can simply follow these links (from one resource to another) or query them integrally if they also have the means to do so. In this specific case, links such as the one proposed will allow for further examinations of both the accuracy of the definitions in the lexicographic resource and the aspects of, for instance, the distribution and frequency of specific senses as found in a body of texts. Thus, lexicographers and corpus linguists can benefit from these connections.

One of the approaches explored with the FrAC module for modelling attestations in corpora (most notably online corpora) is to use the standardized Web Annotation vocabulary. This vocabulary, published in 2017, was developed by W3C. The vocabulary offers terminology to indicate a selection that one wishes to annotate. For the current case, we use a TextPositionSelector to indicate the start and end of our selection within the entire corpus of DOEC. For the sentence in which *gēardagum* occurs, this selection would start at 982592 (i.e., the value embedded as 'byte' in the URL for the DOEC snippet above) and end at 982708. If we were to select solely the token, however, the selection should start 15 characters (or bytes) later and be 9 characters (or bytes) long.

Thus, the selection would start at 982607 and end at 982616. Listing 6 shows the resulting RDF for both options. The body of the annotation is the lexical sense from TOE; its target is the selection of the token (or its sentence) in DOEC. The motivation for the annotation is one of 'identifying', indicating that the lexical sense offers details on the identity of the selection. Selecting the token in DOEC only, rather than its entire sentence, is preferable since it

allows for fine-grained analyses. Additionally, feeding this more accurate starting position to the DOEC interface (i.e., embedding it as 'byte' in the URL) does not pose any issues: The website of the online corpus still presents the user with an appropriate context for this more accurate selection. In conclusion, the use-case of DOEC shows that the Web Annotation vocabulary provides enough expressivity to capture attestations in corpora.

5. Conclusion

In this paper, we introduced the OntoLex-FrAC vocabulary, an OntoLex extension for representation of frequency, attestation and corpus information for the needs of digital lexicography, natural language processing and corpus linguistics. We described its structure, some selected use cases, elementary concepts and fundamental definitions, with a specific focus on frequency and attestations.

The main goal of the paper is to document the progress achieved so far, and even more importantly, to elicit feedback from the language resource community.

The next step is to reach a consensus for representing additional corpus information such as collocations and similarity scores. Another important direction is to apply the model on a larger scale to further test its applicability.

Acknowledgements

This paper is supported by the Horizon 2020 research and innovation programme with the projects Prêt-à-LLOD (grant agreement no. 825182) and ELEXIS (grant agreeement no. 731015). It is also partially based upon work from COST Action CA18209 - NexusLinguarum "European network for Web-centred linguistic data science". We also thank the anonymous reviewers for their helpful comments.

6. References

Cimiano, P., McCrae, J. P., and Buitelaar, P. (2016). Lexicon Model for Ontologies: Community Report.

Declerck, T., McCrae, J., Hartung, M., Gracia, J., Chiarcos, C., Montiel, E., Cimiano, P., Revenko, A., Sauri, R., Lee, D., Racioppa, S., Nasir, J., Orlikowski, M., Lanau-Coronas, M., Fäth, C., Rico, M., Elahi, M. F., Khvalchik, M., Gonzalez, M., and Cooney, K. (2020). Recent developments for the linguistic linked open data infrastructure. In Nicoletta Calzolari, et al., editors, *Proceedings of the Twelfth International Conference on Language Resources and Evaluation (LREC 2020)*. ELRA, ELRA, 5.

Depuydt, K. and de Does, J. (2018). The Diachronic Semantic Lexicon of Dutch as Linked Open Data. In *Proceedings of the Eleventh International Conference on Language Resources and Evaluation (LREC 2018)*, Paris, France, May. European Language Resources Association (ELRA).

diPaolo Healey, A., Wilkin, J. P., and Xiang, X. (2009). Dictionary of Old English Web Corpus.

Khan, A. F. and Boschetti, F. (2018). Towards a Representation of Citations in Linked Data Lexical Resources. In Jaka Čibej, et al., editors, *Proceedings of the XVIII EURALEX International Congress: Lexicography in Global Contexts*, pages 137–147, Ljubljana, Slovenia, July. Ljubljana University Press, Faculty of Arts.

Kilgarriff, A. (1997). "I Don't Believe in Word Senses". *Computers and the Humanities*, 31(2):91–113.

Krek, S., McCrae, J., Kosem, I., Wissek, T., Tiberius, C., Navigli, R., and Sandford Pedersen, B. (2019). European lexicographic infrastructure (elexis). In *Proceedings of the XVIII EURALEX International Congress on Lexicography in Global Contexts*, pages 881–892.

Kučera, H. and Francis, W. N. (1967). *Computational Analysis of Present-day American English*. Brown University Press.

Liddell, H., Scott, R., and Jones, H. S. (1996). *A Greek-English lexicon*. Oxford University Press, 9th edition.

McCrae, J., de Cea, G. A., Buitelaar, P., Cimiano, P., Declerck, T., Gómez-Pérez, A., Gracia, J., Hollink, L., Montiel-Ponsoda, E., Spohr, D., and Wunner, T. (2012). Interchanging lexical resources on the Semantic Web. *Language Resources and Evaluation*, 46(6):701–709.

Peroni, S. and Shotton, D. (2012). Fabio and cito: ontologies for describing bibliographic resources and citations. *Web Semantics: Science, Services and Agents on the World Wide Web*, 17:33–43.

Roberts, J., Kay, C., and Grundy, L. (2000). *A Thesaurus of Old English: In Two Volumes*. Rodopi.

Saur, K. (1998). Ifla study group on the functional requirements for bibliographic records. functional requirements for bibliographic records: final report.

Stolk, S. (2019). A Thesaurus of Old English as linguistic linked data: Using OntoLex, SKOS and lemon-tree to bring topical thesauri to the Semantic Web. In *Proceedings of the eLex 2019 conference*, pages 223–247, oct.

Proceedings of the Globalex Workshop on Linked Lexicography, pages 10–19
Language Resources and Evaluation Conference (LREC 2020), Marseille, 11–16 May 2020
© European Language Resources Association (ELRA), licensed under CC-BY-NC

SynSemClass Linked Lexicon: Mapping Synonymy between Languages

Zdeňka Urešová, Eva Fučíková, Eva Hajičová, Jan Hajič
Charles University, Faculty of Mathematics and Physics
Institute of Formal and Applied Linguistics
Malostranské nám. 25
11800 Prague 1, Czech Republic
{uresova,fucikova,hajicova,hajic}@ufal.mff.cuni.cz

Abstract

This paper reports on an extended version of a synonym verb class lexicon, newly called SynSemClass (formerly CzEngClass). This lexicon stores cross-lingual semantically similar verb senses in synonym classes extracted from a richly annotated parallel corpus, the Prague Czech-English Dependency Treebank. When building the lexicon, we make use of predicate-argument relations (valency) and link them to semantic roles; in addition, each entry is linked to several external lexicons of more or less "semantic" nature, namely FrameNet, WordNet, VerbNet, OntoNotes and PropBank, and Czech VALLEX. The aim is to provide a linguistic resource that can be used to compare semantic roles and their syntactic properties and features across languages within and across synonym groups (classes, or 'synsets'), as well as gold standard data for automatic NLP experiments with such synonyms, such as synonym discovery, feature mapping, etc. However, perhaps the most important goal is to eventually build an event type ontology that can be referenced and used as a human-readable and human-understandable "database" for all types of events, processes and states. While the current paper describes primarily the content of the lexicon, we are also presenting a preliminary design of a format compatible with Linked Data, on which we are hoping to get feedback during discussions at the workshop. Once the resource (in whichever form) is applied to corpus annotation, deep analysis will be possible using such combined resources as training data.

Keywords: Linked Lexicon, Linked Data, Semantics, Syntax, Synonymy, Parallel Corpus

1. Introduction

The aim of the presented research is to create a linked lexicon of bilingual Czech-English synonyms, now openly available in version 1.0 (Urešová et al., 2019). Synonyms are extracted from translated texts of the Prague Czech-English Dependency Treebank corpus. A functionally adequate relationship in terms of translation must exist between the meaning of the English and the Czech verbs, i.e., the English and the Czech verb(s) are considered synonymous in the given context(s) if the translated verb adequately expresses the functional intent of the original. We aim for each synonym class to be characterized both meaning-wise (verb sense(s), semantic roles) and structurally (valency arguments) by linking (mapping) semantic roles and valency members (Role ↔ Argument mapping).

This paper synthesizes previous work on the lexicon to comprehensively describe its version 1.0 published in connection with this paper (and under a new name that reflects future direction from bilingual to multilingual entries), but it also adds - on top of a comprehensive description of lexicon structure and the process of its creation - a number of interannotator agreement evaluation experiments (Sect. 4) and a first attempt at defining a Linked Data scheme for it (Sect. 5).

The paper is structured as follows. In Sect. 2, structure and content of the lexicon are described. The resources used and linked to are presented in Sect. 3. Sect. 4 contains a description of the process by which the lexicon has been created, i.e., the annotation process and interannotator agreement (IAA) analysis. The principles of (re)structuring and (re)formatting the links to Linked Data format are described in Sect. 5, and related work is described in Sect. 6. We summarize our work and outline future plans in Sect. 7.

2. Structure and Content of the Lexicon

The SynSemClass lexicon - formerly CzEngClass, whose previous preliminary versions as well as various aspects of its theoretical basis and the annotation process are described in (Urešová et al., 2019a; Urešová et al., 2018a; Urešová et al., 2018e; Urešová et al., 2018d; Urešová et al., 2018c; Urešová et al., 2018b) - builds upon the PCEDT parallel corpus (Sect. 3.1) and the existing internal resources, namely CzEngVallex, PDT-Vallex, and EngVallex lexicons (Sect. 3.2). On top of that, other lexical databases, namely FrameNet, VerbNet, PropBank, OntoNotes and WordNet (Sect. 3.2) are used as additional sources, and links are annotated and kept between their entries and the SynSemClass entries. The overall scheme of the lexicon with an example of one class entry is depicted in Fig. 1.

Each synonym class contains Czech and English verbs (verb senses) that have similar meaning. The latest version of SynSemClass captures 3515 verb senses with 2027 on the English and 1488 on the Czech side. The synonymous senses are represented as valency frames (of generally different verbs) and they are called Class Members.

Each class is assigned a common set of semantic roles, called a Roleset. A Roleset contains the core "situational participants" common for all the Class Members in one class. When determining Class Membership for a potential candidate verb (sense), the Roleset also serves as a source of context information: if all the semantic roles from the Roleset can be mapped to valency slots (labeled by a "functor" in the valency theory (Panevová, 1974) within the Functional Generative Description, or FGD (Sgall et al., 1986), framework) for the given verb sense as recorded in its valency frame in the appropriate valency lexicon (and vice versa), it is deemed–together with the approximate sense match to the other Class Members–as belonging to

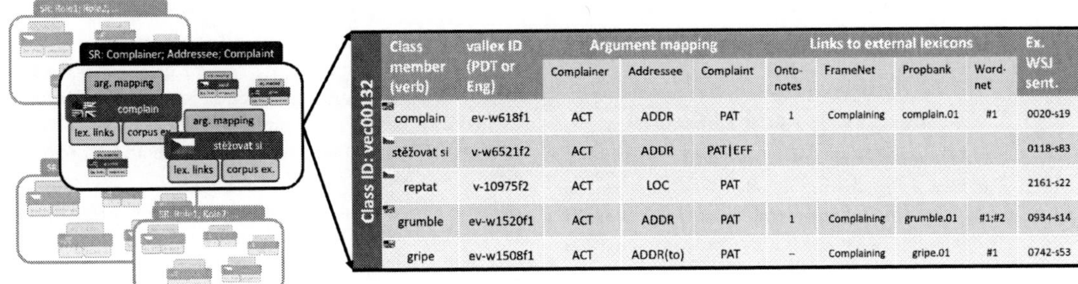

Figure 1: The overall scheme of the SynSemClass lexicon and an example of a class ("complain-stěžovat si")

that synonym class. As a result, each Class Member has its valency frame slots mapped to the semantic roles kept in that class' Roleset.[1] The valency frames of different Class Members of one SynSemClass class are thus "compatible" through the mapping to the Roleset, even if they possibly differ in their argument labels (valency slot functors).

Some typical Rolesets:

- Class "klesnout-decline": Item, Initial_value, Final_value, Difference
- Class "nabídnout-offer": Offerer, Recipient, Entity_offered, Entity_received
- Class "chránit-defend": Defender, Asset_Patient, Harmful_situation

While the role labeling system is still preliminary, we strive to have the names semantically descriptive in nature (i.e., Offerer instead of Agent), and we keep the convention that for better human understanding, we use an underscore for signalling an "or" when the following word is capitalized (as in Asset_Patient), as opposed to a mere use of multiple words to describe the role, in which case the next word is not capitalized (Final_value).

When mapping the roles from a given Roleset, each of the roles must be mapped to "something" from the valency frame of a verb in that class; that "something" may be

- either a member of the valency frame,
- or any other free modification to which the given semantic role might be mapped,
- or a proxy semantic participant (#any, #sb, #sth).

Conversely, each member of the valency frame of a verb listed in the given synonymous class must be mapped to a semantic role from the assigned Roleset.[2] If any member of the valency frame of a potential Class Member of the given synonymous class really cannot be mapped to the chosen Roleset of that class, then that candidate Class Member cannot be included in the class.

Class Members are further linked to the original resources used (the parallel Czech-English treebank and the Czech and English valency lexicons) and also to other external resources (see Sect. 3).

A simplified example of the synonym class "complain–stěžovat si" is shown in Fig. 1. It schematically shows the SynSemClass lexicon on the left with its entries (= classes), and an example synonym class in the form of a table with the additional annotation available for this entry. Most importantly, the table shows the Argument mapping between the roles in the common Roleset for this class (which in this case contains three semantic roles: Complainer, Addressee (of the complaint) and Complaint) and the individual Class Members' arguments from the PDT-Vallex and EngVallex lexicons. While in most cases the mapping is straightforward (as is the case of the valency slot ACT, which is mapped to Complainer for all the Class Members shown in Fig. 1), in some cases there is a need to specify certain restrictions (e.g., restrict the mapping between ADDR and Addressee to the use of the preposition "to") or a combination of arguments (slot names) mapped to a single semantic role (PAT|EFF is mapped to Complaint for the Czech Class Member "stěžovat si"). For more details about this mapping and its annotation, see Sect. 4.3.

The links to external resources follow - for English, they contain the OntoNotes sense number (e.g., 1, or a hyphen if no OntoNotes sense to map to is available for the given verb sense), FrameNet frame name (Complaining), Prop-Bank roleset number (e.g., gripe.01) and WordNet sense number (e.g., #1). Alternatives may exist (e.g., for Word-Net senses - see grumble, which maps to both grumble#1 as well as grumble#2 in WordNet). Czech verbs are linked only to the VALLEX lexicon (Lopatková et al., 2016), and in the future, they will also map to Czech WordNet.

Examples are selected from the available corpora, in this case from the Prague Czech English Dependency Treebank (PCEDT), which is a parallel version of the WSJ part of the Penn Treebank (WSJ section and sentence ID number is used in Fig. 1, see also Sect. 3.1). These examples are selected so that they best characterize the corresponding verb sense as included in the particular class.

The extended version of SynSemClass (Urešová et al., 2019) is openly available in the LINDAT/CLARIN repository[3] contains 145 synonym classes with 3515 verbs fully

---

[1]This 'perfect' 1:1 mapping has to be relaxed in specific cases, see e.g., (Urešová et al., 2018a).

[2]There is only one exception to this rule: If the valency frame of an English Class Member includes a non-obligatory free modification (which is not in line with the FGD rules), it may not (but can) be taken into account in the mapping and when the Roleset is created.

[3]http://hdl.handle.net/11234/1-3125

annotated in Step 2, out of which 57 classes are also annotated in Step 3. For more details on the annotation process and its Steps see Sect. 4.

3. Resources Used and Linked to

In this section, we describe the main corpus used as the source of evidence for creating the SynSemClass lexicon entries (= the synonym classes), and the lexical resources used for both identifying the Class Members as well as linking them to the external lexicons.

3.1. The Corpus

As described in previous papers on this resource (Urešová et al., 2019a; Urešová et al., 2018a; Urešová et al., 2018e; Urešová et al., 2018c; Urešová et al., 2018b), for evidence examples, we use the parallel Prague Czech-English Dependency Treebank 2.0 (PCEDT 2.0) (Hajič et al., 2012). This corpus contains approx. 50 thousand aligned sentence pairs. The English side is the WSJ part of the Penn treebank (Marcus et al., 1993); it has been translated to Czech by professional translators. Each language part is enhanced with a rich manual linguistic annotation in the Prague Dependency Treebank (PDT 2.0) style (Hajič et al., 2006; Hajič et al., 2018) which is based on the Functional Generative Dependency (FGD) framework (Sgall et al., 1986). For the purpose of our work, it is important that the annotation captures aligned surface dependency trees and deep syntactico-semantic (tectogrammatical) trees across the two languages on sentence and node levels. Moreover, at the deep (tectogrammatical) layer, each verb node (occurrence) is assigned a valency frame, also representing a verb sense, by way of using its ID which identifies it in the associated valency lexicons, PDT-Vallex and EngVallex (Sect. 3.2).

3.2. Linked Lexical Resources

When building the synonym classes, we proceed from the PDT-style valency lexicons which are an integral part of the PCEDT. The existing annotation of PCEDT by the valency lexicon entries has helped to seed the SynSemClass lexicon and also to get real-world examples. For Czech verbs, PCEDT uses the Czech valency lexicon called PDT-Vallex (Urešová et al., 2014), (Urešová, 2011), while for English verbs, the English valency lexicon EngVallex (Cinková et al., 2014) is used. The most important links come from the CzEngVallex lexicon (Urešová et al., 2015), (Urešová et al., 2016), a bilingual valency lexicon which combines PDT-Vallex and EngVallex entries and contains not only Czech and English verbs which are translation equivalents to each other but it also captures mapping among their valency arguments.

The individual Class Members in SynSemClass are further mapped to the following external lexical resources: FrameNet (Baker et al., 1998; Fillmore et al., 2003), VerbNet (Schuler, 2006), PropBank (Palmer et al., 2005), senses from OntoNotes Groups (Pradhan and Xue, 2009), English WordNet[4] and Czech Vallex (Lopatková et al., 2016).[5]

---

[4]https://wordnet.princeton.edu
[5]https://ufal.mff.cuni.cz/vallex/3.5

4. Creating the Lexicon

SynSemClass is being built strictly "bottom-up", i.e., from the corpus and existing lexical resources towards the new synonym lexicon. Since the lexicon is a complex resource, we divide its creation and annotation of its entries into three "areas": (1) determining which verbs should go into one class (Class Members), (2) determining the common set of semantic roles for each class and mapping it to valency for each Class Member, and (3) adding links to other existing lexical resources.

These three areas are intertwined and influence each other - for example, while linking a Class Member to the other lexical resources the annotator might realize that the Class Member should go to a different class, or that the class should be split into two, or merged etc., but overall, this "division of work" allows us to describe the structure of the lexicon and the annotation process more clearly.

The tasks to be performed to get full annotation and meet all the objectives in all of the three areas are even more complex. Going "bottom-up", i.e., starting from the PCEDT corpus, we proceed in four steps, interspersing automatic and manual phases.

In the automatic phases, the PCEDT corpus is used to get preliminary Class Membership and valency information for both Czech and English verbs.

In the manual phases, many (sub)tasks are performed for each class, all of them for verbs in both languages (Czech and English):

- pruning the preliminary Class Members in each class, eliminating clear misalignments and/or sense mismatches,

- creation (Step 1) and possible amendment (Steps 2 and 3, see below) of the set of semantic roles for each class (the Roleset),

- linking (mapping) semantic roles to valency members for each verb in the class, with possible restrictions on the semantics of the arguments,

- selecting the most appropriate examples from the corpus to accompany each Class Member,

- adding links to the external lexical resources.

4.1. The Annotation Process

The annotation process has been sequenced into an initial automatic seed selection step (Step 0) and three followup steps (Steps 1-3), each consisting of an automatic phase (pre-assignment of verbs from the aligned parallel corpus to the classes, as populated in the previous step), and a manual pruning and annotation phase (Fig. 2).

We will refer to these Steps later when describing the results, including inter-annotator agreement in the three annotation "areas".

These steps can be briefly described as follows (Fig. 2):

- Step 0: An automatic semi-random selection of 200 Czech verbs (frames or verb senses from the Czech valency lexicon) which provisionally denote class names and form the initial set of classes, and which represent verbs (valency frames) of various frequencies in the parallel PCEDT corpus.

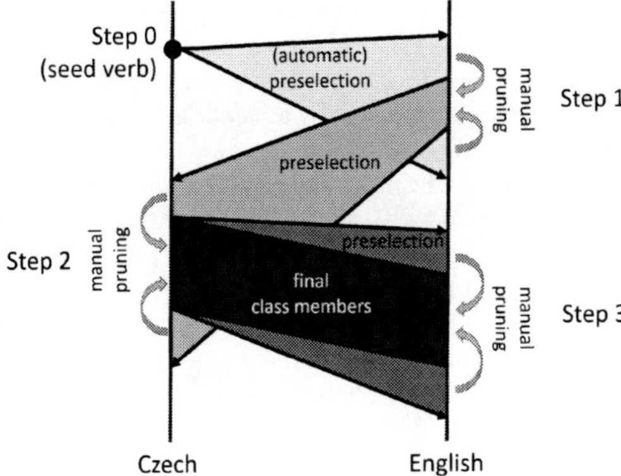

Figure 2: SynSemClass annotation process - major steps

- Step 1: For each of the provisional classes from Step 0 (containing just one Czech verb at this point), English verb translation counterparts have been automatically added based on the PCEDT corpus' (automatic) word alignments. This pre-selection has been followed by the manual phase, when Class Members have been pruned (using a five-point Likert scale, transformed then to binary membership decisions (Sect. 4.2.1)), a common Roleset has been created for the class, argument mapping and external links to English resources have been built as well as mapping restrictions and notes, and the appropriate English examples from the PCEDT have been chosen.

- Step 2: Czech translation counterparts of English verbs retained and annotated in Step 1 have been added in the automatic phase of this Step. Similarly to Step 1, these verbs have then been manually pruned, mappings to their arguments from the Roleset has been established (possibly amending the Roleset when necessary), and this argument mapping, plus restrictions, notes, external links and examples have been added for the newly selected Czech verbs.

- Step 3: English translation counterparts of the Czech verbs retained as Class Members for all the classes remaining after Steps 1 and 2 (after merging certain duplicate classes in the process, as described in (Urešová et al., 2019b)), except for the initial Czech verb from Step 0, have been added. Again, these pre-selected Class Members have been manually pruned, mappings to their arguments from the Roleset have been established (possibly amending the Roleset again when necessary), and argument mapping restrictions, notes, external links and examples have been added for the newly selected English verbs. This third step has been added after inspecting the results of Step 2 - it was apparent that the composition of each class was skewed towards containing more Czech than English verbs, which has been corrected by adding the additional English verbs in this Step. While it might seem that there is now again more English verbs than the Czech ones, manual inspection shows that this is due

to the richer verb vocabulary used in the original text, while the Czech translation has been more uniform. No "Step 4" is thus planned.

In each Step, adjustments in the results of the previous Step(s) have been allowed. Specifically, after Step 2, it was clear that some of the original seeds (Czech verbs from Step 0) have been expanded to very similar or almost identical classes; therefore these classes have then been merged, reducing the overall number of classes. Such global operations, as well as the resolution of any disagreement between the annotators, have been done by a single adjudicator, who might also have modified or better exemplified the issues in the annotation guidelines.

Also, such modifications might further concern the Roleset, mappings of arguments to semantic roles, or the links to the other lexical resources.

The decision which roles to select for a given synonym class cannot be inferred easily from any single Class Member. Often, it is only during the annotation of all additional potential Class Members (as added in Steps 2 and 3) that the semantic character of each Class (and its Class Members) becomes clear, and some amendment has to be done in order to keep consistency at the level of "semantic depth" of the semantic roles (SRs) used. While the SRs are mostly taken from FrameNet, sometimes their labels have to be modified to fit the properties of the synonym class. Currently, there are 123 SRs taken from FrameNet and 49 SRs have a specific SynSemClass label; we are also using some of the ideas from previous work on comparison of semantic roles, such as (Aguilar et al., 2014).

In addition, the Roleset composition and annotation is very closely related to the mapping of valency slots of the valency frame for each Class Member to the individual semantic roles (Sect. 2, Sect. 4.3). It could even change the decisions made during the Class Membership inclusion/exclusion (Sect. 4), since if no mapping between the Roleset and the valency frame can be established, the verb must be excluded from the class.[6]

4.2. Determining Class Membership

4.2.1. Interannotator Agreement

In (Urešová et al., 2018d), the first interannotator agreement experiment was described where 8 annotators were determining Class Membership of the automatically preselected list of English verbal translation equivalents (total of 544 English verbs, as inserted by the automatic phase of Step 1) for 60 of the Czech seed verb senses (as selected in Step 0). In that experiment, the annotators had to prune the English Class Member candidates by checking the corpus examples through the CzEngVallex valency argument alignments, i.e., their usage in context. They could select not only Yes or No, but also a tentative Yes or No (Rather Yes, Rather No) and also a special value "Delete", which was used to signify a total mismatch (wrong underlying corpus alignment, in most cases); they were thus using sort of a 5-point Likert scale, mapped back to binary decisions (with

---

[6]In the actual annotation process, the annotators only report such a case and the final determination of deletion is being done by the adjudicator.

Yes and Rather Yes taken as a positive answer) for the IAA computation.

The agreement for the Class Membership, as described in (Urešová et al., 2018d), was as follows: Of the 544 datapoints the annotators (4 annotators for each decision, in our case) fully agreed in 358 cases (65.8%), which gives a good idea of the adjudication effort needed.[7]

For a pairwise comparison, we have used Cohen's kappa (Eq. 2), see also (Urešová et al., 2018d); macroaveraged over all annotator pairs, $\kappa = 0.44$.

The agreement as measured over all the annotators using Fleiss' kappa was $\kappa = 0.45$. While both the averaged Cohen's kappa as well as the Fleiss' kappa values are low, (Urešová et al., 2018d) also measured deviation from an average value on the full Likert scale used, and that value was surprisingly low (0.36 when the Yes-Rather Yes-...-Delete 5-point scale has been converted to values 4 to 0).

In Steps 2 and 3 (see intro to Sect. 4), we have concentrated on pairwise comparison, limited to three annotators (two of them continuing work from Step 1 and one new annotator). For those classes annotated by two annotators, we have computed mutual F_1 score (Eq. 1) (Jardine and van Rijsbergen, 1971) and Cohen's kappa κ (Eq. 2) (Cohen, 1960):[8]

$$F_1 = \frac{2PR}{P+R},\qquad(1)$$

where P is precision and R recall, and

$$\kappa = \frac{p_o - p_e}{1 - p_e}\qquad(2)$$

where p_o is the observed and p_e the expected probability, as estimated from the annotated data of the pair of annotators. We provide the numbers microaveraged over the n classes each annotator pair worked with, and then macroaveraged over the three pairs of annotators.

In Step 2, three annotators have been pruning the automatically preselected Czech verbs, using the same scale as in Step 1 (except now for Czech verbs). At least seven classes (498 verbs min.) have been double annotated by each pair of annotators, to measure the IAA. The pairwise results are summarized in Tab. 1; the macroaveraged F_1 score is 0.95, and the macroaveraged kappa value is 0.94.

Annotator	A_4	A_5	A_9
A_4	-	0.93 / 0.91	1.0 / 1.0
A_5		-	0.91 / 0.90
A_9			-

Table 1: F_1-measure / Cohen's kappa κ for Class Membership annotation in Step 2 (Czech verbs)

In Step 3, similarly to Step 2, several classes have been selected to double-annotate them to assess IAA, in this case on English verbs (Tab. 2). At least seven classes (169 verbs min.) have been annotated by a pair of annotators. One of the annotators for the multiple annotation experiment was a native speaker.[9] The macroaveraged F_1 score over the three pairs of annotators is 0.82, and the macroaveraged kappa value is 0.52. This is better than in Step 1 (which was also concerned with English verbs).

Annotator	A_4	A_6	A_9
A_4	-	0.79 / 0.52	0.83 / 0.49
A_6		-	0.84 / 0.56
A_9			-

Table 2: F_1-measure / Cohen's kappa κ for Class Membership annotation in Step 3 (English verbs)

It can be seen from these numbers that apparently determining Class Membership for English verbs is harder (results of Steps 1 and 3) than for the Czech verbs (Step 2). A natural explanation would be that Czech native speakers would be better aligned for determining Class Membership for the Czech verbs, but the numbers from Step 3, where one of the annotators was a native speaker of English, suggest that this might not necessarily be the case.

4.3. Mapping Semantic Roles to Valency

As described in Sect. 2, an important part of each synonym class is the Roleset, set of semantic roles that are shared among Class Members. To make sure that these SRs are applicable to all of them, there must exist a mapping between the valency frame slots of each Class Member and the SRs of that class' Roleset. This mapping was also done fully manually, for all the 3515 Class Members in the current version of SynSemClass. For some mapping examples, see Fig. 1 - e.g., the verb "grumble" (more precisely, the valency frame ev-w1502f1 for grumble) in the class "complain–stěžovat si" maps ACT to Complainer, ADDR to Addressee and PAT to Complaint.

4.3.1. Interannotator Agreement

For IAA in the Roleset-to-valency-slot mappings, we have computed a full match between an annotator pair (microaveraged over all verbs in the classes that were annotated by the two annotators), and then also matches for the individual valency slot labels, or functors (ACT, PAT, ADDR, EFF, ORIG, and "other" (all remaining) used in the valency frames). Only fully equivalent mapping of all (valency slot functor $\leftrightarrow$ semantic role) pairs counts as a correct complete match. Only agreement accuracy is computed, as the ratio of a number of complete matches between the two annotators to the number of Class Members considered as valid Class Members by both annotators (valid means that they annotated the Class Member as Yes or Rather Yes when

---

[7]The total agreement has been measured using all labels; i.e., if 3 annotators assigned No and 1 assigned Rather No, it did not count as full agreement.

[8]While Cohen's kappa is routinely used in IAA computation, we were curious how it differs from the F_1 measure, which is used for many tasks in NLP. Please note that there is (naturally) no true gold standard when computing IAA; the F_1 is symmetrical between the two annotators, with Precision and Recall swapped when computed in the opposite direction.

[9]This annotator was new to the project and had to learn the objectives, principles and concrete rules of annotation from the project documentation, but there has been enough learning period to consider the experience on par with the other annotators.

determining its Class Membership).[10] The results are in Tab. 3 and Tab. 4, for Step 2 and Step 3 mappings, respectively.

Annot. pair	A_4-A_5	A_4-A_9	A_5-A_9	Avg.
# of pairs	70	124	84	-
Accuracy	31.4%	78.2%	45.2%	51.6%

Table 3: Accuracy of a full manual match between slot to role mappings, for 3 annotator pairs in Step 2 (Czech verbs)

Annot. pair	A_4-A_6	A_4-A_9	A_6-A_9	Avg.
# of pairs	87	311	91	-
Accuracy	67.8%	87.5%	83.5%	79.6%

Table 4: Accuracy of a full manual match between slot to role mappings, for 3 annotator pairs in Step 3 (English verbs)

The low agreement numbers in Tab. 3 are mainly due to the fact that during Step 2 (when the first set of Czech verbs has been added) not only the mappings, but also the Roleset as created in Step 1 for the initial, mostly English verb set has been often modified, causing a mismatch between the two annotators.[11] Examples include adding or deleting a role, or a partial swap etc. In Step 3 (i.e., after adding another set of English verbs to each class), the Roleset has hardly been ever changed, and only the mapping to valency slots was the cause of mismatches. Thus in this case, we believe that the difference in average agreement (51.6% vs. 79.6%) is not a language issue.

Tables 5 and 6 show the breakdown of the accuracy of the valency slot to role mappings. Only the core argument slots are listed individually, while all other (incl. the special #any, #sb and #sth slots) are grouped together. As expected, the agreement accuracy measure is higher than for the complete match for the whole valency frame, and quite high in general, except for the mix of other non-core valency slots for the Czech verbs added in Step 2 and for the EFF valency slot for English verbs added in Step 3. Since the EFF valency slot corresponds to the third, fourth or fifth argument, as the case may be, we can only speculate that perhaps the EngVallex valency slot labeling might not be consistent enough to allow the annotators understand well its relation to the semantic roles in the given class, and they then therefore differ in their judgment.

4.4. Mapping to Other Lexical Resources

In this section, we evaluate the interannotator agreement in linking the individual class members to external resources, as described in Sect. 3.2, i.e., to VALLEX on the Czech

Annot. pair	A_4-A_5	A_4-A_9	A_5-A_9	Avg.
# of pairs	70	124	84	-
ACT	100%	100%	98.7%	99.6%
PAT	98.3%	98.9%	95.5%	97.6%
ADDR	100%	100%	100%	100%
EFF	100%	100%	86.7%	95.6%
ORIG	N/A	N/A	N/A	N/A
other	86.7%	100%	83.3%	90.0%

Table 5: Accuracy for each valency slot mapping to a semantic role, for 3 annotator pairs in Step 2 (Czech verbs)

Annot. pair	A_4-A_6	A_4-A_9	A_6-A_9	Avg.
# of pairs	87	311	91	-
ACT	100%	99.7%	98.9%	99.5%
PAT	97.5%	99.7%	98.8%	98.7%
ADDR	100%	95.0%	100%	98.3%
EFF	66.7%	33.3%	83.3%	61.1%
ORIG	100%	100%	100%	100%
other	75.0%	96.9%	100%	90.6%

Table 6: Accuracy for each valency slot mapping to a semantic role, for 3 annotator pairs in Step 3 (English verbs)

side (after Step 2), and to FrameNet, WordNet, OntoNotes, VerbNet and PropBank on the English side (after Step 3). The annotators could assign none, one, or more links to an entry in the external resource. Multiple links have been allowed in case they believed that both (or all) such links relate well to the given class member, i.e., in cases where the granularity of the external resource has been finer than the granularity of the PDT-Vallex or EngVallex entries, respectively, in terms of sense distinctions. In the opposite case, when the granularity of PDT-Vallex (or EngVallex) is finer than the external resource entry(ies), the annotators have been asked to simply assign the link to such a more coarse-grained entry, without any special notes or markup. After the lexicon is completed, it will be possible to extract such asymmetric cases by reverting the links.

When comparing the links assigned by two annotators, only a full match (when *all* links agreed, for each external resource individually) counted as agreement, including cases when multiple (or no) links have been assigned by any of the two.

4.4.1. Interannotator Agreement

Interannotator agreement on linking to the external resources has been measured again as a simple agreement rate (mutual accuracy), taken as the ratio on agreed upon links to the total number of class members annotated by a given pair of annotators. External links have only been annotated for valid class members, i.e., those retained after the manual pruning of automatically preselected class members which is always performed first in each Step (Step 2 for Czech and Step 3 for English verbs in this case).

Tab. 7 shows the agreement for linking to VALLEX, the alternative Czech valency lexicon, which is not used in the annotation of the Czech corpora but developed independently (Sect. 3.2). VALLEX, however, uses almost the same principles as PDT-Vallex for sense distinctions as well

---

[10]Due to the high number of combinations of valency slots and semantic roles (e.g., for 3 slots and 3 roles, allowing for combined assignment of more slots to one role, or the possibility to leave out any of them, plus to assign any of #sb, #sth or #any, the number of combinations is (3!)x8=48), kappa value comes out very high due to p_e being very low, and is thus not telling much in terms of the agreement.

[11]However, we did take into account simple label renaming, which has not been considered a mismatch.

as for slot labels, the two features most important here. Only a full match (valency frame ID, or a set of valency frame IDs in case of multiple links) counts as "correct".

Annot. pair	A_4-A_5	A_4-A_9	A_5-A_9	Avg.
# of pairs	70	124	84	-
VALLEX	65.7%	69.4%	71.4%	68.8%

Table 7: Agreement ratio for linking the Czech verbs to the VALLEX lexicon, for 3 annotator pairs in Step 2

While the three pairs of annotators do not differ much in the agreement ratio, it is interesting to observe the relatively low agreement on assigning links to a very closely related resource, possibly caused by the fact that every entry in the VALLEX lexicon has been throughly and widely researched and all possible senses of a given lexeme added, making it both more fine-grained than PDT-Vallex as well as having more senses for each lexeme, including those not found in the underlying corpora. Such a richness made the task of the annotators apparently quite hard.

For the English verbs (as added in Step 3), the results are in Tab. 8.

Annot. pair	A_4-A_6	A_4-A_9	A_6-A_9	Avg.
# of pairs	87	311	91	-
FrameNet	59.8%	60.1%	72.5%	64.1%
WordNet	41.4%	34.4%	27.5%	34.4%
VerbNet	54.0%	57.2%	49.5%	53.6%
PropBank	88.5%	72.0%	80.2%	80.2%
OntoNotes	79.3%	80.4%	91.2%	83.6%

Table 8: Agreement ratio for linking the English verbs to the external lexicons, for 3 annotator pairs in Step 3

As the results show, the agreements ratios vary widely. The relatively high agreement for PropBank and OntoNotes is undoubtedly due to the fact that the EngVallex verb senses come from the same corpus (at least in part), namely the WSJ part of the Penn Treebank, despite the differences in creating the argument structure in ProbBank and the OntoNotes groupings, vs. the valency frames in EngVallex. FrameNet frame assignment agreements, due to the relatively broad nature of FrameNet frames, are somewhat low. VerbNet, even though its classes are definitely broader than the synonym sets in SynSemClass, displays very low agreement, which might be caused by mismatches in the assignment to the single class or subclass in the VerbNet hierarchy.

WordNet links display an extremely low agreement, caused, in our opinion, by the very fine-grained distinctions in WordNet verb senses, which often caused multiple WordNet senses being assigned to a single SynSemClass class member. This leads easily to a disagreement between the annotators due to the fact that an agreement is counted as correct only if all links agree (i.e., linking to WordNet senses #1 and #2 by one annotator and to only sense #2 by the other annotator is a mismatch).

5. Converting to Linked Data

Linked Data is a widespread effort to make data available "in context", i.e., to link them to other data, in our case to lexical resources, in order to use the "knowledge" these links add mutually to the individual resources. Our motivation is to be compatible with such lexicons, e.g., resources available in the ELEXIS[12] project, as describe e.g., in (Declerck et al., 2015).

In the work described so far, we have concentrated on the content creation, including the various links, especially to the existing external lexicons. In order to design the structure for providing the data in Linked Data form, we have used the OntoLex (lemon) format[13]. Content-wise, we have been mostly inspired by (McCrae et al., 2014), since in the treatment of word (verb) senses and the view of ontology it is closest to our approach. Similarly, (Corcoglioniti et al., 2016) has a set of modules for PropBank, FrameNet, VerbNet and NomBank, which we will use as well.

For verbs, as already mentioned in the Introduction section, there is no ontology as we can find, e.g., in the medical domain (e.g., the ICD, or various other classifications schemes in MESH), or biology or other domains. In fact, the idea behind SynSemClass is to build an ontology substitute that could be used for a sort of grounding (at least at the event type level) in data (text) annotation. Thus, we treat a class in SynSemClass as substitute for an ontology unit, similar to the treatment of WordNet synset in (McCrae et al., 2014). Each member of the class is a *sense*, denoted by a concatenation of the verb lemma (usually, infinitive form or a concatenated infinitive form of a MWE in case of e.g., phrasal verbs) and the valency frame ID, which is unique in the whole linked dataset, including across languages (cf. the valency frame ID prefix), for example `confirm-ev-w649f1`, while a *word* (LexicalEntry), even though redundant (because reachable through the link to the valency lexicons) is represented by its lemma concatenated by the word ID, e.g., `confirm-ev-w649`, see Fig. 3. External links are represented as links to the LD versions of WordNet (McCrae et al., 2014) and FrameNet (Bryl et al., 2012), while the links to VerbNet, FrameNet, PropBank frames and OntoNotes sense groupings are represented as URLs (URIs) to their web presence, if it exists in the Unified Verb Index, or as the customary ID with an appropriate lexicon-unique prefix if they do not. While the SynSemClass lexicon does not have a hyponym/hyperonym hierarchy (yet), it will be represented by the *broader* relation as found in SKOS. Grammatical properties (i.e., the mapping between the valency arguments and semantic roles, as a property of each class, will be represented as standard *properties*.

Fig. 3 shows a linked representation of one SynSemClass entry, or more precisely, one sense of the verb *confirm*, identified by its EngVallex reference (`ev-w649f1`). The lower half of the scheme shows the links to external resources, as described above. Please note that each link to each external lexicon can appear multiple times; for example, to simplify the picture, we have left

---

[12]https://elex.is/
[13]https://www.w3.org/2019/09/lexicog

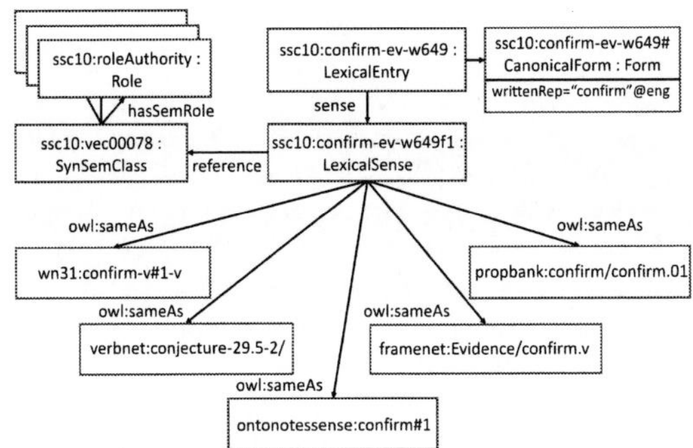

Figure 3: The Linked Data scheme of the SynSemClass lexicon entry (example entry confirm, simplified)

links to WordNet sense `confirm#2` and to two additional FrameNet frames (`Statement` and `Verification`), as identified by the annotators of that entry, and one more VerbNet class (`indicate-78-1-1`). All entries in other languages (Czech, for the moment) will have their own entries, but they will share the reference to the SynSemClass (`ssc10:vec00078` in this case).

6. Related work

We have presented the first version of SynSemClass, a bilingual verbal synonym lexicon linked to several external resources, as an initial step in developing multilingual verbal ontological resource that can link to existing lexical-semantic resources (and resources bordering already on ontologies, such as FrameNet). We are aware of several such projects (or similar ones), such as the Predicate Matrix project (Lacalle et al., 2014), VerbAtlas (Di Fabio et al., 2019) and especially the SemLink work lead by M. Palmer and colleagues (Palmer, 2009; Bonial et al., 2013; Bonial et al., 2012). Our contribution here is the inclusion of valency and its mapping to semantic roles as a major criterion of including a verb (or better, its sense) in a synonym class, while adding the fully manually assigned mapping (linking) to these other resources.

In terms of Linked Data, there has been previous projects, especially for FrameNet, as comprehensively described in (Ide, 2014). WordNet has also several conversion to Linked Data (more precisely, to RDF/OWL), and there is also a description of the model(s) and outstanding issues;[14] previous work on WordNet conversion to Linked Data can be found in `http://xmlns.com/2001/08/wordnet` as well as in (McCrae et al., 2014) (which, among other features, also links to VerbNet).

7. Summary and Future Extensions

Our main contribution is the linking of the (currently) bilingual verbal synonym lexicon in two directions: (a) to deep syntactic information for each verb included (i.e., to the Czech and English valency lexicons), and (b) to existing "popular" lexical resources (i.e., VerbNet, PropBank, OntoNotes groupings, FrameNet and WordNet). We have also presented a suggested mapping to the Linked Data scheme, and shown that all the necessary components are there; this conversion will be physically made once we increase the coverage of SynSemClass and check its consistency (for the moment, the lexicon is available in XML format as an Open Resource).[15]

In the short term, we plan to extend the resource by using both automatic and manual methods and annotation. As shown in this paper, the manual effort involved is relatively large for getting all the components of the lexicon together, and agreement among annotators is not that high, even though it has been improving. Thus the plan is to involve distributional methods (in part using deep learning based on this initial version, e.g., to find more precisely additional synonym candidates in both parallel as well as monolingual texts, including also languages other than Czech and English). We have also started to cooperate on linking the resources from the Unified Verb Index[16] to SynSemClass and vice versa, sharing data in order to minimize the annotation effort needed to enrich both resources.

In the long term, we would like to add connection (including entry to entry links) to additional and newly appearing resources, such as VerbAtlas (as being worked on within the BabelNet project) (Di Fabio et al., 2019), which is in fact very close in goals to the project presented here. This implies adding verbal and event nominals and provide the linking for them, too.

We believe that SynSemClass can be used, already in the current state and coverage, as an evaluation resource for any automated methods and tools for annotation of all three areas: synonym class membership, valency to semantic role mapping, and mapping to external resources.

We also plan to create a textual resource (preferably, a treebank, and ideally, a parallel one or ones) that would be annotated by the classes (and semantic roles associated with these classes) from SynSemClass. Such a resource can then be used to train various NLP tools, from verb sense disambiguation to information extraction to full grounding that would include both entities as well as events/states. In this area, we plan to cooperate with other projects and initiatives that tackle universal or uniform semantic representations, such as the UMR project (Pustejovsky et al., 2019), or the semantic representations that have been used in the CoNLL 2019 MRP Shared Task (Oepen et al., 2019).

8. Acknowledgements

This work has been supported by the GAČR (Grant Agency of the Czech Republic) grants No. GX20-16819X and GA17-07313S. It uses resources hosted by the LINDAT/CLARIN (LINDAT/CLARIAH-CZ) Research Infrastructure, projects No. LM2015071 and LM2018101, supported by the Ministry of Education and Youth of the Czech Republic. The work described herein would not at all be possible without the annotators who have actually made it happen–we would thus like to thank them all: Kathryn S. Conger, Darja Klambotskaya, Vlaďka Krajcsovicsová, Jakub Sláma, Barbora Bulantová, Kateřina Truksasová, Martin Babička, and Alena Straková.

---

[14] `https://www.w3.org/TR/wordnet-rdf`

[15] `http://hdl.handle.net/11234/1-3125`
[16] `https://uvi.colorado.edu`

9. Bibliographical References

Aguilar, J., Beller, C., McNamee, P., Van Durme, B., Strassel, S., Song, Z., and Ellis, J. (2014). A comparison of the events and relations across ACE, ERE, TAC-KBP, and FrameNet annotation standards. In *Proceedings of the Second Workshop on EVENTS: Definition, Detection, Coreference, and Representation*, pages 45–53, Baltimore, Maryland, USA, June. Association for Computational Linguistics.

Baker, C. F., Fillmore, C. J., and Lowe, J. B. (1998). The Berkeley FrameNet Project. In *Proceedings of the 36th Annual Meeting of the Association for Computational Linguistics and 17th International Conference on Computational Linguistics - Volume 1*, ACL '98, pages 86–90, Stroudsburg, PA, USA. Association for Computational Linguistics.

Bonial, C., Feely, W., Hwang, J. D., and Palmer, M. (2012). Empirically Validating VerbNet Using SemLink. In *Seventh Joint ACL-ISO Workshop on Interoperable Semantic Annotation*, Istanbul, Turkey, May.

Bonial, C., Stowe, K., and Palmer, M. (2013). Renewing and revising SemLink. In *Proceedings of the 2nd Workshop on Linked Data in Linguistics (LDL-2013): Representing and linking lexicons, terminologies and other language data*, pages 9 – 17, Pisa, Italy, September. Association for Computational Linguistics.

Bryl, V., Tonelli, S., Giuliano, C., and Serafini, L. (2012). A novel framenet-based resource for the semantic web. *Proceedings of the ACM Symposium on Applied Computing*, 03.

Cohen, J. (1960). A coefficient of agreement for nominal scales. *Educational and psychological measurement*, 20(1):37–46.

Corcoglioniti, F., Rospocher, M., Aprosio, A. P., and Tonelli, S. (2016). PreMOn: a lemon extension for exposing predicate models as linked data. In *Proceedings of the Tenth International Conference on Language Resources and Evaluation (LREC'16)*, pages 877–884, Portorož, Slovenia, May. European Language Resources Association (ELRA).

Declerck, T., Wandl-Vogt, E., Krek, S., and Tiberius, C. (2015). Towards multilingual elexicography by means of linked (open) data. In Jorge Gracia, et al., editors, *Proceedings of the Fourth Workshop on the Multilingual Semantic Web (MSW4) co-located with 12th Extended Semantic Web Conference (ESWC 2015), Portorož, Slovenia, June 1, 2015*, volume 1532 of *CEUR Workshop Proceedings*, pages 51–58. CEUR-WS.org.

Di Fabio, A., Conia, S., and Navigli, R. (2019). VerbAtlas: a novel large-scale verbal semantic resource and its application to semantic role labeling. In *Proceedings of the 2019 Conference on Empirical Methods in Natural Language Processing and the 9th International Joint Conference on Natural Language Processing (EMNLP-IJCNLP)*, pages 627–637, Hong Kong, China, November. Association for Computational Linguistics.

Fillmore, C. J., Johnson, C. R., and L.Petruck, M. R. (2003). Background to FrameNet: FrameNet and Frame Semantics. *International Journal of Lexicography*, 16(3):235–250.

Ide, N. (2014). FrameNet and linked data. In *Proceedings of Frame Semantics in NLP: A Workshop in Honor of Chuck Fillmore (1929-2014)*, pages 18–21, Baltimore, MD, USA, June. Association for Computational Linguistics.

Jardine, N. and van Rijsbergen, C. J. (1971). The use of hierarchic clustering in information retrieval. *Information storage and retrieval*, 7(5):217–240.

Lacalle, M. L. D., Laparra, E., and Rigau, G. (2014). Predicate Matrix: extending SemLink through WordNet mappings. In *Proceedings of the 9th conference on International Language Resources and Evaluation (LREC'14*.

Lopatková, M., Kettnerová, V., Bejček, E., Vernerová, A., and Žabokrtský, Z. (2016). *Valenční slovník českých sloves VALLEX*. Nakladatelství Karolinum, Praha, Czechia.

Marcus, M. P., Santorini, B., and Marcinkiewicz, M. A. (1993). Building a Large Annotated Corpus of English: The Penn Treebank. *COMPUTATIONAL LINGUISTICS*, 19(2):313–330.

McCrae, J. P., Fellbaum, C., and Cimiano, P. (2014). Publishing and Linking WordNet using lemon and RDF. In *Proceedings of the 3rd Workshop on Linked Data in Linguistics, colocated with LREC 2014*, Reykjavik, Iceland.

Oepen, S., Abend, O., Hajic, J., Hershcovich, D., Kuhlmann, M., O'Gorman, T., Xue, N., Chun, J., Straka, M., and Uresova, Z. (2019). MRP 2019: Cross-framework meaning representation parsing. In *Proceedings of the Shared Task on Cross-Framework Meaning Representation Parsing at the 2019 Conference on Natural Language Learning*, pages 1–27, Hong Kong, November. Association for Computational Linguistics.

Palmer, M., Gildea, D., and Kingsbury, P. (2005). The Proposition Bank: An Annotated Corpus of Semantic Roles. *Computational Linguistics*, 31(1):71–106, March.

Palmer, M. (2009). Semlink: Linking PropBank, VerbNet and FrameNet. In *Proceedings of the Generative Lexicon Conference*, page 9–15.

Panevová, J. (1974). On verbal Frames in Functional Generative Description. *Prague Bulletin of Mathematical Linguistics*, 22:3–40.

Pradhan, S. S. and Xue, N. (2009). OntoNotes: The 90% solution. In *Proceedings of Human Language Technologies: The 2009 Annual Conference of the North American Chapter of the Association for Computational Linguistics, Companion Volume: Tutorial Abstracts*, pages 11–12, Boulder, Colorado, May. Association for Computational Linguistics.

Pustejovsky, J., Lai, K., and Xue, N. (2019). Modeling Quantification and Scope in Abstract Meaning Representations. In *Proceedings of the First International Workshop on Designing Meaning Representations*, pages 28–33, Florence, Italy, August. Association for Computational Linguistics.

Schuler, K. K. (2006). *VerbNet: A Broad-Coverage, Com-*

prehensive Verb Lexicon. Ph.D. thesis, University of Pennsylvania.

Sgall, P., Hajičová, E., and Panevová, J. (1986). *The Meaning of the Sentence in its Semantic and Pragmatic Aspects*. D. Reidel, Dordrecht.

Urešová, Z., Fučíková, E., and Šindlerová, J. (2016). CzEngVallex: a bilingual Czech-English valency lexicon. *The Prague Bulletin of Mathematical Linguistics*, 105:17–50.

Urešová, Z., Fučíková, E., Hajičová, E., and Hajič, J. (2018a). Creating a Verb Synonym Lexicon Based on a Parallel Corpus. In *Proceedings of the 11th International Conference on Language Resources and Evaluation (LREC'18)*, Miyazaki, Japan, May. European Language Resources Association (ELRA).

Urešová, Z., Fučíková, E., Hajičová, E., and Hajič, J. (2018b). A Cross-lingual synonym classes lexicon. *Prace Filologiczne*, LXXII:405–418.

Urešová, Z., Fučíková, E., Hajičová, E., and Hajič, J. (2018c). Defining Verbal Synonyms: between Syntax and Semantics. In Dag Haug, et al., editors, *Proceedings of the 17th International Workshop on Treebanks and Linguistic Theories (TLT 2018)*, number 155, pages 75–90, Linköping, Sweden. Universitetet i Oslo, Linköping University Electronic Press.

Urešová, Z., Fučíková, E., Hajičová, E., and Hajič, J. (2018d). Synonymy in Bilingual Context: The CzEng-Class Lexicon. In *Proceedings of The 27th International Conference on Computational Linguistics*, pages 2456–2469, Sheffield, GB. ICCL, ICCL.

Urešová, Z., Fučíková, E., Hajičová, E., and Hajič, J. (2018e). Tools for Building an Interlinked Synonym Lexicon Network. In *Proceedings of the 11th International Conference on Language Resources and Evaluation (LREC'18)*, Miyazaki, Japan, May. European Language Resources Association (ELRA).

Urešová, Z., Fučíková, E., Hajičová, E., and Hajič, J. (2019a). Meaning and Semantic Roles in CzEngClass Lexicon. *Jazykovedný časopis / Journal of Linguistics*, 70(2):403–411.

Urešová, Z., Fučíková, E., Hajičová, E., and Hajič, J. (2019b). Parallel Dependency Treebank Annotated with Interlinked Verbal Synonym Classes and Roles. In *Proceedings of the 18th International Workshop on Treebanks and Linguistic Theories (TLT, SyntaxFest 2019)*, pages 38–50, Paris, France. Université Paris Sorbonne Nouvelle, Association for Computational Linguistics.

Urešová, Z. (2011). *Valenční slovník Pražského závislostního korpusu (PDT-Vallex)*. Studies in Computational and Theoretical Linguistics. Ústav formální a aplikované lingvistiky, Praha, Czechia.

10. Language Resource References

Cinková, Silvie and Fučíková, Eva and Šindlerová, Jana and Hajič, Jan. (2014). *EngVallex - English Valency Lexicon*. LINDAT/CLARIN digital library at the Institute of Formal and Applied Linguistics, Charles University, `http://hdl.handle.net/11858/00-097C-0000-0023-4337-2`.

Jan Hajič and Eva Hajičová and Jarmila Panevová and Petr Sgall and Silvie Cinková and Eva Fučíková and Marie Mikulová and Petr Pajas and Jan Popelka and Jiří Semecký and Jana Šindlerová and Jan Štěpánek and Josef Toman and Zdeňka Urešová and Zdeněk Žabokrtský. (2012). *Prague Czech-English Dependency Treebank 2.0*, `https://catalog.ldc.upenn.edu/LDC2004T25`. Also at LINDAT/CLARIN digital library at the Institute of Formal and Applied Linguistics, Charles University, `http://hdl.handle.net/11858/00-097C-0000-0015-8DAF-4`.

Hajič, Jan and Bejček, Eduard and Bémová, Alevtina and Buráňová, Eva and Hajičová, Eva and Havelka, Jiří and Homola, Petr and Kárník, Jiří and Kettnerová, Václava and Klyueva, Natalia and Kolářová, Veronika and Kučová, Lucie and Lopatková, Markéta and Mikulová, Marie and Mírovský, Jiří and Nedoluzhko, Anna and Pajas, Petr and Panevová, Jarmila and Poláková, Lucie and Rysová, Magdaléna and Sgall, Petr and Spoustová, Johanka and Straňák, Pavel and Synková, Pavlína and Ševčíková, Magda and Štěpánek, Jan and Urešová, Zdeňka and Vidová Hladká, Barbora and Zeman, Daniel and Zikánová, Šárka and Žabokrtský, Zdeněk. (2018). *Prague Dependency Treebank 3.5*. LINDAT/CLARIN digital library at the Institute of Formal and Applied Linguistics, Charles University, `http://hdl.handle.net/11234/1-2621`.

Jan Hajič and Jarmila Panevová and Eva Hajičová and Petr Sgall and Petr Pajas and Jan Štěpánek and Jiří Havelka and Marie Mikulová and Zdeněk Žabokrtský and Magda Ševčíková-Razímová and Zdeňka Urešová. (2006). *Prague Dependency Treebank 2.0*. LDC, number LDC2006T01, `http://hdl.handle.net/11858/00-097C-0000-0015-8DAF-4`.

Urešová, Zdeňka and Štěpánek, Jan and Hajič, Jan and Panevová, Jarmila and Mikulová, Marie. (2014). *PDT-Vallex: Czech Valency lexicon linked to treebanks*. LINDAT/CLARIN digital library at the Institute of Formal and Applied Linguistics, Charles University, `http://hdl.handle.net/11858/00-097C-0000-0023-4338-F`.

Zdeňka Urešová and Eva Fučíková and Jan Hajič and Jana Šindlerová. (2015). *CzEngVallex - Czech English Valency Lexicon*. LINDAT/CLARIN digital library at the Institute of Formal and Applied Linguistics, Charles University, `http://hdl.handle.net/11234/1-1512`.

Urešová, Zdeňka and Fučíková, Eva and Hajič, Jan and Hajičová, Eva. (2019). *SynSemClass 1.0*. LINDAT/CLARIN digital library at the Institute of Formal and Applied Linguistics, Charles University, `http://hdl.handle.net/11234/1-3125`.

Proceedings of the Globalex Workshop on Linked Lexicography, pages 20–28
Language Resources and Evaluation Conference (LREC 2020), Marseille, 11–16 May 2020
© European Language Resources Association (ELRA), licensed under CC-BY-NC

Representing Etymology
in the LiLa Knowledge Base of Linguistic Resources for Latin

Francesco Mambrini, Marco Passarotti
CIRCSE Research Centre, Università Cattolica del Sacro Cuore
Largo Gemelli, 1 - 20123 Milan (Italy)
{francesco.mambrini, marco.passarotti}@unicatt.it

Abstract

In this paper we describe the process of inclusion of etymological information in a knowledge base of interoperable Latin linguistic resources developed in the context of the *LiLa: Linking Latin* project. Interoperability is obtained by applying the Linked Open Data principles. Particularly, an extensive collection of Latin lemmas is used to link the (distributed) resources. For the etymology, we rely on the Ontolex-lemon ontology and the lemonEty extension to model the information, while the source data are taken from a recent etymological dictionary of Latin. As a result, the collection of lemmas LiLa is built around now includes 1,465 Proto-Italic and 1,393 Proto-Indo-European reconstructed forms that are used to explain the history of 1,400 Latin words. We discuss the motivation, methodology and modeling strategies of the work, as well as its possible applications and potential future developments.

Keywords: etymology, linked open data, Latin

1. Introduction

Latin is the most widely attested member of the Italic branch of the Indo-European family, which also includes other cognate languages (such as for instance Oscan, Umbrian and Faliscan) spoken in central and southern Italy before the Roman domination. As the language of Rome, whose authority and influence extended over the Mediterranean as well as a large portion of continental Europe and of the Near East for many centuries, Latin played a role in the cultural and linguistic history of the world that is hard to overestimate. Moreover, as the direct ancestor of the Romance family, several languages of Europe like Spanish, Portuguese, French, Italian and Romanian trace their roots directly to it. As a consequence, a great part of the vocabulary of many modern languages is derived, through inheritance or borrowing, from Latin.

In the present days, large corpora of Latin texts for several million words, belonging to different genres and produced in the span of many centuries, are publicly available on the web.[1] In addition to texts, the internet provides also an extensive selection of digitized dictionaries, including etymological lexica (Mambrini and Passarotti, 2019, 72-3 for an overview). While these resources can be browsed, read and queried from separate interfaces, interaction between them is extremely limited.

Indeed, etymological studies are a very good example of how the lack of interoperability between digital resources imposes limitations to users. Researchers and students of historical linguistics would greatly benefit from the capability to interrogate simultaneously all the dictionaries that discuss the etymology, meaning or synonyms of words, together with corpora that document all the attestations of any given lexical item. However, this experience is precluded by the limits of the publication model currently used for lexica and corpora, which relegates them in the condition of isolated silos.

The adoption of the Linked Open Data (LOD) paradigm for linguistic resources can greatly improve the situation for historical linguistics of Latin. Defined by Berners-Lee with the goal of shifting from a web of document to a web of interconnected data (Berners-Lee, 2006), the LOD principles prescribe, among other things, to use Uniform Resource Identifiers (URIs) as names, preferably in the form of HTTP URLs that can be looked out on the web, and to include links to other URIs so as to provide context for the published data. The advantage of the model for linguistic resources is evident, as in a web of data it becomes "possible to follow links between existing resources to find other, related data and exploit network effects" (Chiarcos et al., 2013, iii). Not by chance, across the last years the research community dealing with the creation and distribution of linguistic resources has been working extensively to build the so-called Linguistic Linked Open Data cloud (LLOD),[2] a collaborative effort pursued by several members of the Open Linguistics Working Group,[3] with the goal of developing a Linked Open Data (sub-)cloud of linguistic resources as part of the wider Semantic Web (McCrae et al., 2016).

In this context, the Ontology-Lexica Community Group has been particularly active in the effort to provide models for the representation of lexica as LOD. The main result of the enterprise is the publication of the Ontolex-lemon model, now a de facto standard for the representation of lexical resources (McCrae et al., 2017).[4]

Ontolex is built around a core module, whose primary element is the Lexical Entry; this class includes all the relevant elements of the lexicon, such as words, multi-word expressions or morphemes like affixes. Lexical entries are connected to forms that represent the grammatical realiza-

---

[1]To give an idea, on March 22, 2019, the (meta-)repository of Latin corpora *Corpus Corporum* (`http://www.mlat.uzh.ch/MLS/`) passed the total of 160 million words with its latest update.

[2]`http://linguistic-lod.org/llod-cloud.`
[3]`https://linguistics.okfn.org/index.html.`
[4]`https://www.w3.org/2016/05/ontolex/.`

tion of the lexical item; one of them can be identified as the canonical "dictionary form", or lemma. From the standpoint of meaning, entries can be linked to concepts in ontologies either directly (through a denotative link) or via a "lexical sense" that reifies the relation between an entity from an ontology (e.g. a concept from DBpedia)[5] and a lexical entry.

The Ontolex-lemon model has been extended to account for a number of linguistic properties of the lexicon, like translation (Gracia et al., 2014) and lexicographic metadata.[6] Most recently, Khan (2018a) proposed an extension of Ontolex, called lemonEty, designed to represent also etymological information linked to lexical entries. The extended Ontolex-lemon model is therefore suitable to represent complex lexicographic information, including etymology, in the Semantic Web; this, in turn, is a step towards interoperability between resources, which, as we saw, is a fundamental *desideratum* for students and researchers in (historical) linguistics.

Other approaches to the task of modeling etymological lexical resources using LOD principles include the endeavor to represent the *Dictionnaire étymologique de l'ancien français* (DEAF) (Städtler et al., 2014) using OntoLex-Lemon (Tittel and Chiarcos, 2018) and the LOD representation, again using Lemon, of the *Tower of Babel (Starling)*, a major etymological database featuring short- and long-range etymological relations (Abromeit et al., 2016).

As for Latin, Bon and Nowak (2013) show how intrinsic wiki concepts, such as namespaces, templates and property-value pairs can be used for linking Medieval Latin dictionaries. The same authors are also among the developers of *medialatinitas.eu*,[7] a Web application that integrates dictionaries, corpora and encyclopaedic resources for Latin in a user-friendly interface, although it does not provide any explicit (and reusable) link between the resources (Nowak and Bon, 2015).

The idea of using the LOD paradigm to integrate not only lexical resources, but also textual corpora and Natural Language Processing (NLP) tools for Latin in the Semantic Web is the guiding principle of the project *LiLa: Linking Latin* (henceforth, LiLa). This paper reports on a large-scale experiment on including the information from a recent etymological dictionary of Latin and Italic languages into the Ontolex-based lexical knowledge base of Latin canonical forms of LiLa. Section 2. summarizes the aims and the current status of LiLa. Section 3. describes the treatment of etymology in the LiLa knowledge base. Particularly, 3.1. presents the source of our etymological data; 3.2. provides more details on the lemonEty ontology that was adopted for the experiment; 3.3. discusses the representation of etymologies as scientific propositions, and 3.4. describes how we integrated the etymological information into the LiLa architecture. Section 4. reports an example of how we can make the etymologies interact with the rest of the linguistic information in LiLa. Finally, Section 5. concludes the paper and outlines directions for future work.

2. LiLa: Linked Open Data for Latin resources

The ERC-funded LiLa project (2018-2023) intends to use the LOD paradigm to build a knowledge base of linguistic resources for Latin, i.e. a collection of several (distributed) data sets described using the same vocabulary of knowledge description and linked together.[8] Ultimately, the goal of LiLa is to exploit the wealth of linguistic resources and NLP tools for Latin developed thus far to the best, in order to bridge the gap between raw language data, NLP and knowledge description (Declerck et al., 2012).

The approach adopted by LiLa rests on two principles. Our initial assumption is that lexicon is the level where interoperability between linguistic resources can be achieved, as texts are made of occurrences of words, lexica and dictionaries describe properties of words, and NLP tools process words. But, in particular for a richly inflected language like Latin, the level of lemma is considered the ideal interface between the different types of resources we intend to link. Lemmatization, defined as the task to reduce the inflected forms of a word to one of them conventionally chosen to be the canonical form (e.g. the first person singular of indicative for verbs), is a layer of annotation common to different kinds or resources. Dictionaries tend to index lexical entries using lemmas. Thesauri organize the lexicon by collecting all related entries, and use lemmas to index them. Digital libraries use lemmas to enable lexical search in corpora. In NLP, lemmatization is also included in many pipelines of annotation.

The core of the LiLa knowledge base is built around a comprehensive collection of Latin forms that can be used as lemmas in lexical or textual resources. As we said, in the Ontolex-lemon model the traditional notion of "lemma" is expressed by the "canonical form" property that links a lexical entry to one (and not more than one) form. Therefore, by modeling our collection of lemmas as Ontolex's forms that are potentially used as canonical forms of lexical entries, we ensure compatibility with any other resource that adopts that ontology. As Ontolex forms are licensed to have multiple written representations, the model is very apt to express any orthographic variation and non-canonical spelling of words, which is particularly important for a language like Latin with more than 2,300 years of written attestation.

The list of lemmas included in LiLa was populated from the comprehensive database of the Latin morphological analyzer Lemlat (Passarotti et al., 2017). Lemlat's database reconciles three reference dictionaries for Classical Latin (Gradenwitz, 1904; Georges and Georges, 1913 1918; Glare, 1982), the entire Onomasticon from Forcellini's *Lexicon Totius Latinitatis* (Budassi and Passarotti, 2016), and the Medieval Latin *Glossarium Mediae et Infimae Latinitatis* by du Cange et al. (1883 1887), for a total of over 150,000 lemmas (Cecchini et al., 2018).

Currently, LiLa includes 190,237 lemmas.[9] The relevant

---

[5]https://wiki.dbpedia.org/.
[6]https://www.w3.org/2019/09/lexicog/.
[7]https://medialatinitas.eu/.

[8]https://lila-erc.eu.
[9]The current total number of lemmas in the LiLa collection is higher than in Lemlat, because LiLa includes also a set of lemmas for deadjectival adverbs and present, future and perfect participles

morphological properties of them (part of speech, gender, inflection type) are described using a specific ontology that we intend to align with OLiA (Chiarcos and Sukhareva, 2015). This collection is what the etymological information is linked to and that ultimately serves as a connection point with the other linguistic resources on Latin.

The portion of LiLa that is based on the list taken from the aforementioned three dictionaries of Classical Latin was also enriched with information on word formation derived from the lexicon of the project *Word Formation Latin* (WFL) (Litta et al., 2016).[10] In LiLa, all the lemmas analyzed in WFL are connected to the derivational morphemes (prefixes and affixes) and the lexical bases that can be isolated in them. Thus, it is possible to browse, for instance, all the canonical forms where the prefix *ad-* is used,[11] or the 12 lemmas that have the same lexical base as the noun *rosa* "rose" (Litta et al., 2019).[12]

3. Etymologies in LiLa

3.1. Data

An etymological dictionary is a lexicon that aims to reconstruct the history of each entry, rather than focusing on aspects of meaning or usage. In this context, etymology is generally intended as the task of documenting the origins of a given lexical item and trace back its transfers across different languages, be it by borrowing (even from genetically unrelated tongues), or in a direct hereditary relation from an ancestor to the target language. In the case of the earliest attested Indo-European languages like Latin, particular stress is put on the latter phenomenon. Historical linguists attempt, whenever it is possible, to investigate the most remote origin, form and meaning of a word in the Proto-Indo-European (PIE) phase, based on the comparative study of the evidence offered by the cognate languages, and/or in the intermediate (also reconstructed) ancestor of a sub-family (like the Proto-Italic, henceforth PIt, for the Italic family). Less frequent, but obviously not less interesting, is the case of words that don't appear to have a plausible Indo-European etymology and are (often, very tentatively) explained as loans from non-Indo-European languages.

The etymological information that we connect to the LiLa knowledge base is taken from the most recent *Etymological Dictionary of Latin and the other Italic Languages* (de Vaan, 2008). The content of the dictionary itself is copyrighted by the publisher; however, the owners (Brill ed.) have clarified to us *per litteras* that information about the reconstructed PIt and PIE forms and their connection to the Latin words can be used, provided that explicit attribution to the author and the publication is given.

The dictionary contains 1,874 entries, which, as it is customary for etymological lexica, do not cover the whole Latin vocabulary. Words created by regular derivation processes internal to a language (e.g. by derivational morphemes) are generally grouped together under whatever word is identified as the most interesting for etymological purposes.[13] So, for instance, the nouns *aedicula* "small house" (formed with the diminutive suffix *-cul*) and *aedilis* "aedile" (a magistrate for public buildings, formed with the suffix *-il*) do not have an entry for themselves in the dictionary, but are instead listed among the derivatives of *aedes* "dwelling-place, temple". Also, the entries are limited to the words that belong to the inherited lexicon of Latin: the loan words (mostly from Ancient Greek), which are especially frequent in the domains of grammar, science and philosophy, are not treated.

In the dictionary by de Vaan (2008), each entry follows a defined structure, in which five layers can be distinguished. The first level provides the lemma, a translation, a minimal historical contextualization (such as the first attestation), some relevant morphological information (part of speech, gender and inflection type), and a series of Latin cognate words (like *aedicula* and *aedilis* for *aedes*). The following sections list the PIt and PIE reconstructed ancestors, together with a set of cognate words attested (or postulated) in the related languages. Finally, the last two paragraphs contain a lengthier discussion of the history of the word and a bibliography.

As per the agreement with the publisher, we modeled only the information about the PIt and PIE reconstructed ancestors in the second level of the structure just described. The goal is to introduce such ancestors into LiLa, by linking them, according to the chosen ontology, to the relevant Latin lemmas of the LiLa's collection.

Of the ca. 1,900 entries in de Vaan (2008), we identified 1,466 that explicitly list a PIE and/or a PIt reconstructed etymology in the paragraph that we targeted for extraction. Another 25 of them belong to an Italic language (mostly Oscan or Umbrian) and are therefore not linkable to LiLa. A final group of 50 entries that we could not properly link are those that discuss the etymology of derivational morphemes; although, as said, LiLa does provide information on prefixes and suffixes, these morphemes are still not represented as lexical entries in our knowledge base, thus making it impossible to use a Ontolex-based model to describe their etymology.

In total, we identified a pool of 1,391 entries from de Vaan (2008) for which etymological information could be linked to a LiLa lemma.

3.2. The model

The Ontolex-lemon Etymological Extension or lemonEty (Khan, 2018a; Khan, 2018b) extends the Ontolex core by introducing a number of classes and properties to encode etymological information about lexical entries.

The first new class is the Etymology itself. The class reifies the whole process of etymological reconstruction as scientific hypothesis; the main advantage of this approach is that it allows to make statements about the etymology itself, such as the attribution to scholars, bibliographical ref-

---

that were automatically built from the Lemlat database. For more details, see Mambrini and Passarotti (2019).

[10] http://wfl.marginalia.it/.

[11] https://lila-erc.eu/data/id/prefix/5.

[12] https://lila-erc.eu/data/id/base/3079.

[13] According to de Vaan (2008, 10), the word chosen for the entry in the dictionary "represents the derivationally most opaque member of a Latin word family". We take this to mean the word whose derivation cannot be explained (or is explained less easily) with the regular Latin word-formation rules.

erences, or belief values, so that the model can theoretically include also discarded hypotheses that are considered not plausible by specialists (see below, Section 3.3.).

Etymologies group together a series of related lexical entries, one of which (identified by the "lemma" of the entry in the etymological dictionary) is the target whose history must be explained. Any lexical item that is introduced only to describe the history of a word and, as a rule, does not belong to the lexicon of a given language, is a member of the Etymon class, a subclass of Ontolex's Lexical Entry. The subclass serves the purpose of maintaining a distinction between the proper lexical entries of a given language and those words (from an ancestor or any other languages or language phase) that are introduced only for the etymological purposes.

Although the hypotheses concerning the origins and histories of words can be quite complex, and may involve transfers of meanings or restructuring of forms, etymologies can in general be conceptualized as sequences of steps from an earlier linguistic stage to a subsequent phase, until the target word is satisfactory explained. Thus, for instance, Lat. *lupus* "wolf" is explained by de Vaan (2008, 353) by posing a passage from PIE *ulk^wo- to PIt *luk^wo- by metathesis, and from the latter to Latin (possibly, via a loan from Sabellic).[14]

The lemonEty extension allows to model such sequences of stages with the help of the class Etymology Link. An Etymology Link reifies the etymological relations between a source (i.e. an expression postulated as the origin of the relation, such as a word in the ancestor language) and a target. In the example quoted above, the etymology of *lupus* implies the existence of three etymology links: PIE > PIt (> Sabellic) > Latin. The links can then be further specified by defining the type of relations that they imply; in the example, the links between PIE and PIt and from PIt to any Italic language imply inheritance, while the one between Sabellic and Latin is a borrowing. The "sub-source" property can also be attached to the link, in order to narrow some specific semantic or morphological properties of the source word that are relevant for the process. So, for instance, a sublink can be used to specify that Italian *lupo* "wolf" is derived from the accusative form (*lupu(m)*) of Latin *lupus*.

Figure 1 reproduces the proposed etymology for *lupus*, as represented in LiLa,[15] with the links from the reconstructed PIE word to the reconstructed PIt and from PIt to Latin.[16]

---

[14]Metathesis is a process of transposition of syllables or phonemes that is fairly common in the history of words: see for instance Italian *coccodrillo* or Spanish *cocodrilo* "crocodile" from Latin *crocodilus*. Note that in historical linguistics the asterisk is the conventional mark for reconstructed forms, i.e. those forms that, although not positively documented, are postulated by applying the comparative method.

[15]https://lila-erc.eu/data/ lexicalResources/BrillEDL/id/etymology/178.

[16]Since, as we said, we decided to limit our work to PIE and PIt etymons, the etymological representation in LiLa at present skips the passage from Sabellic to Latin.

3.3. Etymologies as scientific propositions

An important feature of the lemonEty ontology is that it allows to represent etymologies as a set of propositions about the history of words, which can be properly attributed and described with all properties pertaining to scientific discourse.

The approach that we adopted to model etymologies as scholarly output is based on the CIDOC Conceptual Reference Model (CRM) (Doerr, 2003), a widely adopted formal ontology used for heterogeneous cultural heritage information. In terms of the CIDOC-CRM, etymologies can be considered instances of the class "E89 Propositional Object", which encompasses the "sets of propositions about real or imaginary things and that are documented as single units or serve as topic of discourse";[17] examples of E89 include Maxwell's Equations or Anselm's ontological argument. The property P70 ("documents") can be used to link any "E31 Document" to any entity of the CIDOC CRM.[18] Therefore, the statement expressing that de Vaan's dictionary (an instance sof E31) documents (via the P70 property) an etymology like the one represented in Figure 1 (E89) is a suitable way to encode the bibliographical attribution. This modelization is represented in Figure 2.

In our first experiment, we limited ourselves to this very simple set of statements. However, as PIE reconstruction is a very speculative field, the model can be enhanced to capture more nuances of the sometimes complex domain of etymological argumentation. In the following paragraphs, we propose a possible modelization that, although not (yet) implemented in LiLa, may be advisable in order to make the information that we derived from de Vaan (2008) more interoperable with other etymologies that are published (or that may be published) on the web.

In his discussion on the history of *lupus*, de Vaan (2008, 353) mentions an alternative hypothesis to the one adopted in LiLa (represented in Figure 1), which he considers less persuasive. According to this alternative reconstruction, the word may originate from PIE *ulp-/*lup- "marten" (see Latin *volpes* "fox"), with a semantic shift from the original sense to the one of wolf.

While, as we saw, lemonEty is equiped to express the semantic change from PIE to Latin, we can apply the CRM_{inf} (Argumentation Model) extension of the CIDOC CRM (Stead et al., 2019) to represent the whole process of argumentation that is reflected in the entry of the etymological dictionary.[19] An Etymology, with its attached Etymology Links and Etymons, can be considered an instantiation of a "I4 Proposition Set" as defined by the Argumentation Model. These propositions are then associated to a belief value (for instance, true or false) in instances of the class "I2 Belief".[20] The CRM_{inf} can thus be used to express the

---

[17]http://www.cidoc-crm.org/html/5.0.4/ cidoc-crm.html#E89.

[18]The 'E31 Document' is the class that "comprises identifiable immaterial items that make propositions about reality" (http://www.cidoc-crm.org/html/5.0.4/ cidoc-crm.html#E31).

[19]http://new.cidoc-crm.org/crminf/.

[20]The class I2 "comprises the notion that the associated I4 Proposition Set is held to have a particular I6 Belief Value by a

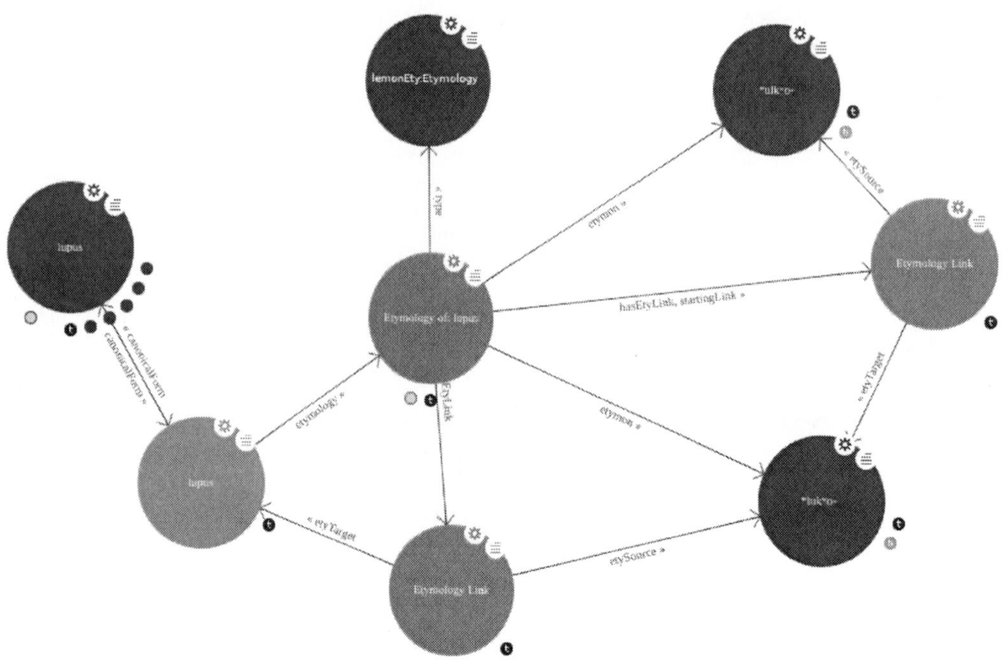

Figure 1: The etymology of *lupus* in LiLa according to the lemonEty model.

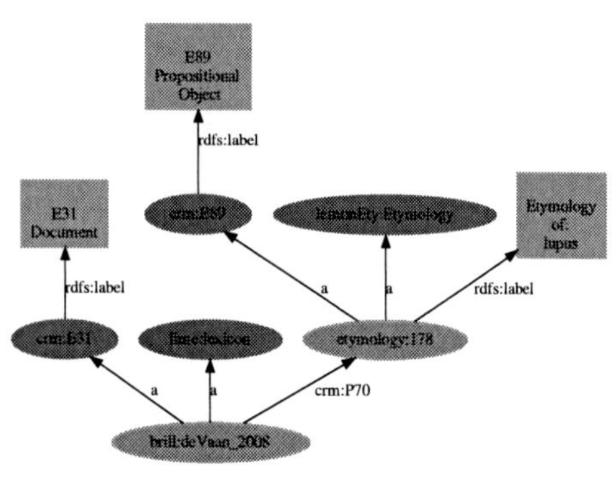

Figure 2: The etymology of *lupus* as an "E89 Propositional Object".

fact that the content of each I4 is considered true or false. Figure 3 illustrates a schematic representation of de Vaan's etymological argumentation about *lupus* according to this model. The whole process of discussion is represented as

an instance of the "I1 Argumentation" class.[21] The conclusions are represented by two beliefs ("J2 concluded that"); on the one hand, the etymology represented in Figure 1 (and not reported in Figure 3) is held to be true, while the second belief is that an alternative explanation (shown here with a single etymology link to PIE $*ulp$-/$*lup$-) is considered less plausible.

For the sake of simplification, Figure 3 adopts a black-and-white model of belief values, where only "True" and "False" are distinguished. de Vaan (2008, 353) uses a much more nuanced language: the accepted explanation is "conceivable", while the alternative entails assumptions that "would require further special pleading". It should be noted that even these assumptions can be encoded using the model suggested here. In Figure 3, the semantic shift required is encoded in the lexical senses attached to the two lexical entries connected via the etymology link; the source is the PIE etymon with the postulated sense of "marten", while the Latin target refers to a different animal (the wolf). The main problem of this etymology, according to de Vaan, is to explain the fact that the root is also continued by Latin *volpes* "fox"; although not shown in Figure 3, it is clear

---

particular E39 Actor. This can be understood as the period of time that an individual or group holds a particular set of propositions to be true, false or somewhere in between" (Stead et al., 2019, 10).

[21] An I1 represets "the activity of making honest inferences or observations. An honest inference or observation is one in which the E39 Actor carrying out the I1 Argumentation justifies and believes that the I6 Belief Value associated with resulting I2 Belief about the I4 Proposition Set is the correct value at the time that the activity was undertaken" (Stead et al., 2019, 10).

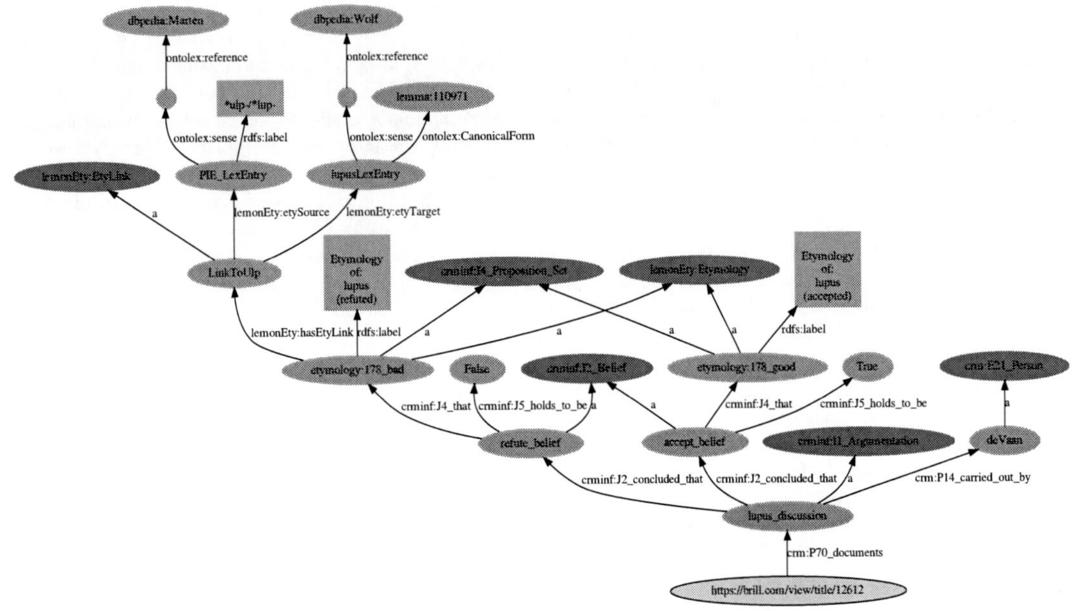

Figure 3: Using CRM$_{inf}$ to model the argumentation about the etymology of *lupus*.

from our previous discussion that the lemonEty model is capable of representing the etymologies of these two words converging to this PIE etymon.

3.4. The linking process

A scrutiny of the 1,391 entries taken from de Vaan (2008) led us to include 2,858 instances of Etymon in LiLa, 1,465 for PIt and 1,393 for PIE. These entries are now grouped in 1,434 etymologies and linked by 2,648 etymology links.

1,400 lexical entries from the Brill dictionary are now connected to a lemma from the LiLa collection. Of these, 1,383 are also linked to an Etymology, while 17 are cognates of other words that share every trait with them (including obviously the history) but the part of speech, like for instance *supra* "over", which is assigned both part of speech adverb and adposition.[22]

In the process of linking, we encountered several cases where the lemma of the dictionary entry matched more than one lemma of the LiLa collection. For instance, the string "pullus" could be matched to three different lemmas of LiLa: one noun ("foal"), and two adjectives, meaning "pure" and "dark-colored" (the latter being the correct lemma for the entry in de Vaan).[23] In all but 13 cases, a manual disambiguation allowed us to identify the correct candidate; most often, as in the case of *pullus*, the information on the part of speech, the inflection class or the deriva-

tional morphology attached to each lemma was sufficient to disambiguate. The other 13 cases either involve errors in the morphological annotation or reflect a greater ambiguity that requires further study.

The connections between the etymons, etymology links and lemmas can be queried using the SPARQL endpoint of LiLa.[24]

4. Using etymologies as linked data

Once that the etymologies are linked with the LiLa lemmas, it becomes possible to cross the information on PIE and PIt derivation with the other resources represented in our knowledge base.

One possible example of a meaningful connection that can be explored is that between etymology and word formation. As we saw, the entries in de Vaan (2008) cover only a portion of the Latin lexicon; some words are listed as cognates and derivatives of the main entry, while many more secondary formations, especially of late attestation, are not mentioned at all. The entry dedicated to *clārus* "loud, bright" in de Vaan (2008, 117-118), for instance, reports six words as Latin cognates, but some other like *clarificatio* "glorification", attested in Ecclesiastical Latin, are not listed. According to the index of Latin forms in de Vaan (2008, 725-765), the dictionary discusses 9,439 Latin words (including affixes).

The information about the derivational morphemes in LiLa may help retrieving the other derivative words that are not explicitly mentioned by de Vaan. Following the model

---

[22] The Ontolex-lemon model requires that in such cases as many lexical entries are created as are the relevant assignments of part of speech.

[23] https://lila-erc.eu/data/id/lemma/120692.

[24] https://lila-erc.eu/sparql.

of Construction Morphology (Booij, 2010), used to represent in LiLa the derivational information provided by WFL (Litta et al., 2019), 36,318 lemmas in the lexical collection of LiLa (corresponding to the section of the analyzer Lemlat optimized for Classical Latin) are linked to the prefixes, the suffixes and the lexical bases that can be distinguished in their internal structure. Thus, the noun *clarificatio* mentioned above is connected to two lexical bases (the one shared with *clarus* and the one shared with *facio* "to make") and the deverbative suffix *-(t)io(n)*.

Lexical bases provide a suitable starting point to investigate the links. As a rule, words that share a lexical base with a lemma of an entry in de Vaan (2008) also share the same etymology. A SPARQL query over LiLa's endpoint returns 1,200 bases out of 3,858 (31.10%) that are linked to at least one lemma of a lexical entry connected to an etymology.

Although these 1,200 bases cover less than a third of the total in LiLa, they link 23,292 lemmas (64% of the lemmas attached to a base). In fact, on average, bases that are connected to a word linked to an etymology group a significantly larger numbers of lemmas (21.01) than those with no link to etymologies (5.36). This may be due to several concurring factors. Some words of PIE origin (such as *facio* "to make", *fero* "to bring" or the numeral *tres* "three") are extremely productive.[25] On the other hand, many loan words, which, as we said, are not discussed by de Vaan (2008) and thus have no etymology link, are usually technical terms that gave origin (if at all) to very few derivatives.

The connection with the lexical bases in the LiLa knowledge base allows us to supplement the list of the ca. 9,400 derivatives with a number of new units ranging from 13,853 new units (assuming all the words in the index of de Vaan are in the results) to a maximum of 23,292 (if no words in the index are in the results). In either case, this represents a significant increase in the coverage of the Latin lexicon.

5. Conclusions and future work

By adopting the Ontolex-lemon model and the lemonEty expansion, and building on the LiLa's original assumption of linking through lemmatization, we were able to include a basic set of etymological connections to our knowledge base of Latin canonical forms. Namely, we introduced a set of etymologies, defined as scientific hypotheses about the inheritance links between Latin words and the reconstructed forms in the PIt and PIE languages. It is now possible to follow the links from the etymologies to the lemmas and, from there, to all the other resources connected to each canonical form.

The potential applications of the (meta)data we created are several and, most importantly, transcend the limits of Latin linguistics. Latin is in fact just one of the many languages that trace their root to PIE. To go back to the example of *lupus* and to name but a few random modern languages, words as different as English *wolf*, Irish *olc*, Czech *vlk*, Albanian *ujk*, Greek *lýkos*, Hindi *vŕk* and Persian *gorg* all originate from the same reconstructed PIE word. Potentially, all lexical databases for Indo-European languages could have etymological links pointing to the same PIE etymon.

In most cases, the precise reconstruction of the form and meaning of a PIE etymon will be extremely controversial. Although this field of research is very speculative, and strong disagreement and incompatible hypotheses are often the rule rather than the exception, we have shown that the ontologies available are capable of modeling, at least broadly, the terms of the scholarly debate and to capture the arguments.

While the information encoded in LiLa is already rich, several directions for future improvement can be outlined. On the one hand, the Latin derivatives of each entry mentioned by de Vaan (2008) and included in the index of 9,439 words mentioned above can be explicitly linked to the main lexical entries as cognates. Also, the etymology of some selected affixes of PIE or PIt origin can be attached to the relevant morphemes by using the Ontolex-lemon model and lemonEty.

Finally, we intend to link the Latin WordNet (LWN) (Minozzi, 2010) to our lemmas, but also to increase its coverage (Franzini et al., 2019). The connection with LWN would allow us to expand the etymology links to trace the sub-links to the senses of Latin lexical entries and the meaning of the PIt and PIE as reconstructed from the comparative evidence. The process of mapping the semantics of etymons would thus produce a similar output to that visualized in Figure 3 for the discarded etymology of *lupus*, with WordNet used as a reference ontology instead of DBpedia.

6. Acknowledgements

We are grateful to Prof. Michiel de Vaan for proposing us to use his work in our project, and to Brill Ed. for granting us the permission to link some of the information contained in the Latin etymological dictionary to LiLa.

This project has received funding from the European Research Council (ERC) under the European Union's Horizon 2020 research and innovation programme - Grant Agreement No 769994.

7. Bibliographical References

Abromeit, F., Chiarcos, C., Fäth, C., and Ionov, M. (2016). Linking the tower of babel: modelling a massive set of etymological dictionaries as rdf. In *Proceedings of the 5th Workshop on Linked Data in Linguistics (LDL-2016): Managing, Building and Using Linked Language Resources*, pages 11–19, Portoroz, Slovenia. European Language Resources Association (ELRA).

Berners-Lee, T. (2006). Linked data. `https://www.w3.org/DesignIssues/LinkedData.html`. Accessed February 13, 2020.

Bon, B. and Nowak, K. (2013). Wikilexicographica. linking medieval latin dictionaries with semantic mediawiki. In *Electronic lexicography in the 21st century: thinking outside the paper. Proceedings of the eLex 2013 conference, 17-19 October 2013*, pages 407–420, Ljubljana and Tallinn. Trojina, Institute for Applied Slovene Studies and Eesti Keele Instituut.

Booij, G. (2010). Construction morphology. *Language and linguistics compass*, 4(7):543–555.

Budassi, M. and Passarotti, M. (2016). Nomen omen. Enhancing the Latin morphological analyser Lemlat with

---

[25]In LiLa, the bases linked to these three lemmas count 688, 367 and 36 lemmas respectively.

an onomasticon. In *Proceedings of the 10th SIGHUM Workshop on Language Technology for Cultural Heritage, Social Sciences, and Humanities (LaTeCH)*, pages 90–94, Berlin, Germany. Association for Computational Linguistics.

Cecchini, F., Passarotti, M., Ruffolo, P., Testori, M., Draetta, L., Fieromonte, M., Liano, A., Marini, C., and Piantanida, G. (2018). Enhancing the latin morphological analyser lemlat with a medieval latin glossary. In *Proceedings of the Fifth Italian Conference on Computational Linguistics (CLiC-it 2018). 10-12 December 2018, Torino*, pages 87–92, Torino. aAccademia University Press.

Chiarcos, C. and Sukhareva, M. (2015). OLiA - Ontologies of Linguistic Annotation. *Semantic Web Journal*, 6(4):379–386.

Chiarcos, C., Cimiano, P., Declerck, T., and McCrae, J. P. (2013). Linguistic linked open data (llod). Introduction and overview. In *Proceedings of the 2nd Workshop on Linked Data in Linguistics (LDL-2013): Representing and linking lexicons, terminologies and other language data*, pages i–xi, Pisa, Italy. Association for Computational Linguistics.

de Vaan, M. (2008). *Etymological Dictionary of Latin: and the other Italic Languages*. Brill, Amsterdam.

Declerck, T., Lendvai, P., Mörth, K., Budin, G., and Váradi, T. (2012). Towards linked language data for digital humanities. In *Linked Data in Linguistics*, pages 109–116. Springer, Berlin.

Doerr, M. (2003). The cidoc conceptual reference module: an ontological approach to semantic interoperability of metadata. *AI magazine*, 24(3):75–75.

du Cange, C. d., Bénédictins de Saint-Maur, Carpentier, P., Henschel, L., and Favre, L. (1883–1887). *Glossarium mediae et infimae latinitatis*. Favre, Niort, France.

Franzini, G., Peverelli, A., Ruffolo, P., Passarotti, M., Sanna, H., Signoroni, E., Ventura, V., and Zampedri, F. (2019). Nunc Est Aestimandum. Towards an evaluation of the Latin WordNet. In Raffaella Bernardi, et al., editors, *Sixth Italian Conference on Computational Linguistics (CLiC-it 2019)*, pages 1–8, Bari, Italy. CEUR-WS. org, CEUR-WS.org.

Georges, K. E. and Georges, H. (1913–1918). *Ausführliches lateinisch-deutsches Handwörterbuch*. Hahn, Hannover.

Glare, P. G. (1982). *Oxford Latin Dictionary*. Oxford University Press, Oxford.

Gracia, J., Montiel-Ponsoda, E., Vila-Suero, D., and Aguado-de Cea, G. (2014). Enabling language resources to expose translations as linked data on the web. In *Proceedings of the Ninth International Conference on Language Resources and Evaluation (LREC'14)*, pages 409–413, Reykjavik, Iceland, May. European Language Resources Association (ELRA).

Gradenwitz, O. (1904). *Laterculi vocum Latinarum: voces Latinas et a fronte et a tergo ordinandas*. Hirzel, Leipzig.

Khan, A. F. (2018a). Towards the Representation of Et-

ymological Data on the Semantic Web. *Information*, 9(12):304, December.

Khan, F. (2018b). Towards the Representation of Etymological and Diachronic Lexical Data on the Semantic Web. In John P. McCrae, et al., editors, *Proceedings of the Eleventh International Conference on Language Resources and Evaluation (LREC 2018)*, Miyazaki, Japan. European Language Resources Association (ELRA). event-place: Miyazaki, Japan.

Litta, E., Passarotti, M., and Culy, C. (2016). Formatio formosa est. building a word formation lexicon for latin. In Anna Corazza, et al., editors, *Proceedings of the third italian conference on computational linguistics (clic–it 2016)*, pages 185–189, Naples. aAccademia University Press.

Litta, E., Passarotti, M., and Mambrini, F. (2019). The treatment of word formation in the LiLa knowledge base of linguistic resources for Latin. In *Proceedings of the Second International Workshop on Resources and Tools for Derivational Morphology*, pages 35–43, Prague, Czechia, September. Charles University, Faculty of Mathematics and Physics, Institute of Formal and Applied Linguistics.

Mambrini, F. and Passarotti, M. (2019). Harmonizing different lemmatization strategies for building a knowledge base of linguistic resources for Latin. In *Proceedings of the 13th Linguistic Annotation Workshop*, pages 71–80, Florence, Italy, August. Association for Computational Linguistics.

McCrae, J. P., Chiarcos, C., Bond, F., Cimiano, P., Declerck, T., de Melo, G., Gracia, J., Hellmann, S., Klimek, B., Moran, S., Osenova, P., Pareja-Lora, A., and Pool, J. (2016). The open linguistics working group: Developing the linguistic linked open data cloud. In *Proceedings of the Tenth International Conference on Language Resources and Evaluation (LREC'16)*, pages 2435–2441, Portorož, Slovenia, May. European Language Resources Association (ELRA).

McCrae, J. P., Bosque-Gil, J., Gracia, J., Buitelaar, P., and Cimiano, P. (2017). The OntoLex-Lemon Model: development and applications. In *Proceedings of eLex 2017*, pages 587–597.

Minozzi, S. (2010). The Latin WordNet project. In P Anreiter et al., editors, *Latin Linguistics Today. Latin Linguistics Today. Akten des 15. Internationalen Kolloquiums zur Lateinischen Linguistik*, pages 707–716, Innsbruck. Institut für Sprachen und Literaturen der Universität Innsbruck.

Nowak, K. and Bon, B. (2015). medialatinitas.eu. towards shallow integration of lexical, textual and encyclopaedic resources for latin. In *Electronic lexicography in the 21st century: linking lexical data in the digital age. Proceedings of the eLex 2015 conference, 11-13 August 2015, Herstmonceux Castle, United Kingdom*, Ljubljana and Brighton. Trojina, Institute for Applied Slovene Studies and Lexical Computing LTD.

Passarotti, M., Budassi, M., Litta, E., and Ruffolo, P. (2017). The Lemlat 3.0 Package for Morphological Analysis of Latin. In Gerlof Bouma et al., editors, *Proceedings of the NoDaLiDa 2017 Workshop on Process-*

ing Historical Language, volume 133, pages 24–31, Gothenburg. Linköping University Electronic Press.

Städtler, T., Dörr, S., Tittel, S., Kiwitt, M., and Möhren, F. (2014). Dictionnaire étymologique de l'ancien français (deaf).

Stead, S., Doerr, M., Ore, C.-E., and Kritsotaki, A. e. a. (2019). Crminf: the argumentation model, version 0.10.1 (draft). `http://new.cidoc-crm.org/crminf/sites/default/files/CRMinf%20ver%2010.1.pdf`. Accessed February 13, 2020.

Tittel, S. and Chiarcos, C. (2018). Historical lexicography of old french and linked open data: transforming the resources of the dictionnaire étymologique de l'ancien français with ontolex-lemon. In *Proceedings of the 6th Workshop on Linked Data in Linguistics: Towards Linguistic Data Science, Co-Located with LREC2018, Miyazaki, Japan*, volume 12.

An automatically generated Danish Renaissance Dictionary
Building a period dictionary by reducing and merging relevant existing dictionary resources

Mette-Marie Møller Svendsen, Nicolai Hartvig Sørensen, Thomas Troelsgård
Society of Danish Language and Literature

The Danish Renaissance Dictionary is part of the project "Music and Language in Danish Reformation Hymns" (2018-21) of which the main goal is to present a digital edition of a series of Danish hymn books from the Lutheran Reformation (officially implemented in 1536). Historically this was a time where many political, social, economical and religious changes were taking place. The Danish language was also experiencing a transitional period, which is of particular interest to this project. Luther's German translation of The New Testament in 1522 motivated the Danish King Christian II to initiate work on a Danish translation (Nielsen 2017). From then on more and more texts in Danish as well as hymns and services in Danish followed. The Reformation encouraged the use of the Danish language, compared to the use of Latin and Low German, and provided a significant boost to the expansion of the vocabulary.

Texts as well as music are digitised and made searchable, and a series of dictionaries relevant to the period, which have only partially been digitised, will be made accessible. Furthermore, for the key texts of the project, the text reader will include an integrated dictionary function that looks up the selected word and presents a generated basic entry – a sort of "sense keywords" – extracted from the project's dictionary sources. Links will also be provided to the full entries of the dictionaries where the selected word is found. The project is funded jointly by the Carlsberg Foundation and the Velux Foundation, and the work takes place at the Society for Danish Language and Literature (DSL).

In this presentation, we will describe how we perform the linking of the dictionaries, and the present stage of our work on processing and presenting data for the "keyword entries" in the Renaissance dictionary.

<u>Dictionary linking</u>
The available dictionary data is highly heterogeneous, as the project dictionaries comprise 12 dictionaries and vocabularies from the time of the Reformation as well as five more recent dictionaries and vocabularies (19th, 20th and 21st century) describing the language of the period. The material each dictionary and vocabulary offers differs greatly in scope and size, but generally (and naturally) the more recent dictionaries are much larger than the early source material. Furthermore, the uneven and sometimes even patchy levels of details and accuracy in the markup of the older dictionaries and vocabularies is another obstacle in the process.

For the linking task, the heterogeneity becomes apparent through a rich variation in spelling across the resources, as well as the provision of part-of-speech information (which is often absent in the older dictionaries), and the choice of base form of the headword. Hence, some resources list verbs in the infinitive, while others use the present tense. For these reasons it became evident that the linking could not be performed in a fully automated way.

The linking is done within a "meta dictionary" that is continuously in development, and which ideally aims at linking all Danish dictionary resources at DSL at entry level. The same meta dictionary is used for linking two modern Danish dictionaries in connection with our tasks in work package WP2 of the ELEXIS project. The work package is centered on dictionary linking across languages and achieving compatible formats for the ensuing meta dictionaries.

The linking of each resource is done in three passes:
1. If a source entry matches a target entry in the meta dictionary, having matching headwords and matching part-of-speech, and neither of them has homographic headwords (of the same part-of-speech) in their respective dictionary, the linking is considered safe and is completed automatically.
2. If one or more possible targets can be found in the meta dictionary, selecting the correct target is done manually using a custom-designed tool called the "Konnektor".
3. If no match can be found, the headword in question is established as a new lemma in the meta dictionary.

For the actual linking we use the tool "Konnektor". Its input is an XML file with a series of sets, each holding the entry to be linked and one or more possible target "meta entries" in the meta dictionary. The targets are organised by prioritising matches in part-of-speech and similarity of the headword, but the overall similarity of the entries is taken into account as well. For the older vocabularies the Latin equivalents are matched as well. The output is the input file, enriched with ID's of the chosen target(s), or with a code denoting that the entry should be established as a new lemma in the meta dictionary.

The "Konnektor" has been an invaluable tool in our linking tasks, but it is still too early in the process to evaluate both the input technique as well as the tool. This is something that will be examined in further detail when we have worked through a larger amount of material during the project.

<u>Generation of keyword entries</u>
The purpose of this task is to generate user-friendly, relatively short and plain entries that collect and condense the information found in a group of linked entries. The aim of these entries is not to present the dictionary content to the user, but simply to give the user an idea of the meaning of the word. Thus, we would ideally like to present a series of definitions or equivalents without evidence, sources, etymology, etc.
As mentioned above, the dictionary sources are quite heterogeneous, and that challenges the generation of the keyword entries. For this reason, we aim to generate content only where the result is meaningful. Thus, if a generated extract is empty, or if it is too complex, we suppress it, and the user will have to follow the link to the actual source entry.
Fig. 1 shows an example of a new entry (*belakke*, 'defame, slander', obsolete in modern Danish) where several definitions/equivalents are extracted. Fig. 2. shows an example (*afladsbrev*, 'letter of indulgence') where no meaningful content could be extracted, thus only presenting links to the source entries (in the yellow link box).

belakke *vb.*

Kristian Sandfelds ordbog til En Ræffue Bog
✦ bagtale

Ordbog over det danske Sprog
✦ tillægge (en) en fejl, mangel (lak); tale ilde om; bagtale.

Kalkars Ordbog
✦ bagtale, laste

Marius Kristensens ordbog til Danske Viser
✦ tilsmudse, bagvaske

Dansk Folkevisekultur 1550-1700
✦ tilsmudse, bagvaske

"belakke" i tidligere dansk
✦ Kalkars Ordbog – "Belakke" *(dansk 1350-1700)*

"belakke" i senere dansk
✦ Ordbog over det danske Sprog *(dansk 1700-1955)*

Fig. 1: An entry with generated content (and additional links to other dictionaries).

afladsbrev *sb.*

Ordet findes ikke i renæssancens ordlister

"afladsbrev" i tidligere dansk
✦ Gammeldansk Ordbog – "aflatsbrev" *(dansk 1100-1450)*
✦ Kalkars Ordbog – "Afladsbrev" *(dansk 1350-1700)*

"afladsbrev" i senere dansk
✦ Ordbog over det danske Sprog – "Afladsbrev" *(dansk 1700-1955)*
✦ Den Danske Ordbog *(dansk 1950-)*

Fig. 2: An entry with no meaningful content for the time period, only links other dictionaries.

<u>Concluding remarks</u>
Currently the dictionary linking, as well as the content extraction and the construction of the website, is a work in progress. We anticipate that both the extraction process and the presentation of the dictionary will improve as soon as we receive feedback from the project's philologists and other users. Furthermore, it is our hope that the enrichment of the meta dictionary will enable us to exploit this data in future projects.

References

Nielsen, Marita Akhøj. *Hvorfor taler vi dansk? Om reformationen og sproget.* København: Eksistensen. 2017.

Svendsen, Mette Marie Møller, Nicolai Hartvig Sørensen & Thomas Troelsgård. "Superordbog og salmesang: ordbogslinkning i praksis" in: *Nordiske studier i leksikografi 15.* Helsinki: Nordisk forening for leksikografi. Expected time of publication: Late 2020.

Proceedings of the Globalex Workshop on Linked Lexicography, pages 33–35
Language Resources and Evaluation Conference (LREC 2020), Marseille, 11–16 May 2020
© European Language Resources Association (ELRA), licensed under CC-BY-NC

Towards an Extension of the Linking of the Open Dutch WordNet with Dutch Lexicographic Resources

Thierry Declerck[1,2]

[1] DFKI GmbH, Multilinguality and Language Technology Lab
[2] Austrian Centre for Digital Humanities and Cultural Heritage at the Austrian Academy of Sciences
[1] Stuhlsatzenhausweg 3, D-66123 Saarbrücken, Germany
[2] Sonnenfelsgasse 19, A-1010 Vienna, Austria
declerck@dfki.de

Abstract

This extended abstract presents on-going work consisting in interlinking and merging the Open Dutch WordNet and generic lexicographic resources for Dutch, focusing for now on the Dutch and English versions of Wiktionary and using the Algemeen Nederlands Woordenboek as a quality checking instance. As the Open Dutch WordNet is already equipped with a relevant number of complex lexical units, we are aiming at expanding it and proposing a new representational framework for the encoding of the interlinked and integrated data. The longer term goal of the work is to investigate if and on how senses can be restricted to particular morphological variations of Dutch lexical entries, and how to represent this information in a Linguistic Linked Open Data compliant format.

Keywords: Dutch WordNet, Lexicography, Linking, OntoLex-Lemon

1. Introduction

Work on interlinking or merging language data for Italian, Spanish and French included in wordnets on the one side and morphological data sets on the other side is documented in (Racioppa and Declerck, 2019). The authors accessed for this experiment Wordnet data that are available at the Open Multilingual Wordnet (OMW, (Bond and Paik, 2012; Bond and Foster, 2013)) portal.[1] OMW brings together wordnets in different languages, harmonizing them in a uniform tabular format that lists synsets IDs and the associated lemmas. OMW is linking those Wordnets to the original Princeton WordNet (PWN, (Miller, 1995; Fellbaum, 1998)). Additionally, XML versions of LMF and *lemon* representations[2] of the data are provided.

The morphological data used in those experiments were taken from updated versions of the MMorph data sets.[3] (Declerck et al., 2019) describe a similar experiment conducted for combining the German data from MMorph with an emerging lexical semantics resource for German.

In all those experiments, the OntoLex-Lemon model (Cimiano et al., 2016)[4] was used for representing the linking and merging of the language data originating from both the Wordnet and the MMorph frameworks.

In our current work we expand this kind of experiments beyond the use of morphologies and consider also full lexical resources.

It has been shown that the access and use of Wiktionary can be helpful in a series of applications. (Kirov et al., 2016), for example, describe work to extract and standardize the data in Wiktionary and to make it available for a range of NLP applications, while the authors focus on extracting and normalizing a huge number of inflectional paradigms across a large selection of languages. This effort contributed to the creation of the UniMorph data (http://unimorph.org/).

BabelNet[5] is integrating Wiktionary data[6] with a focus on sense information, in order to support, among others, word sense disambiguation and tasks dealing with word similarity and sense clustering (Camacho-Collados et al., 2016).

(McCrae et al., 2012b) is directly paving the way for our work, whereas we are upgrading the described approach by the use of OntoLex-Lemon and focusing on establishing relations between senses and morphological forms, and not only between senses and lexical entries.

In our current work, which is dealing with the Dutch language, we consider for the Wordnet side the Open Dutch WordNet (ODWN) and for the lexicographic side the XML dump of the Dutch edition of Wiktionary. We also access the XML dump of the English edition of Wiktionary, in order to extract the descriptions of Dutch nouns included in this edition and to compare them with those proposed in the Dutch edition. When discovering discrepancies between the two, we check manually if a corresponding entry is included in the "Algemeen Nederlands Woordenboek",[7] as a referential point for taking a decision on which data source is to be selected.

---

[1]See http://compling.hss.ntu.edu.sg/omw/ for downloading the resources.

[2]LMF stands for"Lexical Markup Framework", an ISO standard. See (Francopoulo et al., 2006) and http://www.lexicalmarkupframework.org/ for more details. *lemon* stands for "LExicon MOdel for oNtologies". See (McCrae et al., 2012a) and https://lemon-model.net/ for more details.

[3]See (Petitpierre and Russell, 1995).

[4]OntoLex-Lemon is a further development of the *lemon* model. See also https://www.w3.org/2016/05/ontolex/ for more details on the model.

[5]See (Navigli and Ponzetto, 2010) and https://babelnet.org/.

[6]As far as we are aware of, BabelNet integrates only the English edition of Wiktionary, but includes all the languages covered by this edition.

[7]See http://anw.inl.nl/ and (Tanneke Schoonheim, 2010).

2. Open Dutch WordNet

(Postma et al., 2016) describe how the Open Dutch Word-Net (ODWN) combines lexical semantics information and lexical units. This is partially done, as the authors of ODWN had to remove from the predecessor resource, called "Cornetto" (Vossen et al., 2008), a large part of the lexical units, which were owned by a publishing house not willing to publish them as open source. So that "only" around 50,000 full lexical units are associated to the 117,914 ODWN synsets. Those lexical units are originating from the "Referentie Bestand Nederlands" (RBN).[8] In order to replace the removed lexical units, data from public sources, including Wiktionary, were accessed, but this was limited to the "lemmas" that could be associated to a (Dutch) synset to be aligned to a PWN synset. Our aim is thus to add to those lemmas a full lexical description.

ODWN also converted its data to *lemon*, and in our current work we are aiming at upgrading this formal representation to OntoLex-Lemon, the successor of *lemon*, as this new model is designed to also accommodate conceptual lexical data such as those one can find in a wordnets.

3. Wiktionary

Our work consists in accessing lexical data from the XML dump of the Dutch edition of Wiktionary,[9] with a focus for now on Dutch nouns. When we say "XML dump" of Wiktionary, we have to precise that most of the data within the XML encoded general entries are in fact encoded using the MediaWiki markup language, which is more intended for generating a human readable web page. Some of the data is included in such a way that tools are called for generating the information to be displayed in HTML tables, like the (possibly complex) display of inflection of entries.

As mentioned above, we are also accessing the English Wiktionary for Dutch nouns, as there all metadata and definitions etc. are in English, easing thus the comparison between entries of different languages. There are about 52,000 entries for Dutch words in the English Wiktionary.[10] Consulting the Dutch Wiktionary, we see that from the total of 754,631 entries (also called "pages"), 388,786 are about Dutch words (and 11,330 about English words).

A first comparison of both sources for Dutch words shows that there is in general a certain level of congruence of information between them, while the Dutch Wiktionary is more expansive on semantically related words. It might happen that one source is displayed more definitions ("senses") than the other, and this constitutes a challenge for the automatic merging of sense-related information.[11] Also the ways of encoding the lexical information are distinct. So, for the Dutch word "route" (*road*, *way*),

the English Wiktionary encodes the information on Part-of-Speech, gender, plural form(s) and diminutive(s) this way:

```
{{nl-noun|f|-s|pl2=-en|routetje}}
```

while in the Dutch edition the more or less corresponding data is displayed this way:

```
{{-nlnoun-|{{pn}}|[[{{pn}}n]]
[[{{pn}}s]]|bezield=nietgeanimeerd|
          meta=abstract|telbaar=ja}}
{{-noun-|nld}}
'''{{pn}}'''  {{m}}
```

where we can notice that the information on diminutive form(s) is missing, whereas there is some semantic information added.[12]

But it seems that the information on the gender is contradictory, as the English Wiktionary is indicating for the entry the feminine gender, and the Dutch version the masculine gender. Using here the Algemeene Nederlandse Woordenboek (ANW)[13] as a "referee", we see that the word is in fact " mannelijk of vrouwelijk" (*masculine or feminine*), which corresponds to the distribution of genders in Dutch, following which nouns are either of grammatical gender "common" ("feminine or masculine") and "neuter".

So that even within Wiktionary there is a need to harmonize data representation across distinct language-based editions. For this we are currently porting the Wiktionary data into OntoLex-Lemon. This way we can compare, link and merge with lexical data from the ANW[14] and associate those lexical unit with the OntoLex-Lemon encoding of the ODWN synsets.

4. Conclusion

In this extended abstract, we presented current work aiming at adding further lexical data to the Open Dutch Word-Net. This goal requires that we first harmonize all the data sources we are considering, using for this purpose the OntoLex-Lemon model. The longer term goal of our work is to be able to represent the association of senses to morphological variants of lexical entries.

5. Acknowledgements

The presented work is supported by the Horizon 2020 research and innovation programme with the projects Prêt-à-LLOD (grant agreement no. 825182) and ELEXIS (grant agreeement no. 731015). It is also partially supported by the COST Action CA18209 - NexusLinguarum "European network for Web-centred linguistic data science".
We also thank the anonymous reviewers for their helpful comments.

---

[8]The Referentiebestand Nederlands - RBN (Version 2.0.1) (2014) is available at the Dutch Language Institute: `http://hdl.handle.net/10032/tm-a2-n2`. See also (van der Vliet, 2007).

[9]The dumps of Wiktionary can be downloaded at `https://dumps.wikimedia.org/backup-index-bydb.html`. The human readable Dutch version of Wiktionary is accessible at `https://nl.wiktionary.org/wiki/Hoofdpagina`.

[10]Data is taken from `https://en.wiktionary.org/wiki/Wiktionary:Statistics`.

[11]This topic is at the core of a challenge on "Monolingual Word Sense alignment (MWSA)" organized in the context of the ELEXIS project (`https://elex.is/`). See for more details on this challenge: `https://sinaahmadi.github.io/resources/mwsa.html`.

[12]Both human readable entries can be accessed at `https://en.wiktionary.org/wiki/route#Dutch` and `https://nl.wiktionary.org/wiki/route` respectively.

[13]`http://anw.inl.nl/article/route`.

[14]A description of ANW lexical data encoded in OntoLex-Lemon is given in (Tiberius and Declerck, 2017).

6. Bibliographical References

Bond, F. and Foster, R. (2013). Linking and extending an open multilingual Wordnet. In *Proceedings of the 51st Annual Meeting of the Association for Computational Linguistics (Volume 1: Long Papers)*, pages 1352–1362, Sofia, Bulgaria, August. Association for Computational Linguistics.

Bond, F. and Paik, K. (2012). A survey of wordnets and their licenses. In *Proceedings of the 6th Global WordNet Conference (GWC 2012)*, Matsue. 64–71.

Camacho-Collados, J., Pilehvar, M. T., and Navigli, R. (2016). Nasari: Integrating explicit knowledge and corpus statistics for a multilingual representation of concepts and entities. *Artificial Intelligence*, 240:36–64.

Cimiano, P., McCrae, J. P., and Buitelaar, P. (2016). Lexicon Model for Ontologies: Community Report.

Declerck, T., Siegel, M., and Gromann, D. (2019). Ontolex-lemon as a possible bridge between wordnets and full lexical descriptions. In Christiane Fellbaum, et al., editors, *Proceedings of the Tenth Global Wordnet Conference*, pages 264–271, wyb. Stanisława Wyspiańskiego 27 50-370 Wrocław Poland, 7. Oficyna Wydawnicza Politechniki Wrocławskiej, Oficyna Wydawnicza Politechniki Wrocławskiej.

Christiane Fellbaum, editor. (1998). *WordNet: An Electronic Lexical Database*. Language, Speech, and Communication. MIT Press, Cambridge, MA.

Francopoulo, G., George, M., Calzolari, N., Monachini, M., Bel, N., Pet, M., and Soria, C. (2006). Lexical markup framework (lmf). In *International Conference on Language Resources and Evaluation-LREC 2006*.

Kirov, C., Sylak-Glassman, J., Que, R., and Yarowsky, D. (2016). Very-large scale parsing and normalization of wiktionary morphological paradigms. In Nicoletta Calzolari (Conference Chair), et al., editors, *Proceedings of the Tenth International Conference on Language Resources and Evaluation (LREC 2016)*, Paris, France, may. European Language Resources Association (ELRA).

McCrae, J., de Cea, G. A., Buitelaar, P., Cimiano, P., Declerck, T., Gómez-Pérez, A., Gracia, J., Hollink, L., Montiel-Ponsoda, E., Spohr, D., and Wunner, T. (2012a). Interchanging lexical resources on the Semantic Web. *Language Resources and Evaluation*, 46(6):701–709.

McCrae, J., MontielPonsoda, E., and Cimiano, P., (2012b). *Integrating WordNet and Wiktionary with lemon*, pages 25–34. Springer Berlin Heidelberg, Berlin, Heidelberg.

Miller, G. A. (1995). Wordnet: A lexical database for english. *COMMUNICATIONS OF THE ACM*, 38:39–41.

Navigli, R. and Ponzetto, S. P. (2010). BabelNet: Building a very large multilingual semantic network. In *Proceedings of the 48th Annual Meeting of the Association for Computational Linguistics*, pages 216–225, Uppsala, Sweden, July. Association for Computational Linguistics.

Petitpierre, D. and Russell, G. (1995). MMORPH: The Multext morphology program. Multext deliverable 2.3.1, ISSCO, University of Geneva.

Postma, M., van Miltenburg, E., Segers, R., Schoen, A., and Vossen, P. (2016). Open dutch wordnet. In *Proceedings of the Eight Global Wordnet Conference*, Bucharest, Romania.

Racioppa, S. and Declerck, T. (2019). Enriching open multilingual wordnets with morphological features. In Raffaella Bernardi, et al., editors, *Proceedings of the Sixth Italian Conference on Computational Linguistics*. CEUR, 10.

Tanneke Schoonheim, R. T. (2010). Dutch lexicography in progress: the algemeen nederlands woordenboek (anw). In Anne Dykstra et al., editors, *Proceedings of the 14th EURALEX International Congress*, pages 718–725, Leeuwarden/Ljouwert, The Netherlands, jul. Fryske Akademy.

Tiberius, C. and Declerck, T. (2017). A lemon model for the anw dictionary. In Iztok Kosem, et al., editors, *Proceedings of the eLex 2017 conference*, pages 237–251. INT, Trojína and Lexical Computing, Lexical Computing CZ s.r.o., 9.

van der Vliet, H. (2007). The referentiebestand nederlands as a multi-purpose lexical database. *International Journal of Lexicography*, 20(3):239–257.

Vossen, P., Maks, E., Segers, R., and van der Vliet, H. (2008). Integrating lexical units, synsets and ontology in the cornetto database. In European Language Resources Association (ELRA), editor, *Proceedings of LREC 2008, Marrakech*.

Proceedings of the Globalex Workshop on Linked Lexicography, page 36
Language Resources and Evaluation Conference (LREC 2020), Marseille, 11–16 May 2020
© European Language Resources Association (ELRA), licensed under CC-BY-NC

Widening the Discussion on "False Friends" in Multilingual Wordnets

Hugo Gonçalo Oliveira, Ana R. Luís
University of Coimbra, DEI-CISUC, University of Coimbra, CELGA-ILTEC
hroliv@dei.uc.pt, aluis@fl.uc.pt

Abstract

Cognates are words that have similar meaning and spelling in two or more languages (Carroll, 1992), such as *impossible* (English) and *impossível* (Portuguese) or *education* (English) and *educação* (Portuguese). Although Portuguese is a Romance language and English is a Germanic language, they share an extraordinary high number of cognates which are essentially of Latin and Greek origin (Domíngues, 2008).

Portuguese and English also have *false friends*, namely pairs of words that appear similar but have a different meaning. Examples include *push* (English) and *puxar* (Portuguese), meaning 'to pull'; *library* (English) and *livraria* (Portuguese), meaning 'bookshop'; or *beef* (English) and *bife* (Portuguese), meaning 'steak'. Among them, some pairs of words are 'partial' *false friends* as they may have different meanings only in some contexts. Examples include *medicine* (English), which is cognate with *medicina* (Portuguese), but can also mean 'substance used to treat an illness'; or *figure* (English), which is cognate with *figura* (Portuguese), but can also mea 'number'.

Cognates have been successfully identified with Natural Language Processing techniques using methods such as orthographic similarity and semantic similarity, combined with machine learning (Bradley & Kondrak, 2011). While the identification of cognates has made much progress, the identification of *false friends* is still an under-researched area. But available studies show that it is an area from which other areas that support Natural Language Processing, including the development of computational lexical resources, could benefit (Hefler, 2017; Castro, Bonanata & Rosá, 2018).

Focusing on wordnets for different languages, and towards multilingual processing, two main strategies have been adopted for alignment with the Princeton WordNet (Fellbaum, 1998): the expand or the merge approach (Vossen, 2002). In both cases, *false friends* can be a source of errors, either in the application of automatic steps (e.g., for automatic translation) or simply due to a lack of knowledge of the people involved, influenced by orthographic similarity.

For instance, with a quick search in the Portuguese wordnet OpenWordNet-PT (Paiva, Rademaker & Melo, 2012) a few errors of this kind are identified. In Table 1, we present some of them, with the id and the words of the English synset, followed by the words of the aligned Portuguese synset, followed by a brief explanation of the problem. Although the focus of this exploratory exercise was on Portuguese and English, such problems are common among other pairs of languages.

Motivated by these problems, we aim to open a discussion on the potential benefits of further research on *false friends* in the development of wordnets and other multilingual linked resources. Possible tasks to tackle could exploit lists of *false friends* from the literature for cleaning multilingual wordnets. A simple thing to do would be to remove *false friends* from linked synsets, or even to remove the connection between those synsets. Moreover, an RDF property could perhaps be used for explicitly

linking pairs of lexical items, in different languages, that are *false friends*. Besides enabling other lines of research, this information could also be considered in further expansions of the wordnet.

Synset ID	Portuguese	English	Explanation
02275799-v	*pretender*	*pretend*	*pretend* (EN) means 'deceive', while *pretender* (PT) means 'want, intend
02374914-a	*simpático*	*sympathetic*	*sympathetic* (EN) means 'showing compassion', while *simpático* (PT) means 'nice, friendly'
00074558-v	*constipar*	*constipate*	*constipate* (EN) is related to 'difficulty in emptying the bowels', while *constipar* (PT) means 'getting a cold'
10661216-n	*estrangeiro*	*stranger*	*stranger* (EN) is a person who is unkown, while *estrangeiro* (PT) is a 'foreigner'

Table 1 : False friend-related issues in OpenWordNet-PT

Keywords: false friends, cognates, multilingual wordnets

Bibliographical References

Bradley, H. and Kondrak, G. (2011). Clustering Semantically Equivalent Words into Cognate Sets in Multilingual Lists. *Proceedings of the 5th International Joint Conference on Natural Language Processing*, pp. 865–873.

Carroll, S. (1992). On cognates. *Second Language Research* 8 (2), 93–119

Castro, S., Bonanata. J. and Rosá, A. (2018). A High Coverage Method for Automatic False Friends Detection for Spanish and Portuguese. Proceedings of the Fifth Workshop on NLP for Similar Languages, Varieties and Dialects, 29–36.

Domínguez, P. (2008). Semantics and Pragmatics of False Friends. New York, London: Routledge.

Fellbaum, C. (1998). WordNet: An Electronic Lexical Database (Language, Speech, and Communication). The MIT Press.
Hefler, M. (2017). False Friends between English and Italian. Submitted in partial fulfilment of the requirements for the B.A. in English Language and Language, University of Rijeka.

Paiva, V. D., Rademaker, A., & Melo, G. D. (2012). OpenWordNet-PT: An open Brazilian wordnet for reasoning. COLING 2012.

Vossen, P. (2002). EuroWordNet: general document.

Proceedings of the Globalex Workshop on Linked Lexicography, pages 37–44
Language Resources and Evaluation Conference (LREC 2020), Marseille, 11–16 May 2020
© European Language Resources Association (ELRA), licensed under CC-BY-NC

Pinchah Kristang: A Dictionary of Kristang

Luis Morgado da Costa

Interdisciplinary Graduate School – Global Asia,
Nanyang Technological University, Singapore
lmorgado.dacosta@gmail.com

Abstract

This paper describes the development and current state of *Pinchah Kristang* – an online dictionary for Kristang. Kristang is a critically endangered language of the Portuguese-Eurasian communities residing mainly in Malacca and Singapore. *Pinchah Kristang* has been a central tool to the revitalization efforts of Kristang in Singapore, and collates information from multiple sources, including existing dictionaries and wordlists, ongoing language documentation work, and new words that emerge regularly from relexification efforts by the community. This online dictionary is powered by the Princeton Wordnet and the Open Kristang Wordnet – a choice that brings both advantages and disadvantages. This paper will introduce the current version of this dictionary, motivate some of its design choices, and discuss possible future directions.

Keywords: kristang, online dictionary, wordnet, portuguese-malay creole, endangered language

1. Introduction

Pinchah Kristang (lit. to cast a net over Kristang) was officially launched, in Singapore, at the First Kristang Language Festival, in May 2017, by then Singapore's Deputy Prime Minister, Mr. Teo Chee Hean. This Festival celebrated the culmination of over a year of successful language revitalization efforts by *Kodrah Kristang* (lit. Awaken, Kristang) – a grassroots initiative with the goal of revitalizing Kristang in Singapore.

Pinchah Kristang is an open-source online bilingual dictionary (English-Kristang) and it is powered by the Open Kristang Wordnet – an ongoing project, supported by an eclectic team of trained linguistics, heritage speakers, students and community volunteers.

The main goals of this dictionary include both documenting and helping disseminate this beautiful endangered language. Building this dictionary is a great way to better understand, document and revitalize Kristang and, by making it accessible through an online interface, it has also been a great way to give back and empower the community to remember and use their language.

The remainder of this paper will start by providing an introduction to Kristang and its revitalization efforts in Singapore, followed by a discussion of *Pinchah Kristang*'s stages of development. It will conclude with some notes on the current state of the project, followed by a discussion of concerns and future directions.

1.1. Kristang

Kristang is a critically endangered creole language, spoken mainly by Portuguese-Eurasian communities in Malacca and Singapore. Although estimates concerning the number of speakers is a sensible topic, it is generally agreed that the number of speakers does not go beyond the lower thousands, in both Singapore and Malaysia.

According to Pillai et al. (2017), in Malacca, Kristang is estimated to be spoken fluently by only about half of the residents at the Portuguese Settlement, which has approximately 800–1000 residents. In Singapore, where the situation is much direr, it is estimated that fewer than 100 families use Kristang daily, and only a very small percentage is still passing it down to younger generations. It is also generally agreed that the number of speakers in both countries has seen a steady decline (Nunes, 1999; Martens Wong, 2017). Kristang is known by many different names, including: Bahasa Geragau, Bahasa Serani, Luso-Malay, Malacca Creole, Malaccan, Malaqueiro, Malaquenho, Malaquense, Malaquês, Malayo-Portuguese, Malaysian Creole Portuguese, Papia Cristao, Papia Kristang, Portuguese Patois, Português de Malaca, and Serani.[1] For the remainder of this paper, we will refer to it as Kristang. Kristang, referring to both the language and its people (Hancock, 2009; Baxter, 2005), is the name most recognized by the community speaking this language in Singapore, where this project had its birth.

Kristang is originally derived from Malay and Portuguese, having its roots in the beginning of the 16th century with the arrival of the Portuguese to Malacca. At the same time, most likely caused by the inflow of people and cultural exchange through the Portuguese maritime exploration, there is evidence to suggest that Kristang is also related to number of other Portuguese Creoles, sharing commonalities with other languages and creoles from Africa, India, Southeast Asia, and Southern China (Nunes, 1999; Fernández, 2012; Baxter, 2012; Nunes, 2012)

Since the fall of Malacca to the Dutch, in the mid-17th century, the Kristang community has survived through roughly three more centuries of colonial occupation by both the Dutch and the English empires. This was accompanied by a mixture of other languages that also influenced Kristang. According to a few studies (Baxter and Bastos, 2012; Pillai et al., 2015), traces of Chinese, Indian, Malay, Dutch, Sri Lankan, Filipino and English language elements are evident in Kristang.

Kristang is a Subject-Verb-Object (SVO) language, with its vocabulary largely derived from Portuguese, with heavy influence from Malay and light influence from several other languages, notably Dutch and English. Its grammar and phonology are closely related to Malay.

---

[1] https://www.ethnologue.com/language/mcm

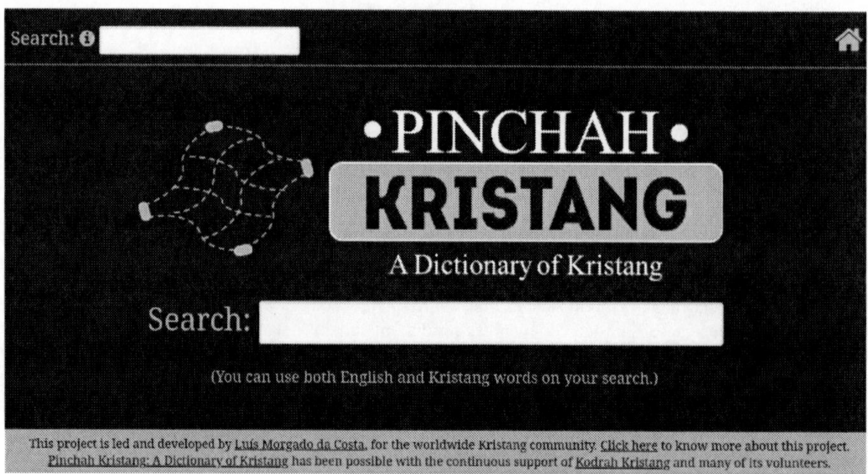

Figure 1: Screenshot of *Pinchah Kristang*'s Welcome Page

1.2. *Kodrah Kristang*: **Revitalization in Singapore**

Pinchah Kristang was developed within the larger context of *Kodrah Kristang*, an initiative to revitalize Kristang in Singapore. *Kodrah Kristang* (lit. Awaken, Kristang) is an initiative founded by Kevin Martens Wong, that started to take form in early 2015. The sole purpose of this initiative is to work with the community to reawaken the language and bring it back to a healthy level of use.

Kodrah Kristang has published and maintains a revitalisation plan[2] that describes the long-term plans, goals and projects to revitalize the Kristang language in Singapore, up to the year 2045 CE. Following this plan, the *Kodrah Kristang* team has launched a number of initiatives including free classes for children and adults, freely available audio and vocabulary courses, musical performances in Kristang, public talks, social media presence, as well as TV and radio interviews. These initiatives have reached thousands of people around the world, and have also greatly increased public awareness of this endangered language in Singapore.

1.2.1. *Jardinggu*: **Relexification Effort**

A specific project that is closely related to this dictionary is the relexification effort led by *Kodrah Kristang*, known as *Jardinggu* – from the concatenation of *jarding* (garden) and *linggu* (language), meaning 'Language Garden'.

The primary goal of *Kodrah Kristang* is to encourage more people to learn and speak Kristang. Many young people, however, do not see the value in learning a language that is not ready for the modern age, and that lacks words for concepts that are important today, like 'website', 'cell phone' and 'wifi'. Similar to what has happened in other languages, such as Hawaian or Alutiiq (Kimura and Hawaiian Lexicon Committee, 2009), *Kodrah Kristang* created a language incubator that engages and invites the community to actively create new words that are missing from Kristang's known lexicon. New word suggestions are presented to the com-

munity, who votes to accept or reject them as part of the language. This is a flexible and continuous process. And, ultimately, only a long term analysis will be able to determine which words were picked up by speakers.

However, in an effort to both document and facilitate the use of newly coined words, the Open Kristang Wordnet (and, by default, *Pinchah Kristang*) includes theses words with a temporary status. These words have a special status within the dictionary and may, at a later stage, be removed or substituted by different words that receive greater acceptance.

2. Development of *Pinchah Kristang*

Pinchah Kristang's online interface is a simple web application powered by Python, Flask,[3] and SQLite3. It is heavily inspired by the Open Multilingual Wordnet (Bond and Foster, 2013, OMW), and its interface is being built in tandem with the most recent OMW codebase [4] – reusing many of its core structure and functionalities, including the database design, but completely diverging in its user interface.

Figure 1 shows the welcome page of of Pichah Kristang. The online dictionary uses a simple bilingual search interface, where both English and Kristang can be used in searches. In addition, it is also enabled by SQLite3's GLOB clause, allowing simple regular expression searches such as the use of wildcards (e.g. the search 'cat*' will match any words that start with 'cat').

2.1. The Dictionary Data

At its core, *Pinchah Kristang* is powered by the Princeton Wordnet (Fellbaum, 1998, PWN), along with two other wordnets - the Open Kristang Wordnet and the Extended Kristang Wordnet. The reason for using two Kristang wordnets is simple: creating and curating a high quality wordnet is extremely time consuming. The Open Kristang Wordnet is a standard wordnet, being developed by linguists and trained volunteers. On the other hand, the Extended Kristang Wordnet is a lemma-to-lemma dictionary mapping dis-

---

[2]https://kodrahkristang.files.wordpress.com/2017/02/kaminyu-di-kodramintu-v2.pdf

[3]https://flask.palletsprojects.com/en/1.1.x/
[4]https://github.com/globalwordnet/OMW/

guised in the form of a wordnet to be able to share the same online platform. In the following sections, the origin and structure of the dictionary data will be discussed in further detail.

2.2. Data Gathering

Given the endangered and fragmentary status of Kristang, there is a lack of competent speakers from whom to draw consistent lexicographic knowledge. As such, our dictionary is actively collating and validating this necessary lexicographic knowledge using multiple different sources. These sources include:

1. paper dictionaries and word-lists made available through both published works (including but not limited to: Baxter and de Silva (2004), Marbeck (2011) and Scully and Zuzarte (2004)); and through families or individuals who have kept notes about the language;

2. linguistic publications concerning Kristang, which often contain either wordlists or elicited language data that has been glossed (see, for example, Hancock (1970), Baxter (1988), and Avram (2013));

3. language documentation work, lead by *Kodrah Kristang* or its affiliates. This includes work done by Michael Erlewine and his EL3212 2017 course in Field Methods in Linguistics (which focused on Kristang), at the National University of Singapore. This course piloted the data collection and entry into this wordnet using OMWEdit (Morgado da Costa and Bond, 2015);

4. new words and senses that are produced by *Jardinggu*, the Kristang lexical incubation project, introduced above, in Section 1.2.1;

2.3. The Open Kristang Wordnet

The Open Kristang Wordnet was built using the 'expansion approach' (Vossen, 1998), where the structure of another wordnet is used as pivot. In this approach, building a wordnet is essentially a translation effort – conserving the structure of the pivot wordnet and translating individual nodes of the hierarchy, which can easily be done incrementally (i.e. usually starting by a subset of frequent concepts). The Princeton Wordnet (Fellbaum, 1998) is, by far, the most frequently used pivot for wordnet projects around the world.

As previously mentioned, this project drew large inspiration on the work of OMW – possibly the best example of the benefits provided by developing wordnets using the 'expansion approach'. For many years, the OMW has linked dozens of open wordnets using PWN as the pivot structure. However, a change to the way the OMW operates was recently introduced with the creation of the Collaborative Interlingual Index (Bond et al., 2016, CILI) – an open, language agnostic, flat-structured index that links wordnets across languages without imposing the hierarchy of any single wordnet. Through CILI, multiple projects are now able to link to each other and to contribute directly to the set of CILI's concepts without the penalty of being frozen within an imposed structure.

Perhaps not surprisingly, CILI was initially created using the full set of concepts provided by the PWN (i.e. all PWN concepts have a direct link to CILI). As such, the quickest and easiest way to link a new wordnet to CILI is still to use the expansion approach with PWN's hierarchy as pivot – and this is what the Open Kristang Wordnet is doing.

2.3.1. Linking and Validation

With the help of all data sources described above, a master word list of aligned Kristang and English lemmas was compiled (and continues to be updated regularly). Depending on the source, extra information such as part-of-speech, full definitions and alignments to other languages such as Portuguese and Malay is, sometimes, available. Currently, this master list contains 15,435 word alignments between English and Kristang. It is important to note, however, that many of these alignments are not unique, as different sources often provide the same or similar information.

The first step to create our wordnet was done using a custom script to project all available English alignments onto PWN and generate a list of all candidate senses based on the data we have collected. This script is able to leverage multiple levels of information (e.g. language alignments, part-of-speech, number of overlaps per concept, etc.) to generate a ranked list of candidate senses. A full description of this script is, unfortunately, outside the scope of this paper.

A total of 51,077 candidate senses, spanning over 19,445 unique synsets were generated using the process described above. This data has, since then, been in a continuous process of validation by multiple members of *Kodrah Kristang* core team and some of its higher fluency students. This validation process consists of determining, with a high degree of certainty, if a candidate sense is attested in Kristang or not. Each candidate sense has three possible states: rejected (i.e. there is no evidence that this sense is available in the language); accepted (i.e. this sense has been confirmed to exist in the language, albeit with varying degrees of usage frequency); undetermined (i.e. it is possible that this sense exists in the language, but there is not enough evidence to confirm this at the moment, and requires further documentation work).

Out of the 51,077 candidate senses generated by our method: 8,382 ($\sim$16.4%) have been rejected; 7,011 ($\sim$13.7%) have been accepted; and 3,692 ($\sim$7.2%) were left undetermined – a total of 19,085 ($\sim$37.4%) candidate senses have been checked.

Table 1 provides a summary of the data currently contained in the Open Kristang Wordnet. It currently includes slightly more than 5,300 synsets, with just over 7,000 senses. About 97.5% of all concepts have been hand-linked to CILI (i.e. 2.5% do not have a mappeable concept in CILI).

POS	Synsets	%	Words	%	Senses	%
Noun	2,969	55.3	2,248	61.5	3,860	55.1
Verb	1,195	22.3	426	11.6	1,447	20.6
Adjective	1,005	18.7	834	22.8	1,435	20.5
Adverb	171	3.2	127	3.5	231	3.3
Non-ref	26	0.5	22	0.6	38	0.5
	5,366		3,657		7,011	

Table 1: Statistics for Open Kristang Wordnet

The Open Kristang Wordnet is currently supported both

in the new WN-LMF format[5] and the tab-separated-value (TSV) format used by the original OMW specifications.

2.4. The Extended Kristang Wordnet

As mentioned above, building and curating a wordnet can be extremely time consuming. The Open Kristang Wordnet is only roughly one third of the way from checking the 51,000 generated candidate senses. And even though the order with which senses are checked tries to maximise the revitalization efforts (e.g. giving priority to checking senses that are currently used in the Kristang classrooms), using only one third of the data would greatly diminish the usefulness of the online dictionary.

The Extended Kristang Wordnet solves this issue by creating a flat wordnet linking all English-Kristang lemma pairs that were not yet covered by the Open Kristang Wordnet manual efforts. Strictly speaking, the Extended Kristang Wordnet is only a wordnet in the sense that it makes use of the WN-LMF format to create English-Kristang word pairings. This wordnet is not linked to CILI (or any other wordnet) and, as such, it has no hierarchy, and is unable to leverage on PWN's data to further populate the dictionary with data other than basic English lemmas (e.g. full English definitions are not available).

Currently, the Extended Kristang Wordnet introduces 6,887 extra concepts, linking 6,883 Kristang Lemmas to 7,972 English Lemmas. Since these word-pairs come from various sources of data, most often from simple wordlists, the Extended Kristang Wordnet does not contain parts-of-speech information – making it very difficult to provide any kind of structured statistics for this resource.

As the manual efforts of the Open Kristang Wordnet continue to manually check all the data, the size of the Extended Kristang Wordnet will slowly decrease. The purpose of the Extended Kristang Wordnet is merely to bridge coverage issues, and it will cease to exist as soon as the Open Kristang Wordnet finishes the validation process of the existing data.

3. Current state of *Pinchah Kristang*

This dictionary project is still in active development, and it is primarily maintained by one of the core members of *Kodrah Kristang*. It is important to note that both *Kodrah Kristang* and this dictionary are fully run on a voluntary basis and, as such, it is most definitely slower than what would be expected from funded/staffed projects.

Currently, *Pinchah Kristang* is a strictly bilingual dictionary (see discussion below about plans to further expand this). Whenever available, English data is provided by the PWN. Despite being powered by wordnets, *Pinchah Kristang* is currently hiding some of the more complex features available in a wordnet (e.g. the rich semantic hierarchy) – which is done with user friendliness in mind. Most users are either learners or heritage speakers trying to remember forgotten words. As such, overloading the dictionary with linguistic information irrelevant to these users would impose a toll on usability.

Nevertheless, the fact that the dictionary is powered by wordnets is still somewhat clear. Let's compare Figure 2 and Figure 3 below:

Figure 2 shows the search results for the lemma 'gatu' ('cat', in Kristang). Since this lemma is completely unambiguous, only one entry is shown. In this case, this entry has been linked to the PWN. The Kristang lemma is shown to the left (highlighted in yellow), and it is accompanied by the English lemmas provided by the PWN. The part-of-speech and the definition are also provided.

Figure 3, on the other hand, shows the search results for the lemma 'cat'. These results are a bit more verbose. The PWN presents nine senses for the lemma 'cat' – including the senses for the domestic cat, and the verbal sense synonymous with 'to vomit'. Both these entries have a linked Kristang sense, which appear on the left column ('gatu' and 'gumitah', respectively). The seven other English sense of the lemma 'cat' do not have any Kristang lemmas linked to them. This is currently shown by a question mark in place of the Kristang lemma. Clicking on this question mark on will redirect the user to *KlaiFalah* (lit. 'how to say'), an initiative under *Jardinggu*, the Kristang Lexical Incubator, where users can request and suggest new words to be created. In this platform, users are able to inquire about senses that are still missing from the dictionary. These senses might already exist in the language, but the data was not yet collected, or it might be considered by the lexical incubator program – which works with the community to create a new word for the missing sense. As this process is done outside the scope of this dictionary project, it will not be discussed here in further detail.

Lastly, Figure 3 shows a tenth sense (in the second line) with is a match for the lemma 'cat' but in Kristang. One of the existing data sources lists *cat* as a Kristang word for 'pain'. However, as it can be seen from the lack of part-of-speech and definition, this Kristang lemma belongs to the Extended Kristang Wordnet. As of this moment, this use is not yet attested beyond a written source and, as such, it has not been linked to the PWN. This is also a good example to show how the single search input form matches both English and Kristang lemmas.

4. Concerns and Future Directions

This section will focus on specific points of concern for this project, and outline some of the future directions the project is likely to take.

4.1. Non-English Concepts

A problem that is common to many wordnets that followed the 'expand' approach, is the difficulty in breaking away from the preexisting structure of the pivot project – in our case, CILI / the Princeton Wordnet.

It is not surprising, therefore, that we share these same concerns. There are many concepts that are not currently represented in Open Kristang Wordnet for the simple reason that these concepts do not have an English counterpart in the PWN. Some of these concepts are culturally specific, such as *kari debal* or *pang susi* – two of the most charismatic recipes of Kristang cuisine – and would not be expected to exist in PWN. But some other basic concepts are also missing due to way Kristang lexifies certain concepts that are treated compositionally in English. This happens, for example, with *dosora* (two o'clock) and *desora* (ten o'clock) –

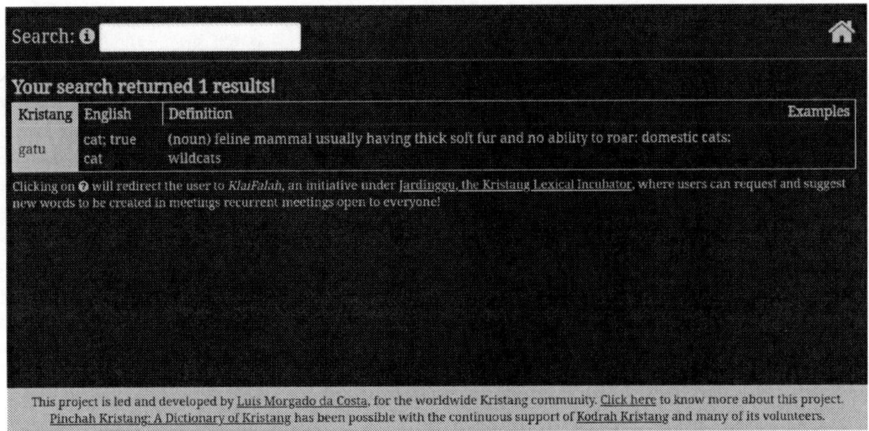

Figure 2: Screenshot of Pinchah Kristang's Search Results for 'gatu'

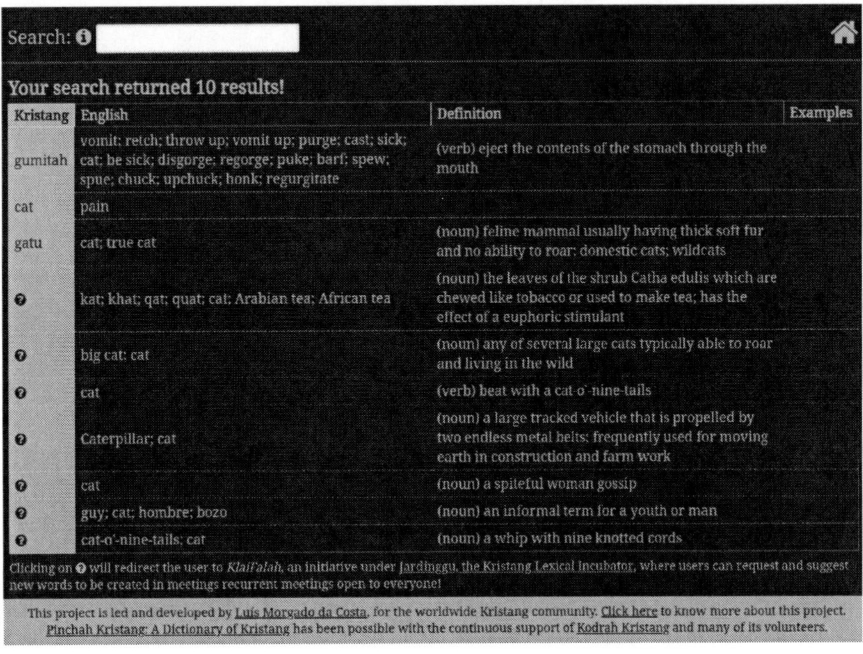

Figure 3: Screenshot of *Pinchah Kristang*'s Search Results for 'cat'

which are deemed compositional in English (ten + o'clock), and hence do not have a concept in PWN.

Currently, this problem is mitigated by the use of the Extended Kristang Wordnet – which provides these Kristang words and translations to the dictionary, but lacks more structured data such as the part-of-speech or a definition.

Moving forward, the solution for this is for this project to be fully integrated within CILI (Bond et al., 2016), and gain the ability to suggest new concepts that necessary to adequately represent Kristang.

4.2. Relexification

Another topic of concern to this dictionary project is the decision to support the relexification efforts of *Kodrah Kristang*, which has been briefly introduced above, in Section 1.2.1. Even though supporting these efforts without the guarantee that a word has permanently entered the language may seem rash at first glance, it is important to note that *Pinchah Kristang*'s main goal is to support Kristang's revitalization. In addition, for all practical purposes, these new words enter the language once they are voted in by the community – even if with a temporary status. And despite the real chance that some of these words might end up substituted by new words in the future, these new words may still see usage before they are deprecated, in favor of different words. One of *Pinchah Kristang*'s goals is also to help disseminate these new words, with the hope of updating Kristang's vocabulary to modern times.

Ultimately, *Jardinggu* is a parallel effort towards Kristang's revitalization, with its own procedures and coordination. And lists of newly created words, notes on how the words were created, and their respective voting results are stored outside this dictionary. For this reason, and even though these new words hold a special status in the dictionary data, the current interface does not show the provenance of any of its senses (including words created by the relexification efforts). This decision might, however, be revised in the future – organically accompanying and responding to the ways the lexical incubator operates.

4.3. Examples and Corpus Integration

Pinchah Kristang has also started working on further supporting the documentation and revitalization of Kristang through the creation of a sense-tagged example corpus. Even though a wordnet is capable, in principle, to better disambiguate different senses and their usages (i.e. when compared to a simple bilingual word-list, which is the form of most dictionaries), this is not always enough. Having an example corpus, that provides users with clear usage examples of each sense is, to some extent, essential to full-fledged dictionary projects. Many wordnet projects have pioneered this line of thinking, and built their wordnets in parallel with an example corpus or, in the best case scenario, a sense-tagged example corpus. *Pinchah Kristang* will follow in their footsteps, and is currently working on a sense-tagged example corpus to enrich its user-experience.

4.4. Orthographic Variation

Since Kristang has rarely been recorded in written form over the course of its history, it never acquired a standard written form broadly accepted by its multiple communities. Orthographic and phonetic influences from geographical or cultural proximity with Kristang communities has resulted in wide orthographic variation in the language. Portuguese, Malay and English orthographies have all left a mark on Kristang orthography in Singapore. For example, Baxter and de Silva (2004) lists 'dog' as *kachoru*, where the word-medial consonant /ʧ/ follows the Portuguese or English orthographic system, while Marbeck (2011) lists it as *kacoru*, with the same /ʧ/ consonant spelled as it would be in Malay – both phonetically equivalent. Similarly, *kuelu* (Marbeck, 2011) and *kwelu* (Scully and Zuzarte, 2004) for 'rabbit' closely resembles Malay orthography, while the variant spelling *coelho* (Scully and Zuzarte, 2004) undoubtedly mimics Portuguese orthography.

The prevalence of metathesis in certain consonant clusters is another related problem. Examples of this include '-dr-' (*kodrah* and *kordah* for 'to wake up'), '-tr-' (*kotri* and *korti* for 'town' or 'city'), and '-br-' (*ebra* and *erba* for 'grass'). These are not, however, phonetically equivalent – posing a new level of complexity that should, at least, be acknowledged by *Pinchah Kristang*.

Pinchah Kristang aims to recognize all variant spellings included in existing dictionaries as well as others widely used by speakers in Singapore. Currently, these are all listed as different senses. In the future *Pinchah Kristang* will move towards the representation of a canonical form with multiple spelling variations. The canonical form will be orthography used by *Kodrah Kristang*, wich follows the orthography proposed by Baxter and de Silva (2004). Only senses that have the same phonetic realization will be merged (e.g. *kachoru* and *kacoru*, meaning 'dog') but not in cases of metathesis (e.g. *ebra* and *erba*, both meaning 'grass'). The current reasoning to deal with metathesis in a different way than plain orthographic variation comes from the fact that metathesis introduces phonetic differences – which is more closely tied to the identity of the speakers. And while we believe there is little hurt in moving towards standardization of the written form (since most of the variation comes from the fact that a written form never really existed), standardizing phonetic variation would impose stronger claims over how the language should be used. We want to move away from politicizing the language as much as possible.

4.5. Pronunciation and Phonetic Representation

In keeping with the role of supporting the documentation and revitalization efforts of Kristang, *Pinchah Kristang* will soon also include both voice recordings and phonetic representation (i.e. IPA) for some or all of our wordnet senses. These efforts are being pursued in tandem with language documentation interviews, that have provided hundreds of individual, segmented sense pronunciation recordings (sometimes by more than one speaker).

4.6. Linked Etymology

Largely inspired by projects such as the Etymological Wordnet (Melo, 2014) and the World Loanword Database (Haspelmath and Tadmor, 2009, WOLD), it would be extremely interesting to leverage on CILI and other linked wordnets (through the OMW) to study and integrate information concerning possible etymologies of Kristang lemmas in *Pinchah Kristang*.

Currently, the OMW includes large wordnets for the two most important languages from which Kristang vocabulary derives, Portuguese (de Paiva and Rademaker, 2012) and Malay (Mohamed Noor et al., 2011), along with a number of wordnets for other languages that are known to have contributed to the Kristang lexicon, namely English (Fellbaum, 1998), Dutch (Postma et al., 2016), Mandarin Chinese (Wang and Bond, 2013) and Cantonese (Sio and Costa, 2019). Missing from this list are, unfortunately, languages such as Hokkien, Hindi, Tamil and Sanskrit – all known to have influenced Kristang's lexicon.

The plan to use other wordnets to explore and link etymologies of Kristang senses could end up making our bilingual dictionary into a small multilingual dictionary, where languages of interest could be shown alongside relevant senses. Since this would most certainly be extremely time consuming, it would perhaps be interesting to employ semi-automatic methods to measure similarity between Kristang senses and all languages of interest.

4.7. Towards a Multilingual Dictionary

In line with what was discussed in the section above, even prior to having full-fledged etymological links between wordnets, the possibility of adding both Portuguese and Malay as parallel data in the dictionary is currently under discussion. Strictly from a dictionary standpoint, this would be relevant, as it would allow other communities (namely Portuguese and Malay speaking communities) to use the dictionary and get acquainted with Kristang. However, from a revitalization point-of-view, this might also bring certain challenges concerning language identity and 'purity'. As discussed in Section 4.4, on orthographic variation, certain dictionaries (and this is also true for individual people within the community) like to align themselves to either Malay or Portuguese spelling (even when this introduces orthographic ambiguity or a more opaque orthography). Language and identity cannot easily be dissociated, and missteps concerning these topics might impose constraints towards healthy revitalization of Kristang. *Pinchah Kristang* is currently monitoring this possibility, and it will align its design to best serve the Kristang community.

5. License and Release Notes

This dictionary is freely available online[6] and its main objective is to help the documentation and dissemination efforts of *Kodrah Kristang*, by collating information that would otherwise be dispersed and at a risk of being lost.

We want to encourage others to use our work, to work towards the further improvement of Kristang and its communities, to avoid replication of efforts, and to inspire other endangered communities to work towards their language preservation. For this reason, all work developed for *Pinchah Kristang*: A Dictionary of Kristang and the Open Kristang Wordnet are developed under a Creative Commons Attribution 4.0 International[7] (CC BY 4.0) license.

6. Acklowledgments

Ultimately, this is a project for and by the Kristang community (and their friends). And the current state of the dictionary and the wordnet would not have been possible without the volunteered hours of many who dedicated their time to this project. In particular, we would like to thank the many volunteers who helped with many forms of data entry and validation[8], as well as all permanent members and participants of the *Jardinggu* meetings; we would also like to thank Michael Erlewine and his 2017 class of EL3212 Field Methods in Linguistics, at the National University of Singapore, for piloting data collection and entry into this wordnet.

7. Bibliographical References

Avram, A. A. (2013). The Dutch lexical contribution to three Asian Portuguese Creoles // Contribuição lexical do holandês para três crioulos de base portuguesa da Ásia. *PAPIA-Revista Brasileira de Estudos do Contato Linguístico*, 23(1):51–74.

Baxter, A. N. and Bastos, A. (2012). A closer look at the post-nominal genitive in asian creole portuguese. *Ibero-Asian creoles: Comparative perspectives*, 46:47–79.

Baxter, A. N. and de Silva, P. (2004). *A dictionary of Kristang (Malacca Creole Portuguese) with an English-Kristang finderlist*. Number 564, Series B. Pacific Linguistics, The Australian National University, Australia.

Baxter, A. N. (1988). *A Grammar of Kristang (Malacca Creole Portuguese)*. Number 95, Series B. Pacific Linguistics, The Australian National University, Australia.

Baxter, A. N. (2005). Kristang (Malacca Creole Portuguese) –A long-time survivor seriously endangered. *Estudios de sociolingüística*, 6(1):1–37.

Baxter, A. N. (2012). Vestiges of etymological gender in malacca creole portuguese. *Pidgins and Creoles in Asia*, 38:115–149.

Bond, F. and Foster, R. (2013). Linking and extending an open multilingual wordnet. pages 1352–1362, Sofia.

Bond, F., Vossen, P., McCrae, J. P., and Fellbaum, C. (2016). Cili: the collaborative interlingual index. In *Proceedings of the Global WordNet Conference*, volume 2016.

de Paiva, V. and Rademaker, A. (2012). Revisiting a Brazilian wordnet. In *Proceedings of the 6th Global WordNet Conference (GWC 2012)*, Matsue.

Christiane Fellbaum, editor. (1998). MIT Press, Cambridge, MA.

Fernández, M. A. (2012). Nenang, nino, nem não, ni no. *Ibero-Asian Creoles: Comparative Perspectives*, 46:205–237.

Hancock, I. F. (1970). Some dutch-derived items in Papia Kristang. *Bijdragen tot de Taal-, Land-en Volkenkunde 126*, (3):352–356.

Hancock, I. F. (2009). The portuguese creoles of malacca. *Revue roumaine de linguistique*, 54(3-4):295–306.

Martin Haspelmath et al., editors. (2009). *WOLD*. Max Planck Institute for Evolutionary Anthropology, Leipzig.

Kimura, L. and Hawaiian Lexicon Committee. (2009). Indigenous new words creation perspectives from alaska and hawai 'i. *Indigenous Language Revitalization: Encouragement, Guidance and Lessons Learned*, pages 121–139.

Marbeck, J. M. (2011). *Commemorative Bahasa Serani Dictionary*. Adil Enterprise, Malaysia.

Martens Wong, K. (2017). Bos Papiah Kristang? (Do You Speak Kristang?): A Eurasian Linguistic Legacy. In *Singapore Eurasians: Memories, Hopes and Dreams*, pages 369–379. World Scientific.

Melo, G. D. (2014). Etymological wordnet: Tracing the history of words. In Nicoletta Calzolari (Conference Chair), et al., editors, *Proceedings of the Ninth International Conference on Language Resources and Evaluation (LREC'14)*, Reykjavik, Iceland, May. European Language Resources Association (ELRA).

Mohamed Noor, N., Sapuan, S., and Bond, F. (2011). Creating the open Wordnet Bahasa. In *Proceedings of the 25th Pacific Asia Conference on Language, Information and Computation (PACLIC 25)*, pages 258–267, Singapore.

Morgado da Costa, L. and Bond, F. (2015). Omwedit - the integrated open multilingual wordnet editing system. In *Proceedings of the 53rd Annual Meeting of the Associ-*

---

ation for Computational Linguistics and the 7th International Joint Conference on Natural Language Processing of the Asian Federation of Natural Language Processing, System Demonstrations (ACL 2015), pages 73–78, Beijing, China.

Nunes, M. (1999). The use of kristang in the portuguese settlement of malacca. *Journal of Modern Languages*, 12:147–158.

Nunes, M. P. (2012). Traces of superstrate verb inflection in makista and other asian-portuguese creoles. *Ibero-Asian Creoles: Comparative Perspectives*, 46:289–326.

Pillai, S., En, C. M., and Baxter, A. N. (2015). Vowels in malacca portuguese creole. *Research in Language*, 13(3):248–265.

Pillai, S., Phillip, A., and Soh, W.-Y., (2017). *Revitalizing Malacca Portuguese Creole*, pages 1–17. Springer International Publishing, Cham.

Postma, M., van Miltenburg, E., Segers, R., Schoen, A., and Vossen, P. (2016). Open Dutch WordNet. In *Proceedings of the Eight Global Wordnet Conference*, Bucharest, Romania.

Scully, V. and Zuzarte, C. (2004). *The Most Comprehensive Eurasian Heritage Dictionary: Kristang-English / English-Kristang*. SNP International, Singapore.

Sio, J. U.-S. and Costa, L. M. D. (2019). Building the Cantonese Wordnet. In *Proceedings of the Tenth Global Wordnet Conference*, Wroclaw, Poland.

Vossen, P. (1998). A multilingual database with lexical semantic networks. *Dordrecht: Kluwer Academic Publishers. doi*, 10:978–94.

Wang, S. and Bond, F. (2013). Building the chinese open wordnet (cow): Starting from core synsets. In *Sixth International Joint Conference on Natural Language Processing*, pages 10–18.

Proceedings of the Globalex Workshop on Linked Lexicography, pages 45–52
Language Resources and Evaluation Conference (LREC 2020), Marseille, 11–16 May 2020
© European Language Resources Association (ELRA), licensed under CC-BY-NC

Building Sense Representations in Danish by Combining Word Embeddings with Lexical Resources

Ida Rørmann Olsen[1], Bolette S. Pedersen[2], Asad Sayeed[3]
Centre for Language Technology, University of Copenhagen[1,2],
Department of Philosophy, Linguistics, and Theory of Science, University of Gothenburg[3]
Emil Holms Kanal 2, 2300 Kbh S[1,2], Renströmsgatan 6, 412 55 Gothenburg[3]
idaroermannolsen@gmail.com, bspedersen@hum.ku.dk, asad.sayeed@gu.se

Abstract

Our aim is to identify suitable sense representations for NLP in Danish. We investigate sense inventories that correlate with human interpretations of word meaning and ambiguity as typically described in dictionaries and wordnets *and* that are well reflected distributionally as expressed in word embeddings. To this end, we study a number of highly ambiguous Danish nouns and examine the effectiveness of sense representations constructed by combining vectors from a distributional model with the information from a wordnet. We establish representations based on centroids obtained from wordnet synsets and example sentences as well as representations established via a clustering approach; these representations are tested in a word sense disambiguation task. We conclude that the more information extracted from the wordnet entries (example sentence, definition, semantic relations) the more successful the sense representation vector.

Keywords: Danish, wordnet embeddings, word sense disambiguation

1. Introduction

The effective handling of sense ambiguity in Natural Language Processing (NLP) is an extremely challenging task, as is well described in the literature (Kilgarriff, 1997; Agirre and Edmonds, 2006; Palmer et al., 2004; Navigli and Di Marco, 2013; Edmonds and Kilgarriff, 2002; Mihalcea et al., 2004; Pradhan et al., 2007).

In this paper, we focus on a lower-resourced language, Danish, with the hypothesis that if we can compile sense inventories that *both* correlate well with human interpretations of word meaning *and* are well-reflected statistically in large corpora, we would have made a first and important step towards an improved and useful sense inventory: not too fine-grained, but still capturing the essential meaning differences that are relevant in language processing. We investigate this hypothesis by building sense representations from word embeddings using wordnet-associated data.

In order to assess the performance of the proposed model, we study a number of Danish nouns with very high meaning complexity, i.e., nouns that are described in lexica as being *extremely* polysemous. We apply a central semantic NLP task as our test scenario, namely that of *word sense disambiguation* (WSD). For lower-resourced languages, obtaining performance better than a majority-class baseline in WSD tasks is very difficult due to the extremely unbalanced distribution of senses in small corpora. However, the task is an ideal platform for achieving our goal of examining different approaches to sense representation. Our aim is both to support a data-driven basis for distinguishing between senses when compiling new lexical resources and also to enrich and supplement our lexical resource with distributional information from the word embedding model.

In the following, we carry out a series of experiments and evaluate the sense representations in a WSD lexical sample task. For the experiments, we represent wordnet synset information from the Danish wordnet, DanNet (Pedersen et al., 2009), in a word embedding model. We test five different Bag-Of-Words (BOWs) combinations—defined as 'sense-bags'—that we derive from the synsets, including information such as example sentence, definition, and semantic relations. Generally speaking, the synsets incorporate associated concepts via semantic relations which lexicographers have chosen as being the defining relation for each particular concept. This approach sheds light on the extent to which the hand-picked words in the synsets are actually representative of the processed corpus data.

It is not possible at this stage to evaluate an unsupervised word sense induction (WSI) system for Danish with curated open-source data. However, with a knowledge-based system, where the sense representations are linked to lexical entries, it is possible to evaluate with the semantically annotated data available for Danish, the SemDaX Corpus (Pedersen et al., 2016). This corpus is annotated with dictionary senses.

The paper is structured as follows: Section 2 describes Danish as a lower-resourced language and presents existing semantic resources that are available for our task. In Section 3, we present related work, and in Section 4 we describe our five experiments in detail. Section 5 and 6 describe and discuss our results, and in Section 7 we conclude and outline plans for future work.

2. Danish as a lower-resourced language

Semantic processing of lower-resourced languages is a challenging enterprise typically calling for combined methods of applying both supervised and unsupervised methods in combination with language transfer from richer-resourced languages. For Danish we have now a number of standard semantic resources and tools such as a wordnet and SemDaX corpus, a framenet lexicon (Pedersen et al., 2018b), several word embedding models (Sørensen and Nimb, 2018), and a preliminary sense tagger (Martinez Alonso et al., 2015). However, the size and accessibility of the resources as well as the evaluation datasets accompanying them typically constitute a bottleneck.

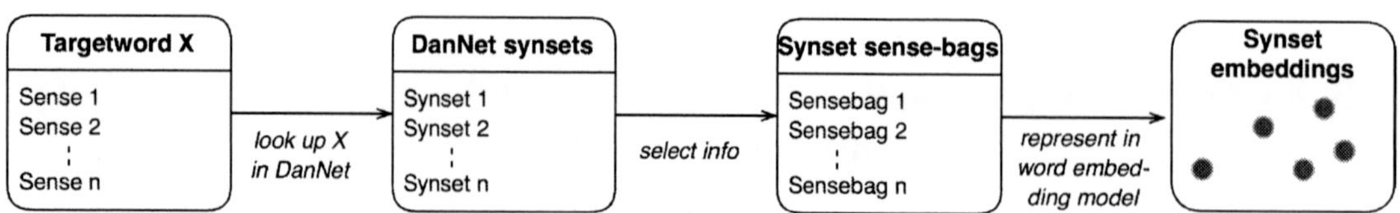

Figure 1: The method used to build the synset embeddings.

For instance, the wordnet, DanNet, which contains 65,000 synsets, is open-source, but the links from DanNet to the complete sense inventory of The Danish Dictionary is not. Our work requires this key, which necessitated connecting the dictionary labels to DanNet synsets through cumbersome manual compilation.[1]

3. Related Work

Both supervised and unsupervised methods to represent words and word senses have been widely explored in NLP, especially given the popularity of word embeddings. Unsupervised approaches to obtain not only word embeddings, but also sense embeddings (such as SenseGram (Pelevina et al., 2017), Adagram (Bartunov et al., 2016), and Neelakantan et al. (2014)) do not rely on existing large datasets; they are are thus suitable for lower-resourced languages. A downside is that the induced senses are not humanly readable or easy to link to lexical resources; this limits their applicability.

An incorporation of valuable high-quality resources, e.g., wordnets, in unsupervised methods can augment the sense representations with additional lexical information, especially for non-frequent word senses. The combination of contextual and knowledge-based information can be established by joint training (Faralli et al., 2016; Johansson and Nieto-Piña, 2015; Mancini et al., 2017), or by post-processing normal word embeddings (Rothe and Schütze, 2017; Bhingardive et al., 2015; Chen et al., 2014; Pilehvar and Collier, 2016; Camacho-Collados et al., 2016). Alternatively, Saedi et al. (2018) successfully converted a semantic network (WordNet) into a semantic space, where the semantic affinity of two words is stronger when they are closer in the semantic network (in terms of paths). They tested the resulting representations in a semantic similarity task and found a significant improvement compared to a regular word2vec space. The study also indicated that the more semantic relations included from the semantic network, the better the result.

Bhingardive et al. (2015) detected the most frequent senses by comparing the target word embedding in a word embedding model with constructed sense representations based on synset information represented in a word embedding model. Our work is also related to Ustalov et al. (2018) who proposed a synset-averaged sense-embedding approach to WSD for an under-resourced language (Russian). They evaluate the system's clustering on a gold-standard with an average number of word senses of 3.2

(Panchenko et al., 2018). Their results show that the task of building unsupervised sense embeddings this way is remarkably difficult.

We estimate the quality of the sense representations in a lexical sample WSD task. The contribution of this paper is therefore a study on these methods for Danish data evaluated on a WSD task and not for most frequent sense detection or on a gold standard. The work provides a detailed investigation of which information types from DanNet improve our WSD results, and with more focus on the role of example sentences than seen in related work.

4. Five word embedding experiments

For a number of years up to now, embeddings have been ubiquitous in computational approaches to numerous NLP tasks. While word embeddings, such as word2vec (Mikolov et al., 2013), have been central in NLP research touching on lexical semantics, other forms of embeddings, from character to paragraph to multimodal, have proven to be flexible, often multi-purpose forms of linguistic representation. Our overall idea is to build sense representations in vector spaces with information of associated words extracted from a lexical resource, namely wordnet. We make use of word embeddings to construct a sense representation, a *synset embedding*. The wordnet synset information (i.e., words) associated to a given sense of a word is collected in a synset "sense-bag". The synset sense-bag is used to construct a unified sense representation, the *synset embedding*, inside a word embedding model. See Figure 1.

Note that for each synset, DanNet provides both the hand-picked related concepts (as illustrated in Figure 2), one handpicked example sentence where the sense is used in context, and (part of) the sense definition from The Danish Dictionary.

For example, a particular synset sense-bag of the polysemous Danish targetword *model* (approximately the same concept as in English)—in the sense of a representation of something (sometimes on a smaller scale) consists of the example sentence: *"Færgen er en model i 1:4"* and the synset members *Effekt, videnskab, fremstille, figur, afprøve, gengive, pynte, arbejdsmodel, gine, globus, globus, mockup, modelbygning, modelfly, skalamodel, skibsmodel, modeljernbane, modelbil, modelskib, modeltog, kirkeskib* [2].

---

[1] We build the sense representations with DanNet, but our evaluation data, SemDaX, is annotated with dictionary labels. The Danish Dictionary is not fully available for research.

[2] "The ferry is a model 1:4", Effect, science, produce, figure, test, represent, decorate, working model, gine, globus, mock-up, model building, airplane model, scale model, ship model, traintrack model, car model, ship model, train model, church ship

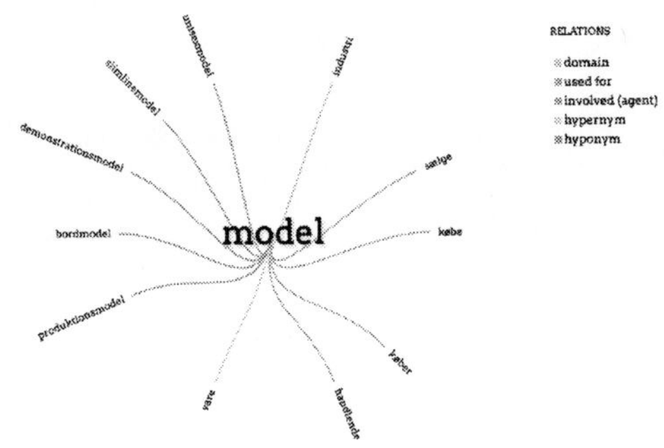

Figure 2: A synset of the targetword *model* (as in a model in industrial production). Semantic relations on the right.

In addition, the synset sense-bag of *model* in the sense of a schematic description or illustration of an abstract, complicated thing or relation, has the example sentence *"Watson og Crick fremsatte deres model af DNA-molekylet som en dobbeltspiral, der kan visualiseres som en vredet stige"* and the synset members *Anskueliggørelse, videnskab, atommodel, forklaringsmodel*[3].

First, we construct synset embeddings represented in a word embedding model by unifying information extracted from DanNet for each sense of the target nouns. These synset embeddings are tested in a WSD task using cosine similarity. Second, we apply the synset embeddings to sense-tag new unannotated data via a clustering approach. By doing this, we build more corpus-influenced synset embeddings (i.e. synset embeddings not exclusively built from wordnet information) and, at the same time, also obtain training data of a proper size to benefit of the advantages of machine learning models for future WSD experiments. See details of the method in section 4.1.

The method will work when there is a correspondence between how words in the knowledge-base for the given lexical resource (DanNet) are distributed across senses and what the distributional information of the words looks like in the word embedding model. If the words associated for each sense in DanNet are important for the concept's use in language, then the collection of those words in the word embedding model is reasonable, since such a model represents word similarity based on the distribution of words used in data.

The approach can be seen as highly scalable since the sense representations can be obtained without full annotation of a training corpus and is applicable for all word entries included in the input resource. The method would therefore be applicable also to other lower-resourced languages.

It should be emphasized that we test our approach *both* on a set of some of the most polysemous words found in Danish *and* operate on the most fine-grained version of the applied evaluation data (the SemDaX Corpus). Working with this corpus, Pedersen et al. (2018a) suggested a principled

approach to sense clustering. In that work, the coarsest sense granularity level proved to be most operational (in a WSD task), obtaining the highest inter-annotator agreement score. In our work, however, we choose the finest level of granularity to access the potential of the method when tested on a really hard task.

4.1. Experiment Details

We collect various synset information in synset sense-bags, and each word sense representation (synset embedding) is the centroid of the word embeddings from the corresponding sense-bag. The word embeddings originate from the word2vec word embedding model described in section 4.3., and the constructed synset embeddings live within that same vector space. The synset information varies for each experiment.

More precisely, a synset sense-bag is a set, $B = \{w_1, \ldots w_n\}$, where n is the number of words in B and the w's are the words selected[4] from the synset information. Each word, w_i in B, can be represented by a word vector $\overrightarrow{W_i}$ in the word embedding model. These word vectors in B are averaged into a mean vector, $\overrightarrow{M}$, where $\overrightarrow{M} = \frac{\sum \overrightarrow{W_i}}{n}$. $\overrightarrow{M}$ is the resulting synset embedding of the given synset sense-bag, B. Therefore, for each sense of each targetword we can collect a synset sense-bag, B, from DanNet and construct a synset embedding, $\overrightarrow{M}$, with the word embedding model. The extracted information from DanNet contain only words (not numbers). The words are not weighted when constructing the synset embedding with their word embeddings. Multi-word terms are treated as multiple words under word tokenization (these instances are rarer in Danish, than in English). In doing this, we examine whether the selected knowledge-based information from DanNet in combination with the distributional representation of the words in the synset sense-bags can construct appropriate sense representations.

Four types of synset sense-bags for building synset embeddings are tested:

1. Local synset members: Collection of hypernyms, hyponyms, synonyms, near-synonyms, used-for and made-by semantic relations, together with the bag-of-words (BOW) of the word sense definition.

2. Example sentence: BOW from the example sentence using the sense in context.

3. Example sentence+: BOW collection of local raw example sentence *and* raw example sentences from the hypo- and hypernym synsets.

4. Combination: All collections from exp. 1-3 put together *and* the BOW of definitions of hypo- and hypernyms.

A fifth and final synset embedding is tested, in which the best performing synset embedding above is used as a seed in the k-means algorithm (Lloyd, 1982) to auto-tag unannotated example context sentences by a clustering approach:

---

[3] *"Watson and Crick presented their model of a DNA molecule like a double-spiral, that can be visualized like a twisted latter"*, *visualization, science, atom model, explanation model.*

[4] Selected according to the given experiment.

5. <u>Cluster centroid</u>: Centroid of clustered context vectors

The idea is to tune the synset embeddings by adding more data than merely information from DanNet. The seeds bootstrap the resulting clusters to a category, and since each target word has a set number of senses (synset embeddings), the number of clusters per target word is pre-set. See figure 3 for a visualization. The new and unlabelled example context sentences are extracted from Korpus DK[5] and are simply word tokenized, lowercased, stripped of punctuation, considered as a BOW, and represented in the word embedding model (with the same method as decribed above for constructing synset embeddings from sense-bags). Around 1000 example sentences are extracted per targetword. We apply the K-means algorithm from the cluster package[6] included in the module Scikit-Learn (Pedregosa and Varoquaux, 2011) from Python. We set the parameter of number of clusters ($n\_clusters$) to the number of synset embeddings constructed for the current target word and set the synset embeddings as initial cluster centers (*init*).

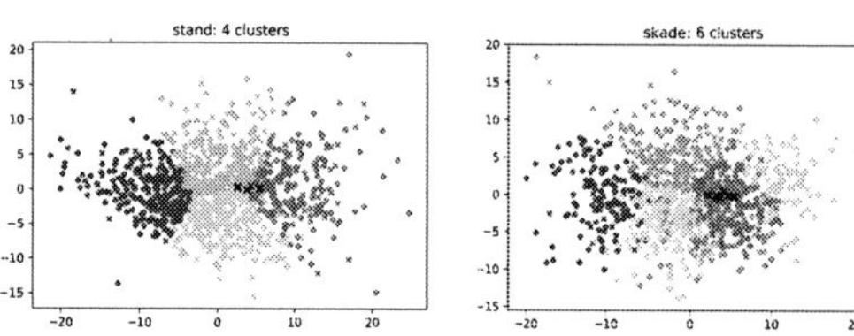

Figure 3: A 2D plot of resulting clusters of the Korpus DK example sentences for *stand* and *skade*, which have 4 and 6 synsets, and therefore 4 and 6 clusters, respectively. The black crosses are the seeds. Dimensionality reduction with PCA.

4.2. Evaluation Method

WSI systems and sense embeddings have typically been evaluated by comparing to a gold standard or in a WSD task measuring the quality by performance. In our approach, we implicitly seek to find a gold standard for word sense representations, and the quality of the developed sense representations are measured here by performance in a WSD task.

Computational semantic analysis systems are typically evaluated on the data sets from the ongoing series of SemEval, the International Workshop on Semantic Evaluation (Kilgarriff and Palmer, 2000). The evaluation data produced for SemEval 2013 task 13: *Word Sense Induction for Graded and Non-graded Senses3* is the standard data used to test WSI systems and sense embeddings. Our evaluation data, SemDaX, contains unranked sense annotations, and annotators were asked to assign one sense to the given instance.

Three test sentences from SemDaX for the Danish target-word *model* (approximately similar concept as in English) are shown below.

- *Og så havde vi kursister den luksus også at have fire fantastiske modeller at arbejde med[7]*

- *Men sådan er prisklassen konkret, og de fleste modeller bliver ofte kun produceret i et meget lille antal[8]*

- *Jeg bryder mig ikke om ordet model[9]*

It has been observed in the SemDaX corpus that almost all discrepancies among annotators were due to underspecified examples, i.e., examples where the precise word sense could not be deduced from the isolated corpus excerpt alone (Pedersen et al., 2018a). In order to account for this fact, all diverging annotations in the data set are considered to be correct (and unranked). The systems applied do not detect groups of relevant senses; they merely rank by similarity and pick the most similar sense. Since the annotated data do not contain ranked senses, and our word sense representation system does not choose a set (or cluster) of relevant senses, a direct comparison with the systems developed for SemEval 2013 task 13 with the same measures is not straightforward.

As indicated above, there might be multiple (correct) classes per instance. The combination of classes might change at every instance. We make use of an accuracy score that counts a "miss" for each instance where the system fails to identify any human-labelled sense, and a "hit" whenever it guesses at least one that matches a human label[10]. It should be noted that the system has "an advantage" in cases where annotators disagree (since more that one value is considered correct) so the results need to be analyzed together with the inter-annotator agreement. This measure is equally generous to the baselines as it is to the systems we tested.

WSD is done by maximizing the cosine similarity between the synset embeddings and the given test sentence represented as a context vector within the word embedding model. The test sentence context vector is the mean vector of the sentence considered as a bag-of-word vectors. The highest-similarity sense representation is chosen.
We apply three baselines:

- **Extended Lesk (E-lesk)**: WSD by cosine similarity between the centroid of the BOW from the wordnet definition of the word sense, and the evaluation text instance vector. (Banerjee and Pedersen, 2002)

- **Random**: WSD by chance

---

[5]A clustering of the annotated sentences in the evaluation data, SemDax, would be more precise, but would not be a scalable approach relying on as little annotated data as possible.

[6] `https://scikit-learn.org/stable/modules/generated/sklearn.cluster.KMeans.html`

[7]*and we as participants then had the luxury of having four fantastic models to work with*

[8]*But that is how the price level actually is, and most models are produced in a very limited amount*

[9]*I do not like the word model*

[10]We tested the Kullback-Leibler divergence score as an alternative "soft" evaluation measure to incorporate the fact that there can be multiple correct answers, but the human distributions are far more "spiky" than the normalized system scores, leading to statistically insignificant differences between systems.

Target words	Synsets	Annotated senses (incl. idiomatic expressions)
Ansigt (*face*)	6	16
Blik (*look, glace, tin*)	6	8
Hold (*team, side, gang*)	8	10
Hul (*hole, gap, leek*)	13	22
Kort (*card, map, plan*)	10	21
Lys (*light, candle, lamp, glare*)	16	30
Model (*model, pattern, type, design*)	8	9
Plade (*plate, sheet, disc*)	13	13
Plads (*room, space, square, post*)	10	21
Skade (*harm, injury, damage, magpie, ray*)	6	12
Slag (*battle, stroke, cape, roll*)	15	28
Stand (*state, condition, shape, booth, stand*)	4	11
Stykke (*piece, part, length, paragraph*)	16	22
Top (*top, peak, apex*)	5	12
Vold (*violence, bank*)	7	10
Kontakt (*contact, switch, touch*)	7	9
Selskab (*company, party, association*)	9	11

Table 1: Target words with number of DanNet synsets (column 1) and number of senses actually encountered in the data (column 2). Some senses encountered in the annotated data are merged and link into the same synset, the reason for which we see the difference in numbers across columns.

- **Most frequent sense (MF)**

The MF as default is usually a very hard baseline to beat, in particular for the most polysemous part of the vocabulary, as we are doing here. See discussion of this in section 6.

4.3. Materials

DanNet: The Danish wordnet, DanNet, was compiled semi-automatically from the Danish dictionary *Den Danske Ordbog* (Hjorth and Kristensen, 2005). These two resources are therefore highly related and possible to link. The 65,000 synsets in DanNet are interrelated via 325,000 semantic relations. All synsets are assigned an ontological type, a corresponding supersense, and come with a definition and an example sentence. The DanNet information extracted are word collections: either words from relevant synsets (i.e., related concepts), or words from the synset example sentences and definition sentence considered as a BOW. The BOW (i.e. the synset sense-bag) is unified and represented as a centroid in the word embedding model according to the method described in 4.1.

Evaluation data: As previously mentioned, the words of interest in our work are 17 of the most polysemous Danish nouns. These words were handpicked by language experts for lexical sample studies as they are both extremely polysemous, yet frequent. See Table 1. The SemDaX corpus is a subpart of the 45 million words CLARIN Reference Corpus (Asmussen, 2012) and consists of different text types. We extract from SemDaX the 6,012 sentences containing our polysemous target nouns. These are annotated with dictionary senses by 2-6 annotators (advanced students and researchers). There are 355 sentences per target noun on average, and the more polysemous a word, the more sentences are included. For the WSD task, we include the window of 5 context words around the target noun in each annotated sentence. The text is simply lowercased and punctuation is removed. As mentioned above, every test sentence is considered as a BOW and represented as a centroid in the word embedding model (similarly as the synset sense-bags).

Note, the nouns are highly ambiguous, so a Krippendorf's α agreement of 0.80 is hard to reach here. The work of Pedersen et al. (2018) finds an agreement of 0.67 useful, which is mostly met in the agreement statistics. For relatively fine-grained sense inventories, a lower agreement score is acceptable.

The word embedding model is created by the Society for Danish Language and Literature (Sørensen and Nimb, 2018). They used the Gensim package (Řehůřek and Sojka, 2010) to train a Word2Vec model (Mikolov et al., 2013) on a corpus of roughly 920 million running words. The corpus had 6.3 million token types, where 5 million occurred less than 5 times. The dimensions of the CBOW word embeddings are 500, a window size of 5, and a threshold for rare words at 5.

Korpus DK: is a corpus [11] of different text types in Danish, and has a size of 56 million words. It consists of relatively recent language and mostly every-day language use. For each target noun, around 1000 sentences containing that noun are extracted. A window of 5 words and no normalization is chosen in line with the pre-processing of other data in this project. Every sentence is considered as a BOW and represented as a centroid in the vector space.

Software packages: With Python (van Rossum, 1995) we used the Sci-kit Learn package (Pedregosa and Varoquaux, 2011), the NLTK package (Bird et al., 2009) and SciPy (Jones et al., 2001).

Data mapping: As mentioned in the introduction, a key from dictionary senses in the evaluation data to DanNet was manually created. For 17 target nouns with 19.1 dic-

---

[11] https://ordnet.dk/korpusdk

tionary senses on average, where 15.6 senses on average was apparent in the annotated data, 159 links are found, with an average on 9.4 senses per word. See Table 1 for an overview across target words. The number of DanNet senses is slightly smaller than that of the dictionary. This is for the most part due to the many idiomatic expressions in the dictionary which are not (as they normally are not) included in the wordnet. To avoid leaving these instances out, the dictionary labels of the target noun in the figurative expressions are merged with the synset that corresponds to the literal sense of the noun. This follows the principle of annotation of idiomatic expressions (without a dictionary entry) or other figurative speech in the work of Pedersen et al. (2018a) where the annotation process is described.

5. Results

The results for all experiments are shown in Table 2. Except for the cluster centroid experiment, the results show steady improvements from .21 to .34 and exceed the random and E-lesk baseline at .13 and .16, respectively. However, the performance does not reach the MF sense baseline at .56 (discussed in Section 6.).

Sense representation	Acc.	Acc. ex. MF
1. Synset members	.21	.28
2. Example sentence	.26	.29
3. Example sentence+	.29	.31
4. Combination	**.34**	.36
5. Cluster centroid	.19	.22
Random	.13	.15
E-lesk	.16	.23
MF	.56	-

Table 2: WSD results

When excluding the MF class in the data and the corresponding synset embedding , the experiments actually perform slightly better and show the same steady improvements (again, except for exp. 5). Interestingly, when working with less frequent senses, the performance of exp. 1 seems to be the most improved.

6. Discussion

The best results for WSD with cosine similarity are achieved when combining all components (exp. 4): hypernyms, hyponyms, synonyms, near-synonyms, used-for, made-by semantic relations together with BOW word sense definition, the BOW example sentence, as well as and the BOW example sentences from hypo- and hypernym synsets. The more features used, the better the performance.

Synset richness: The size of and shared proportion of information of the synsets seems to be important for the sense representations in experiment 4, where the example sentence information for experiment 2-3 works best for homonyms. Experiment 4 performs worse than experiment 2, in particular in the case of the words *hold*, and *vold*, but also for *slag*, *stand*, *kontakt*, and *selskab*. Investigation of the synset member size for *hold* shows that almost half of the synsets only have one concept associated with it in DanNet, namely one hypernym. This is rather little information for establishing a synset embedding, and further, hypernyms tend to be more general and thus less informative.

Level of polysemy: Annotators report that the sentences often lack context and that the senses are highly polysemous (Pedersen et al., 2018a). Worst results from the system are found for *lys* which has a high number of senses (16), but no huge evaluation advantage since the inter-annotator agreement is relatively high (.81). Also, though the sense number is high, the senses are related in meaning and the differences are often very subtle. The target nouns *lys* and *kort* both share word form with common adjectives in Danish, which possibly affects the word embeddings. This could explain why the system performs worse for these words. The words that generally are disambiguated most satisfactorily are *blik*, *hold*, *stand*, *top* and *selskab*. All of these words have low overlap in the DanNet synsets, are homonyms, or have non-subtle sense differences.

For the word *top* and especially *stand*, the performance of experiment 4 is higher than for the other words. This might be due to the low number of senses of these words: *stand* has 4 senses, and *top* has 5, where the average number of senses is 9.4. Also, *stand* is often annotated with the same sense (and high inter-coder agreement) which suggests that there is one highly dominant sense.

In experiment 1-4, the WSD of *blik* also works well compared to the other words considering the performance of the most frequent sense. This word has a relatively low inter-annotator agreement and "only" 6 senses, which could be an explanation. This word is also a case of homonymy (i.e., unrelated meanings) which is foreseen to increase the distance between the sense embeddings in the word embedding model.

Idiomatic expressions: These expressions are relatively static in appearance. A BOW of an idiomatic expression as a sense representation vector will most likely disambiguate a corresponding context vector correctly. (See discussion of *face* below.) Now they are merged with the literal sense used in the expression, which creates bias and imprecise mapping between dictionary senses and DanNet synsets.

Clusters: Experiment 5 was motivated by the hypothesis that the best synset embeddings from former experiments might work as seeds for the clustering of more example sentence data, where the cluster centroids could function as a new synset embedding. However, the results prove otherwise, suggesting that the construction of the synset embeddings does not have clear enough information as a base for clustering.

A qualitative investigation of the sentences in the clusters confirms the results. There are patterns that begin to emerge. The target word *ansigt (face)* has 6 senses. The non-literal senses were captured in the least satisfactory way: the clusters for *face as a manifestation/appearance of a thing or phenomenon*, and *face as the character/nature of a person* contained many instances of the literal and simplest sense of *face*. The clusters of this literal sense proved to be the best and had fewer non-literal senses, although they still contained several errors. This sense was often mixed with *face as an expression/state of mood*, which actually can also be hard for annotators to distinguish between. The cluster of *face* as a *face-like front of an object* contains mostly non-literal senses: the DanNet synset only contains *form* (same as in English) as the related lexeme and no words about persons or physiological words. This cluster contains mostly sentences about God and the Bible, which could be because the clustering algorithm followed that gradient. Finally, *face as a public profile/known face* performs relatively well and captures most instances where *kendt ansigt (known face)* and *ansigt udadtil (public/outward face)* appears in the sentence.

MF sense is hard to beat: As mentioned previously, beating a majority classifier is in general very difficult, and even more difficult when dealing with a lower-resourced language such as Danish. Our experiments indeed confirm this; however, it should be emphasized that we examine the performance of the approach when tested on the hardest task available: the most polysemous nouns in Danish. In other words, our model is expected to perform considerably better on closer-to-average polysemy words.

7. Conclusion

This study set out to determine the possibility of building appropriate sense representations for Danish by combining word embeddings with synset information from the Danish wordnet. The rationale is to combine corpus evidence with senses outlined by humans. We represented the data in a word embeddings space and tested the process in a very hard WSD task. Thousands of example sentences were auto-tagged by sense clustering,

As expected, wordnet-associated data proves to be quite informative for the WSD task. Generally speaking, the more semantic relations and information included from the wordnet, the better the results. However, the word sense representation system has room for improvement, in that the most-frequent baseline is not yet overcome in these unbalanced datasets.

Nevertheless, our sense representation system produces promising results. The best synset embeddings in our study are able to disambiguate well above chance, considering the highly polysemous selection of test words in mind (almost 20 senses on average). We expect performance to increase when handling Danish vocabulary items with closer-to-average polysemy.

For future work, we plan to enrich the synset information with data from The Danish Thesaurus, and we foresee that these enriched data could potentially improve our model. Additionally, the technique of Nieto-Piña and Johansson (2018), linking word sense embedding models to lexical resources, is interesting and could be relevant for future improvements.

Finally, it would be interesting in future to experiment with the granularity level of senses, with the exclusion of idiomatic expressions from the WSD task, and with using our sense-based word clusters to create new evaluation materials.

8. Acknowledgements

This work is partly funded by the H2020 Infraria project ELEXIS and by the Swedish Research Council project 2014-39 that funds the Center for Linguistics Theory and Studies in Probability (CLASP).

9. Bibliographical References

Agirre, E. and Edmonds, P. (2006). Word Sense Disambiguation: Algorithms and Applications. *Text Speech and Language Technology*, 33(33):384.

Asmussen, J. (2012). CLARIN-Referencekorpus. *Sprogteknologisk Workshop October 31.*

Banerjee, S. and Pedersen, T. (2002). An Adapted Lesk Algorithm for Word Sense Disambiguation Using WordNet. In *Computational Linguistics and Intelligent Text Processing: Third Initernational Conference, CiCLing*, pages 136–145, Mexico City, Mexico.

Bartunov, S., Kondrashkin, D., Osokin, A., and Vetrov, D. (2016). Breaking sticks and ambiguities with adaptive skip-gram. In *Proceedings of the International Conference on Artificial Intelligence and Statistics (AISTATS)*, Cadiz, Spain.

Bhingardive, S., Singh, D., and Murthy, R. (2015). Unsupervised Most Frequent Sense Detection using Word Embeddings. In *Proceedings of the 2015 Conference of the North American Chapter of the Association for Computational Linguistics: Human Language Technologies*, pages 1238–1243.

Bird, S., Loper, E., and Klein, E. (2009). *Natural Language ToolKit (NLTK) Book*. O'Reilly Media Inc.

Camacho-Collados, J., Pilehvar, M. T., and Navigli, R. (2016). NASARI: Integrating explicit knowledge and corpus statistics for a multilingual representation of concepts and entities. *Artificial Intelligence*, 240:36–64.

Chen, X., Liu, Z., and Sun, M. (2014). A Unified Model for Word Sense Representation and Disambiguation. In *Proceedings of EMNLP*, pages 1025–1035, Doha, Qatar.

Edmonds , P. and Kilgarriff, A. (2002). Introduction to the special issue on evaluating word sense disambiguation systems. *Natural Language Engineering*, 8:279 – 291, 12.

Faralli, S., Panchenko, A., Biemann, C., and Ponzetto, S. P. (2016). Linked Disambiguated Distributional Semantic Networks. In *The 15th International Semantic Web Conference (ISWC)*, pages 56–64, Kobe, Japan.

Hjorth, E. and Kristensen, K. (2005). *Den Danske Ordbog*. Gyldendal, Copenhagen, 1 edition.

Johansson, R. and Nieto-Piña, L. (2015). Embedding a Semantic Network in a Word Space. *Naacl-2015*.

Jones, E., Oliphant, T., Peterson, P., and others. (2001). SciPy: Open source scientific tools for Python.

Kilgarriff, A. and Palmer, M. (2000). Introduction to the special issue on SENSEVAL. *Computers and the Humanities*.

Kilgarriff, A. (1997). "I don't believe in word senses". *Computers and the Humanities*.

Lloyd, S. (1982). Least squares quantization in pcm. *IEEE Transactions on Information Theory*, 28(2):129–137, March.

Mancini, M., Camacho-Collados, J., Iacobacci, I., and Navigli, R. (2017). Embedding Words and Senses Together via Joint Knowledge-Enhanced Training. In *Proceedings of the 21st Conference on Computational Natural Language Learning (CoNLL 2017)*, pages 100–111, Vancouver, Canada. Association for Computational Linguistics.

Martinez Alonso, H., Johannsen, A., Olsen, S., Nimb, S., Sørensen, N., Braasch, A., Søgaard, A., and Pedersen, B. (2015). Supersense tagging for danish. In *Proceedings of the 20th Nordic Conference of Computational Linguistics NODALIDA 2015*, volume 109. Linköping University Electronic Press. Der er ikke overensstemmelse mellem det ISSN-nr der står på proceedings og det der findes i databasen.

Mihalcea, R., Chklovski, T., and Kilgarriff, A. (2004). The senseval-3 english lexical sample task. *Senseval-3: Third International Workshop on the Evaluation of Systems for the Semantic Analysis of Text*, 01.

Mikolov, T., Chen, K., Corrado, G., and Dean, J. (2013). Efficient Estimation of Word Representations in Vector Space. pages 1–12.

Navigli, R. and Di Marco, A. (2013). Clustering and Diversifying Web Search Results with Graph-Based Word Sense Induction. *Computational Linguistics*, 39(3):709–754.

Neelakantan, A., Shankar, J., Passos, A., and McCallum, A. (2014). Efficient non-parametric estimation of multiple embeddings per word in vector space. In *Proceedings of the 2014 Conference on Empirical Methods in Natural Language Processing (EMNLP)*, pages 1059–1069, Doha, Qatar. Association for Computational Linguistics.

Nieto-Piña, L. and Johansson, R. (2018). Automatically Linking Lexical Resources with Word Sense Embedding Models. In *Proceedings of SemDeep-3, the 3rd Workshop on Semantic Deep Learning*, pages 23–29, Santa Fe, New Mexico, USA.

Palmer, M., Babko-Malaya, O., and Dang, H. (2004). Different sense granularities for different applications. In *Proceedings of the 2nd Workshop on Scalable Natural Language Understanding Systems*, Boston, MA. HTL/NAACL.

Panchenko, A., Lopukhina, A., Ustalov, D., Lopukhin, K., Arefyev, N., Leontyev, A., and Loukachevitch, N. (2018). Russe'2018: A shared task on word sense induction for the russian language. 03.

Pedersen, B. S., Nimb, S., Asmussen, J., Sørensen, N. H., Trap-Jensen, L., and Lorentzen, H. (2009). Dannet: The challenge of compiling a wordnet for Danish by reusing a monolingual dictionary. *Language Resources and Evaluation*, 43(3):269–299.

Pedersen, B., Braasch, A., Johannsen, A., Martinez Alonso, H., Nimb, S., Olsen, S., Søgaard, A., and Sørensen, N. (2016). The semdax corpus - sense annotations with scalable sense inventories. In *Proceedings of the 10th conference of the Language Resources and Evaluation Conference*, pages 842–847. European Language Resources Association.

Pedersen, B. S., Aguirrezabal Zabaleta, M., Nimb, S.,

Olsen, S., and Rørmann, I. (2018a). Towards a principled approach to sense clustering – a case study of wordnet and dictionary senses in Danish. In *Proceedings of Global WordNet Conference 2018*, pages 1–8, Singapore. Global WordNet Association.

Pedersen, B., Nimb, S., Søgaard, A., Hartmann, M., and Olsen, S. (2018b). A danish framenet lexicon and an annotated corpus used for training and evaluating a semantic frame classifier. In *Proceedings of the 11th edition of the Language Resources and Evaluation Conference, Miyazaki, Japan*. European Language Resources Association.

Pedregosa, F. and Varoquaux, G. (2011). *Scikit-learn: Machine learning in Python*.

Pelevina, M., Arefyev, N., Biemann, C., and Panchenko, A. (2017). Making Sense of Word Embeddings. (2012).

Pilehvar, M. T. and Collier, N. (2016). De-conflated semantic representations. In *Proceedings of EMNLP*, Austin, Texas.

Pradhan, S. S., Loper, E., Dligach, D., and Palmer, M. (2007). Semeval-2007 task 17: English lexical sample, srl and all words. In *Proceedings of the 4th International Workshop on Semantic Evaluations*, SemEval '07, pages 87–92, Stroudsburg, PA, USA. Association for Computational Linguistics.

Řehůřek, R. and Sojka, P. (2010). Software Framework for Topic Modelling with Large Corpora. In *Proceedings of the LREC 2010 Workshop on New Challenges for NLP Frameworks*, pages 45–50, Valletta, Malta, 5. ELRA.

Rothe, S. and Schütze, H. (2017). Autoextend: Combining Word Embeddings with Semantic Resources. *Computational Linguistics*, 43:3:593–617.

Saedi, C., Branco, A., António Rodrigues, J., and Silva, J. (2018). WordNet Embeddings. In *Proceedings of the 3rd Workshop on Representation Learning for NLP*, pages 122–131, Melbourne, Australia. Association for Computational Linguistics.

Sørensen, N. H. and Nimb, S. (2018). Word2Dict - Lemma Selection and Dictionary Editing Assisted by Word Embeddings. *Proceedings of the 18th EURALEX International Congres: Lexocography in Global Contexts*, pages 819–827.

Ustalov, D., Teslenko, D., Panchenko, A., Chernoskutov, M., Biemann, C., and Ponzetto, S. P. (2018). An Unsupervised Word Sense Disambiguation System for Under-Resourced Languages. In *Proceedings of the Eleventh International Conference on Language Resources and Evaluation (LREC-2018)*, Miyazaki, Japan, 4.

van Rossum, G. (1995). Python tutorial. Technical Report CS-R9526, Centrum voor Wiskunde en Informatica (CWI), Amsterdam, 5.

Proceedings of the Globalex Workshop on Linked Lexicography, pages 53–60
Language Resources and Evaluation Conference (LREC 2020), Marseille, 11–16 May 2020
© European Language Resources Association (ELRA), licensed under CC-BY-NC

Towards a Swedish Roget-Style Thesaurus for NLP

Niklas Zechner, Lars Borin
Språkbanken Text/Department of Swedish
University of Gothenburg, Sweden
{niklas.zechner, lars.borin}@gu.se

Abstract

Bring's thesaurus (Bring) is a Swedish counterpart of Roget, and its digitized version could make a valuable language resource for use in many and diverse natural language processing (NLP) applications. From the literature we know that Roget-style thesauruses and wordnets have complementary strengths in this context, so both kinds of lexical-semantic resource are good to have. However, Bring was published in 1930, and its lexical items are in the form of lemma–POS pairings. In order to be useful in our NLP systems, polysemous lexical items need to be disambiguated, and a large amount of modern vocabulary must be added in the proper places in Bring. The work presented here describes experiments aiming at automating these two tasks, at least in part, where we use the structure of an existing Swedish semantic lexicon – Saldo – both for disambiguation of ambiguous Bring entries and for addition of new entries to Bring.

Keywords: lexicon, word sense disambiguation, topic detection

1. Introduction[1]

1.1. Lexical Semantic Resources for NLP

Lexical-semantic knowledge sources are a stock item in the language technologist's toolbox, having proved their practical worth in many and diverse natural language processing (NLP) applications.

Although lexical semantics and the closely related field of lexical typology have long been large and well-researched branches of linguistics (see, e.g., Cruse 1986; Goddard 2001; Murphy 2003; Vanhove 2008), the lexical-semantic knowledge source of choice for NLP applications is Word-Net (Fellbaum, 1998b), a resource which arguably has been built largely in isolation from the linguistic mainstream and which thus is somewhat disconnected from it.

However, the English-language Princeton WordNet (PWN) and most wordnets for other languages are freely available, often broad-coverage lexical resources, which goes a long way toward explaining their popularity and wide usage in NLP as due at least in part to a kind of streetlight effect.

For this reason, we should also explore other kinds of lexical-semantic resources as components in NLP applications. This is easier said than done, however. The PWN is a manually built resource, and efforts aiming at automatic creation of similar resources for other languages on the basis of PWN, such as Universal WordNet (de Melo and Weikum, 2009) or BabelNet (Navigli and Ponzetto, 2012), although certainly useful and laudable, by their very nature will simply reproduce the WordNet structure, although for a different language or languages. Of course, the same goes for the respectable number of manually constructed word-nets for other languages.[2]

1.2. Roget's *Thesaurus* and NLP

While wordnets completely dominate the NLP field, outside it the most well-known lexical-semantic resource for English is without doubt Roget's *Thesaurus* (also alter-

nately referred to as "Roget" below; Roget 1852; Hüllen 2004), which appeared in its first edition in 1852 and has since been published in a large number of editions all over the English-speaking world. Although – perhaps unjustifiedly – not as well-known in NLP as the PWN, the digital version of Roget offers a valuable complement to PWN (Jarmasz and Szpakowicz, 2004), which has seen a fair amount of use in NLP (e.g., Morris and Hirst 1991; Jobbins and Evett 1995; Jobbins and Evett 1998; Wilks 1998; Kennedy and Szpakowicz 2008).

There are indications in the literature that Roget-style thesauruses can provide an alternative source of lexical-semantic information, which can be used both to attack other kinds of NLP tasks than a wordnet, and even work better for some of the same tasks, e.g., *lexical cohesion, synonym identification, pseudo-word-sense disambiguation*, and *analogy problems* (Morris and Hirst, 1991; Jarmasz and Szpakowicz, 2004; Kennedy and Szpakowicz, 2008; Kennedy and Szpakowicz, 2014).

An obstacle to the wider use of Roget in NLP applications is its limited availability. The only free digital version is the 1911 American edition available through Project Gutenberg.[3] This version is obviously not well suited for processing modern texts. Szpakowicz and his colleagues at the University of Ottawa have conducted a number of experiments with a modern (from 1987) edition of Roget (e.g., Jarmasz and Szpakowicz 2004; Kennedy and Szpakowicz 2008, but as far as we can tell, this dataset is not generally available, due to copyright restrictions. The work reported by Kennedy and Szpakowicz (2014) represents an effort to remedy this situation, utilizing corpus-based measures of semantic relatedness for adding new entries to both the 1911 and 1987 editions of Roget.

In order to investigate systematically the strengths and weaknesses of diverse lexical-semantic resources when applied to different classes of NLP tasks, we would need access to resources that are otherwise comparable, e.g., with respect to language, vocabulary and domain coverage. The

---

[1]Parts of the introduction reproduced from Borin et al. (2015).

[2]See the *Global WordNet Association* website: <http://globalwordnet.org>.

[3]See <http://www.gutenberg.org/ebooks/22> and Cassidy (2000).

resources should also ideally be freely available, in order to ensure reproducibility as well as to stimulate their widest possible application to a broad range of NLP problems. Unfortunately, this situation is rarely encountered in practice; for English, the experiments contrasting WordNet and Roget have indicated that these resources are indeed complementary. It would be desirable to replicate these findings for other languages and also using lexical-semantic resources with different structures (WordNet and Roget being two out of a large number of possibilities).

This is a central motivation for the work presented here, the ultimate goal of which is to develop automatic methods for producing or considerably facilitating the production of a Swedish counterpart of Roget with a large and up-to-date vocabulary coverage. This is not to be done by translation, as in previous work by de Melo and Weikum (2008) and Borin et al. (2014). Instead, an existing but largely outdated Roget-style thesaurus will provide the scaffolding, where new word senses can be inserted, drawing on the formal structure of an existing Swedish semantic lexicon, Saldo (Borin et al., 2013). Saldo was originally conceived as an "associative thesaurus" (Lönngren, 1998), and even though its organization in many respects differs significantly from that of Roget, there are also some commonalities. Hence, our hypothesis is that the structure of Saldo will yield a good measure for the semantic relatedness of word senses. Saldo is described in Section 2.2 below.

2. The Datasets

2.1. Bring's Swedish Thesaurus

Sven Casper Bring (1842–1931) was the originator of the first and so far only adaptation of Roget's *Thesaurus* to Swedish, which appeared in 1930 under the title *Svenskt ordförråd ordnat i begreppsklasser* 'Swedish vocabulary arranged in conceptual classes' (referred to as "Bring" or "Bring's thesaurus" below). The work itself consists of two parts: (1) a conceptually organized list of Roget categories; and (2) an alphabetically ordered lemma index.

Like in Roget, the vocabulary included in Bring is divided into slightly over 1,000 "conceptual classes". A "conceptual class" corresponds to what is usually referred to as a "head" in the literature on Roget. Each conceptual class consists of a list of words (lemmas), subdivided first into nouns, verbs and others (mainly adjectives, adverbs and phrases), and finally into groups. In the groups, the distance – expressed as difference in list position – between words provides a rough measure of their semantic distance.

Bring thus forms a hierarchical structure with four levels:

(1) conceptual class (Roget "head")
(2) part of speech
(3) group
(4) lemma (word sense)

Since most of the Bring classes have corresponding heads in Roget, it should be straightforward to add the levels above Roget heads/Bring classes to Bring if needed. There are some indications in the literature that this additional structure can in fact be useful for calculating semantic similarity (Jarmasz and Szpakowicz, 2004).

Bring's thesaurus is made available in two digital versions by Språkbanken Text (the text division of the National Swedish Language Bank) at the University of Gothenburg, both versions under a Creative Commons Attribution License:

Bring (v. 1): A digital version of the full contents of the original 1930 book version (148,846 entries).[4]

Blingbring (v. 0.2), a version of Bring where obsolete items have been removed and the remaining entries have been provided with word sense identifiers from Saldo (see section 2.2), providing links to most of Språkbanken Text's other lexical resources. This version contains 126,911 entries.[5]

The linking to Saldo senses in the current Blingbring version (v 0.2) has not involved a disambiguation step. Rather, it has been made by matching lemma-POS combinations from the two resources. For this reason, Blingbring includes slightly over 21,000 ambiguous entries, or about 4,800 ambiguous word sense assignments (out of about 43,000 unique lemma-POS combinations).

The aim of the experiments described below has been to assess the feasibility of disambiguating these ambiguous linkages automatically, and specifically also to evaluate Saldo as a possible knowledge source for accomplishing this disambiguation. The longer-term goal of this work is to develop good methods for adding modern vocabulary automatically to Bring from, e.g., Saldo, thereby hopefully producing a modern Swedish Roget-style resource for the NLP community.

2.2. Saldo

Saldo (Borin et al., 2013) is a large (137 thousand entries and 2 million word forms) morphological and lexical-semantic lexicon for modern Swedish, freely available (under a Creative Commons Attribution license).[6]

As a lexical-semantic resource, Saldo is organized very differently from a wordnet (Borin and Forsberg, 2009). As mentioned above, it was initially conceived as an "associative thesaurus". Since it has been extended following the principles laid down initially by Lönngren (1998), this characterization should still be valid, even though it has grown tremendously over the last decade.

If the fundamental organizing principle of PWN is the idea of full synonyms in a taxonomic concept hierarchy, the basic linguistic idea underlying Saldo is instead that, semantically speaking, the whole vocabulary of a language can be described as having a center – or core – and (consequently) a periphery. The notion of *core vocabulary* is familiar from several linguistic subdisciplines (Borin, 2012). In Saldo this idea is consistently applied down to the level of individual word senses.

The basic lexical-semantic organizational principle of Saldo is hierarchical. Every entry in Saldo – representing a word sense – is supplied with one or more semantic descriptors, which are themselves also entries in the dictionary. All entries in Saldo are actually occurring words or

---

[4]`<https://spraakbanken.gu.se/eng/resource/bring>`

[5]`<https://spraakbanken.gu.se/eng/resource/blingbring>`

[6]`<https://spraakbanken.gu.se/eng/resource/Saldo>`

conventionalized or lexicalized multi-word units of the language. No attempt is made to fill perceived gaps in the lexical network using definition-like paraphrases, as is sometimes done in PWN (Fellbaum, 1998a, 5f). A further difference as compared to PWN (and Roget-style thesauruses) is that Saldo aims to provide a lexical-semantic description of *all* the words of the language, including the closed-class items (prepositions, conjunctions, interjections, etc.), and also including many proper nouns.

One of the semantic descriptors in Saldo, called *primary*, is obligatory. The primary descriptor is the entry which better than any other entry fulfills two requirements: (1) it is a semantic neighbor of the entry to be described and (2) it is more central than it. However, there is no requirement that the primary descriptor is of the same part of speech as the entry itself. Thus, the primary descriptor of *kniv* 'knife (n)' is *skära* 'cut (v)', and that of *lager* 'layer (n)' is *på* 'on (p)'. Through the primary descriptors Saldo is a single tree, rooted by assigning an artifical top sense (called PRIM) as primary descriptor to the 41 topmost word senses.

That two words are semantic neighbors means that there is a direct semantic relationship between them (such as synonymy, hyponymy, meronymy, argument-predicate relationship, etc.). As could be seen from the examples given above, Saldo includes not only open-class words, but also pronouns, prepositions, conjunctions etc. In such cases closeness must sometimes be determined with respect to function or syntagmatic connections, rather than ("word-semantic") content.

Centrality is determined by means of several criteria: frequency, stylistic value, word formation, and traditional lexical-semantic relations all combine to determine which of two semantically neighboring words is to be considered more central.

For more details of the organization of Saldo and the linguistic motivation underlying it, see Borin et al. (2013).

Like Roget, Saldo has a kind of topical structure, which – again like Roget, but different from a wordnet – includes and connects lexical items of different parts of speech, but its topology is characterized by a much deeper hierarchy than that found in Roget. There are no direct correspondences in Saldo to the lexical-semantic relations making up a wordnet (minimally synonymy and – part-of-speech internal – hyponymy).

Given the (claimed) thesaural character of Saldo, we would expect a Saldo-based semantic similarity measure to work well for disambiguating the ambiguous Blingbring entries.

3. The Experiments

The experiments described below represent a continuation of an earlier effort, reported on by Borin et al. (2015), where both a corpus-based and a lexicon-based classifier was applied to the disambiguation problem, reaching accuracies of 69% and 78%, respectively. The lexicon-based representations used in the earlier experiment utilized only one of several possible aspects of the lexical structure of Saldo, and in the experiments reported here we conduct a more detailed investigation of if and how more of Saldo's structure could be used for this purpose. While these earlier experiments use machine learning, that is, statistical methods, the

approach we use here is much simpler and arguably non-statistical. As we will see, it is sometimes possible to get better results with methods simpler than the conventional. There is still a possibility of combining this type of method with a machine learning approach, either in parallel or sequentially, but we leave this for future work.

The evaluation data used for the experiments are the same as in Borin et al. (2015), and we reproduce the data preparation procedure from that paper here for convenience.

The Blingbring data were downloaded from Språkbanken Text's website and a sample of ambiguous Bring–Saldo linkages was selected for manual disambiguation.

An initial sample was drawn from this data set according to the following principles:[7]

- The sampling unit was the class+part of speech-combination, i.e., *nouns in class 12*, *verbs in class 784*, etc.
- This unit had to contain at least 100 lemmas (actual range: 100–569 lemmas),
- out of which at least 1 must be unambiguous (actual range: 56–478 unambiguous lemmas),
- and at least 4 had to be ambiguous.
- From the ambiguous lemmas, 4 were randomly selected (using the Python function random-sample).

The goal was to produce an evaluation set of approximately 1,000 items, and this procedure yielded 1,008 entries to be disambiguated. The disambiguation was carried out by one of the authors. In practice, it deviated from the initial procedure and proceeded more opportunistically, since reference often had to be made to the main dataset in order to determine the correct Saldo word sense. On these occasions, it was often convenient to (a) either disambiguate additional items in the same Bring class; and/or (b) disambiguate the same items throughout the entire dataset.

1,368 entries were disambiguated for the experiments, out of which about 500 came out of the original sample.

For this experiment, a few of those were removed for various anomalies, most commonly because the Bring words are inflected forms and so not directly listed as lemmas in Saldo. This leaves 1317 entries. The degree of ambiguity in this gold standard data is shown in the second column of Table 1, while the third column shows the degree of ambiguity in the full Blingbring dataset containing 44,615 unique lemma-POS combinations.

4. Method and Results

There are two tasks we would like to accomplish. First, there are a number of entries in Bring which are ambiguous, in that they are not associated with one specific Saldo sense. We want to figure out for each of them which of the possible senses is the correct one. Second, there are many entries in Saldo which are not represented in Bring, which we would like to add, so we need to find for each of the Saldo senses which (one or more) of the Bring categories they fit in.

---

[7]These should be seen as first-approximation heuristic principles, and not based on any more detailed analysis of the data. We expect that further experiments will provide better data on which to base such decisions.

# senses/	GS data:	Blingbring:
entry	# entries	# entries
1	9	39,275
2	739	4,006
3	304	873
4	147	286
5	71	102
6	11	31
7	13	18
8	15	10
9	6	3
10	2	6
11	0	5

Table 1: Word-sense ambiguity in the gold standard data and in Blingbring

For the first task, we can easily look up which senses in Saldo are associated with the lemmas used in Bring, which already narrows it down to a usually quite small number of possible senses. Most Bring entries have only one possible sense; those are of course not ambiguous and therefore not included in this task. Of the ambiguous ones, most have only two possible senses.

The second task is more difficult. Rather than just a small number of options, we now need to distinguish between several thousand categories. The same sense can also be present in more than one category. In principle, entries in Bring are also ordered in such a way that more similar words are generally closer together. This is difficult to quantify, so we will neither make use of it nor consider it for output.

4.1. Method

Both Bring and Saldo have connections between entries. In Bring, they are arranged in classes and groups; in Saldo, they have primary and secondary descriptors. To predict whether a sense is a good fit for a Bring group, we compare the established entries in the same group with Saldo entries related to the sense at hand.

To compare the different types of relationships between senses in Saldo, we can borrow terminology from family relations. We let the primary descriptor of a sense be its "mother", a secondary descriptor its "father". A sense which has this one as its primary or secondary is its "daughter" or "son", respectively. Senses sharing a primary or secondary descriptor are "sisters" or "brothers", respectively. In the otherwise rare case where the mother of one sense is the father of another, we will call them "cross siblings". Terms like parent, aunt, etc. should follow by analogy.

Many of the Saldo senses have no secondary descriptors, and are therefore ignored when considering "brothers" etc. We also ignore any secondary descriptor which is inte..1 'not'; this links a lot of words which are negations but otherwise have nothing in common.

4.2. Disambiguating Senses of Entries Already Present in Bring

4.2.1. Method

We start with the list of 1317 manually disambiguated Bring entries, as described in Section 3, and find all the Saldo senses which correspond to the same lemma. Both Bring and Saldo give us information on part of speech, although in different forms. In principle, the correct sense could have been listed as having a different part of speech, but we find that this is never the case; consequentially, we remove as candidates all the senses where the part of speech is not the same as that stated in Bring.

The average number of remaining senses is 2.8, and the maximum is 10. This means that if we were to guess a sense at random, we would get an accuracy of 36%. But although the senses in Saldo are not ordered by any formal criterion, they have a tendency to be listed with the more common first. If we choose the first listed sense, we actually get 63% correct. We consider that to be our baseline for accuracy.

Now we process for each of the ambiguous entries each of the possible senses, by considering related senses and seeing if they are present in the same Bring category. To do that, we have to choose on the one hand which type of relations we are considering, and on the other hand which of the two Bring categories to count – classes (the larger) or groups (the smaller).

It quickly becomes clear that some of the relations are stronger indicators than others. For example, if a descriptor of the sense in question is present in the group, that is a very strong indicator, but on the other hand, it only happens in a small percentage of the cases. Conversely, a sense with a shared descriptor appearing in the class is much more common, but is a less strong indicator that this is the correct sense.

This gives us an advantage over a simple discrimination method: We can decide not to make a choice on some cases. If we can get a very high accuracy on, for example, half the entries, that may be much better than just getting a 50% accuracy on all the entries.

It seems therefore like a sensible approach to start with the most accurate but least thorough method, and then apply different methods in turn. That is, if the first method finds a match, that will be our guess, otherwise we move on to the next. If there are several matches, the algorithm stops at the first match, meaning that we get the first listed of the alternatives. If none of the methods work, we also revert to picking the first listed sense.

4.2.2. Results and Discussion

Table 2 and Figure 1 show the results. We can either spot a small number of entries with high accuracy, or a larger number of entries with lower accuracy.

One example of an ambiguous word is *mask*, which shows up in several different groups in Bring. The word has at least two unrelated senses, both nouns: mask..1 translates as 'worm', mask..2 as 'mask'. In our test set, there are three occurrences of what should be mask..2, in the classes AMUSEMENT, DEFENSE, and COVERING. The first is correctly identified because of a son sense; maskerad..1 'masquerade' is in the same group, and has mask..2 as its

Relation	This step %		So far %	
	Tried	Acc	Tried	Acc
father in group	1	100	1	100
mother in group	14	94	14	94
daughter in group	19	90	31	92
son in group	3	80	33	91
grandparent in group	5	85	37	91
sister in group	23	91	51	91
cross sibling in group	9	66	56	89
brother in group	3	60	58	88
sister in class	39	76	74	85
cross sibling in class	29	64	81	83
brother in class	2	80	82	83
father in class	0	100	82	83
mother in class	14	61	84	83
grandparent in class	11	73	86	83
daughter in class	10	72	87	82
son in class	2	75	88	82
first listed option	100	59	100	80

Table 2: Methods for disambiguating Bring entries, and their accuracies, sequentially applied

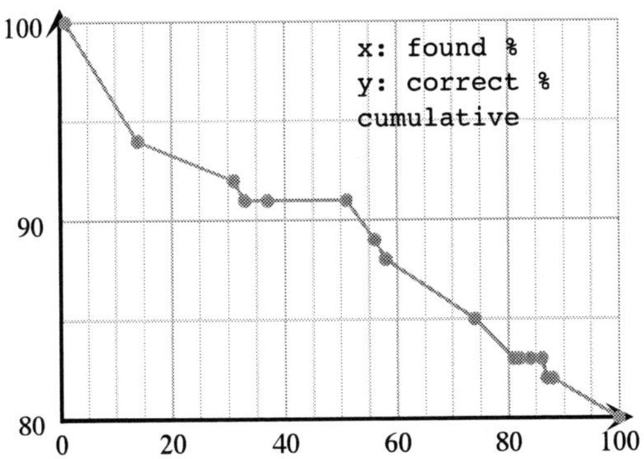

Figure 1: Coverage and accuracy for different methods of disambiguation

secondary descriptor. The second is correctly identified because of a sister sense; överdrag..1 'textile cover' is in the same group, and they share the primary descriptor täcka..1 'cover'. The third is wrongly identified as mask..1 'worm', because of a cross sibling sense; päls..1 'fur' is in the group, and djur..1 'animal' is both the primary descriptor of mask..1 and a secondary descriptor of päls..1.

Generally, most of the failed words, and indeed most of the words altogether, are more closely related senses than this – sometimes clearly distinct but etymologically related senses, including metaphors, such as tomhänt..1 'with empty hands' and tomhänt..2 'with nothing to offer', sometimes with only subtle differences, such as samling..1 'collection', samling..2 'arrangement', and samling..3 'group'.

One obvious alternative approach is to give points for each relative spotted, and check which sense gets the most points. A simple test of this shows no noticeable improvement; further comparison has to be left for future work.

There are other potential extentions to this methods that we could have tried: Reordering the relations, trying additional relations, considering the distance between entries in Bring, considering how far from the root node an entry is in Saldo, looking for combinations of multiple relations occurring in the same category... But preliminary tests show no indication that the real accuracy would be affected by more than a minute amount, and so we leave out further micromanagement to avoid overfitting.

Another possible addition worth considering would be to check the actual frequencies of the senses, and use those instead of the order in Saldo to make the default choice. But without a very large amount of text data, we would not want to rely on the assumption that not only most words but most senses in the dictionary are accurately represented. Manually sense-disambiguated data is somewhat scarce, and we would also not want to rely on automatically sense-disambiguated data; unlike many other applications, we are not interested in the per-token accuracy, but rather the per-lemma accuracy, which is clearly lower, since the sense disambiguation will also be less accurate for less common words.

Relation	Count in sample		Avg. per group		
	True	False	True	False	Ratio
mother	468	3376	0.0969	0.0004	221.2
father	58	694	0.0120	0.0001	133.4
sister	1688	20134	0.3494	0.0026	133.8
brother	635	10465	0.1314	0.0014	96.8
cross sibling	527	10097	0.1091	0.0013	83.3
daughter	701	3156	0.1451	0.0004	354.4
son	130	1651	0.0269	0.0002	125.7
grand-parent	151	5270	0.0313	0.0007	45.7
aunt/ uncle	2313	65570	0.4788	0.0085	56.3
cousin	6753	418069	1.3978	0.0542	25.8

Table 3: Number of occurrences of different relations, for a sample of 10,000 entries

4.3. Adding New Senses to Bring

Now we turn to the second task, in which we want to take senses which are not present in Bring and add them in the correct group. We use the same principles here, looking for groups containing Saldo-relatives of the sense in question. Is it reasonable to think that a sense will have more relatives in the correct category than in other categories? We test this by counting some types of relatives in different categories. For 10,000 unambiguous entries in Bring, we count the relatives in true groups (that is, any group containing an entry using the same sense), compared with those in false groups (groups which do not contain such an entry). Table 3 shows the results.

We see that there are indeed considerably more relatives in the correct groups. For example, a group that contains a given sense x will on average contain 0.13 of its brothers, but a group that does not contain x contains only 0.0014 of its brothers.

Does this mean that we can apply the same method as before, and classify any group containing close relatives of x as likely true groups for x? Unfortunately not, since in this task we have far more options to choose from. Of the sense/group combinations in this sample, there are approximately 1600 times as many false ones. So while the mother sense is about 200 times more likely to be found in a true group than a false group, a group containing the mother sense is still 8 times more likely to be a false group.

Instead, we revisit the idea of a scoring system, counting multiple relatives in the same group. This did not seem to improve the sense disambiguation task noticeably, but it might work better here. As we see in Table 3, the more distant relatives have generally less impressive numbers, and preliminary testing also shows that they do not significantly improve results. We limit the method to parent, child and sibling senses, and give one point for each relative.

For each of the Saldo senses associated with an unambiguous Bring entry, we compare it with each of the 7714 Bring groups. For each sense/group combination, we note the score, and whether the group contains the sense itself or not. This tells us the distribution of scores, that is, how many sense/group combinations were given each score.

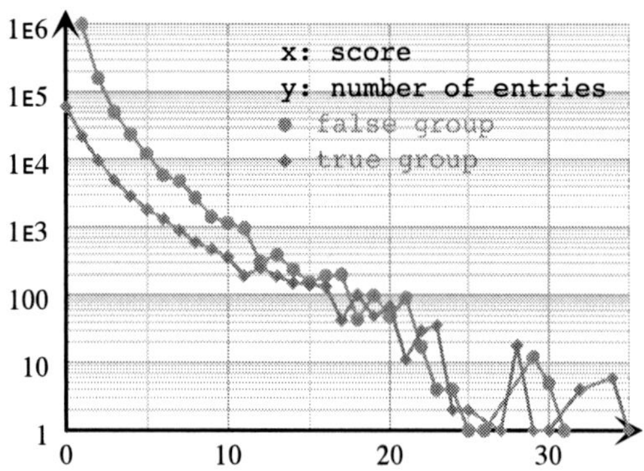

Figure 2: Distribution of scores for true and false groups

4.3.1. Results and Discussion

We find that 24% of the entries were "correctly" classified, that is, the highest-scoring group was a true group. Note that this includes entries which did not get any points in any groups. This in itself is hardly enough accuracy to be useful.

Figure 2 shows the distribution of scores, separately for true and false groups. (Note that one point is outside the graph; there were 30 1E6 false groups with score 0.) Our hope was that for high enough scores, the true groups would outnumber the false, so that beyond a certain score limit we might have a decent accuracy. As we see in the graph, the false groups remain higher at least up to score 10; after that, the smaller number of data points make the graph more erratic. Figure 3 shows the percentage of true groups for each score. The blue curve shows the percentage of true groups among

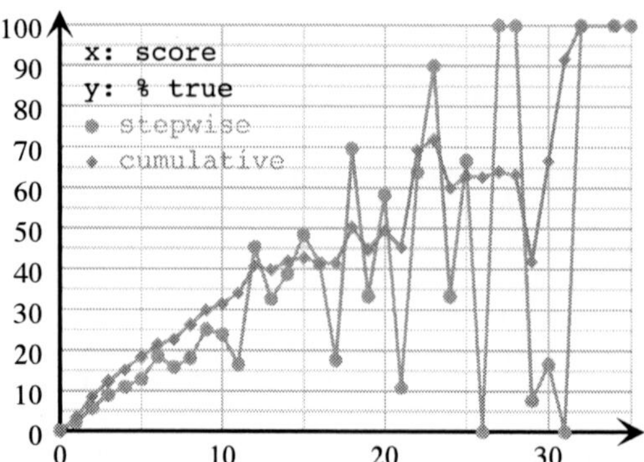

Figure 3: Percentage of true groups for each score. The blue line is for exactly this score, the orange is for at least this score

those with exactly this score, and the orange curve shows the percentage among groups with this score or higher. We see that the percentage does increase noticeably in the lower part. Already beyond 10 or so, the results are less reliable, but the general trend seems to be increasing.

If we were to set a score limit and assign senses to groups if they reach that limit, the orange curve would describe the accuracy of that method. As far as we can tell, this would reach an accuracy around 30% at 10 points. Unfortunately, this method would not be satisfactory. First, an accuracy of 30% is not good enough. Second, the method would only attempt a very small number of words; only one in 200,000 sense/group combinations score at least 10 points.

On average, each word in Bring appears in 2.88 categories, but we would be satisfied for now with finding just one for each new word. Since the automatic methods are not accurate enough, we need to try semi-automatic methods. What if we set a lower score limit, and manually go though the categories with a sufficient score? If we could narrow it down to a list of ten or even a hundred candidate groups instead of the full list of 7714, that would be very helpful.

With a score limit of just 1, the accuracy is 3.5%, and the recall is 43.6% (that is, out of all the true groups, we will find 43.6% by looking at those with at least 1 point). With a score limit of 2, the accuracy is 8.4% and the recall 22.7%. This may be better than nothing, but still not overwhelming. Instead, we can choose to list the suggested groups in order of decreasing score, and see how many groups we would on average need to look at to find a true group. Figure 4 shows the result.

We see that while 24% are found in the first guess, 43% are found in the first 5, and 50% in the first 10. That should at least be enough to reduce the workload of an annotator. Even if the first few listed groups are not correct, it might also give the annotator an idea of where to look – other groups in the same class would presumably be more likely than more distant ones.

5. Conclusions

We have shown that using the relations from Saldo to disambiguate or classify words in Bring is viable as a tool,

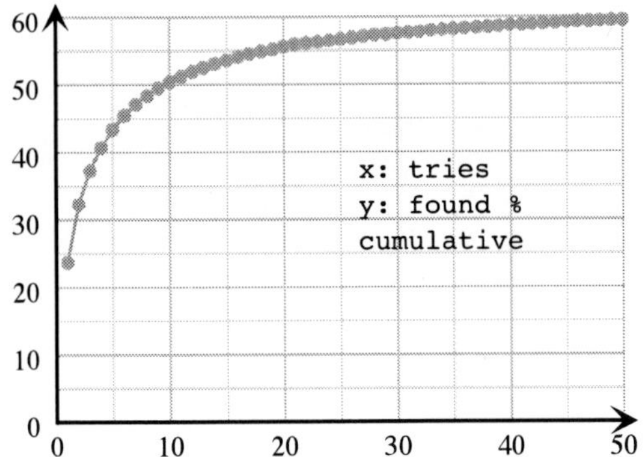

Figure 4: Percentage of entries for which a true group is found within a given number of groups, starting from the highest-scoring

even if the accuracy is not high enough to rely solely on this method. For disambiguation of already existing entries, we can get an accuracy or 80% for the entire list, and higher for a subset; this may be considered acceptable in itself, or it can be seen as a starting point for manual annotators. For classifying new senses, the accuracy is not good enough for automatic annotation, but it can reduce the number of possible groups a manual annotator would have to look through by a factor of several hundred.

It is important to note that the correct answer here is somewhat subjective. There may be cases where a different sense would be just as reasonable, and perhaps more importantly, there are many cases where more than one sense would fit in the same category. Some of the words in Bring are clear homographs, so the senses are very different and should clearly be in different categories, but others may be more closely related senses. This means that the accuracies we see here might be overly pessimistic.

Given more time and resources, it would be possible to extend the manual annotation which we have used as our gold standard. Having more than one annotator might give us a better picture of just how subjective the annotation is, and an approach where for each included sense we also classify the other senses of the same word would perhaps clarify whether the accuracy is actually better than it seems.

It is also possible to combine the approach presented here with other automatic methods, whether commonplace machine learning methods or something else, which is something we intend to do in the future. All the same, we have shown that these transparent, conceptually simple, and relatively fast methods are also quite viable.

6. Acknowledgements

This work has been conducted as part of the effort to construct and develop a Swedish national research infrastructure in support of research based on language data. This infrastructure – *Nationella språkbanken* (the Swedish National Language Bank) – is jointly funded for the period 2018–2024 by the Swedish Research Council (grant number 2017-00626) and its 10 partner institutions.

7. Bibliographical References

Borin, L. and Forsberg, M. (2009). All in the family: A comparison of SALDO and WordNet. In *Proceedings of the Nodalida 2009 Workshop on WordNets and other Lexical Semantic Resources*, Odense.

Borin, L., Forsberg, M., and Lönngren, L. (2013). SALDO: a touch of yin to WordNet's yang. *Language Resources and Evaluation*, 47(4):1191–1211.

Borin, L., Allwood, J., and de Melo, G. (2014). Bring vs. MTRoget: Evaluating automatic thesaurus translation. In *Proceedings of LREC 2014*, pages 2115–2121, Reykjavík. ELRA.

Borin, L., Nieto Piña, L., and Johansson, R. (2015). Here be dragons? The perils and promises of inter-resource lexical-semantic mapping. In *Semantic Resources and Semantic Annotation for Natural Language Processing and the Digital Humanities. Workshop at NODALIDA 2015*, pages 1–11, Linköping. LiUEP.

Borin, L. (2012). Core vocabulary: A useful but mystical concept in some kinds of linguistics. In Diana Santos, et al., editors, *Shall we play the Festschrift game? Essays on the occasion of Lauri Carlson's 60th birthday*, pages 53–65. Springer, Berlin.

Cassidy, P. (2000). An investigation of the semantic relations in the Roget's Thesaurus: Preliminary results. In *Proceedings of CICLing 2000*, pages 181–204.

Cruse, D. A. (1986). *Lexical semantics*. Cambridge University Press, Cambridge.

de Melo, G. and Weikum, G. (2008). Mapping Roget's Thesaurus and WordNet to French. In *Proceedings of LREC 2008*, Marrakech. ELRA.

de Melo, G. and Weikum, G. (2009). Towards a universal wordnet by learning from combined evidence. In *Proceedings of the 18th ACM Conference on Information and Knowledge Management (CIKM 2009)*, pages 513–522, New York. ACM.

Fellbaum, C. (1998a). Introduction. In Christiane Fellbaum, editor, *WordNet: An electronic lexical database*, pages 1–19. MIT Press, Cambridge, Mass.

Christiane Fellbaum, editor. (1998b). *WordNet: An electronic lexical database*. MIT Press, Cambridge, Mass.

Goddard, C. (2001). Lexico-semantic universals: A critical overview. *Linguistic Typology*, 5:1–65.

Hüllen, W. (2004). *A history of Roget's Thesaurus: Origins, development, and design*. Oxford University Press, Oxford.

Jarmasz, M. and Szpakowicz, S. (2004). *Roget's Thesaurus* and semantic similarity. In Nicolas Nicolov, et al., editors, *Recent Advances in Natural Language Processing III. Selected papers from RANLP 2003*, pages 111–120. John Benjamins, Amsterdam.

Jobbins, A. C. and Evett, L. J. (1995). Automatic identification of cohesion in texts: Exploiting the lexical organization of Roget's Thesaurus. In *Proceedings of Rocling VIII*, pages 111–125, Taipei.

Jobbins, A. C. and Evett, L. J. (1998). Text segmentation using reiteration and collocation. In *Proceedings of the 36th ACL and 17th COLING, Volume 1*, pages 614–618, Montreal. ACL.

Kennedy, A. and Szpakowicz, S. (2008). Evaluating *Roget's* thesauri. In *Proceedings of ACL-08: HLT*, pages 416–424, Columbus, Ohio. ACL.

Kennedy, A. and Szpakowicz, S. (2014). Evaluation of automatic updates of *Roget's Thesaurus*. *Journal of Language Modelling*, 2(2):1–49.

Lönngren, L. (1998). A Swedish associative thesaurus. In *Euralex '98 proceedings, Vol. 2*, pages 467–474.

Morris, J. and Hirst, G. (1991). Lexical cohesion computed by thesaural relations as an indicator of the structure of text. *Computational Linguistics*, 17(1):21–48.

Murphy, M. L. (2003). *Semantic relations and the lexicon.* Cambridge University Press, Cambridge.

Navigli, R. and Ponzetto, S. P. (2012). BabelNet: The automatic construction, evaluation and application of a wide-coverage multilingual semantic network. *Artificial Intelligence*, 193:217–250.

Roget, M. P. (1852). *Thesaurus of English Words and Phrases.* Longman, London.

Martine Vanhove, editor. (2008). *From polysemy to semantic change: Towards a typology of lexical semantic associations.* Jon Benjamins, Amsterdam.

Wilks, Y. (1998). Language processing and the thesaurus. In *Proceedings National language Research Institute*, Tokyo. Also appeared as Technical report CS–97–13, University of Sheffield, Department of Computer Science.

Proceedings of the Globalex Workshop on Linked Lexicography, page 61
Language Resources and Evaluation Conference (LREC 2020), Marseille, 11–16 May 2020
© European Language Resources Association (ELRA), licensed under CC-BY-NC

"Design and development of an adaptive web application for OLIVATERM"

Mercedes Roldán Vendrell
UNIVERSIDAD DE JAÉN
mroldan@ujaen.es

ABSTRACT

An Excellency Research Project called "Terminology of olive oil and trade: China and other international markets" (P07-HUM-03041) was initiated under my management in 2008, financed by the Andalusian regional government, the Junta de Andalucía. The project, known as "OLIVATERM", had two main objectives: on the one hand, to develop the first systematic multilingual terminological dictionary in the scientific and socio-economic area of the olive grove and olive oils in order to facilitate communication in the topic; on the other, to contribute to the expansion of the Andalusia's domestic and international trade and the dissemination of its culture. The main outcome of the research was the *Diccionario de términos del aceite de oliva* (DTAO – *Dictionary of olive oil terms*) (Roldán Vendrell, Arco Libros: 2013). This dictionary is currently the main reference source for answering queries and responding to any doubts that might arise in the use of this terminology in the three reference languages (Spanish, English and Chinese). It has received unanimous acknowledgement from numerous specialists in the sphere of Terminology, including most especially Maria Teresa Cabré (UPF), Miguel Casas Gómez (UCA- *Ibérica 27 (2014)*: 217-234), François Maniez (Université de Lyon), Maria Isabel Santamaría Pérez and Chelo Vargas Sierra (UA), Pamela Faber (UGR), Joaquín García Palacios (USAL), and Marie-Claude L'Homme (Université de Montréal).

The DTAO is well-known in the academic area of Terminology, but has not reached many of the institutions and organizations (domestic and international), translators, journalists, communicators and olive oil sector professionals that could benefit from it in their professions, especially salespeople, who need (fortunately, with an ever greater frequency) information on terminology in the book's target languages for their commercial transactions. That is why we are currently working on a multichannel technological solution that enables a greater and more efficient transfer to the business sector: the design and development of an adaptive website (*responsive web design*) that provides access to the information in any usage context. We believe that access must be afforded to this valuable reference information on a hand-held device that enables it to be looked up both on- and offline and so pre-empt situations in which it is impossible to connect to the internet. The web application's database will therefore also feed a series of mobile applications that will be available for the main platforms (iOS, Android). This tool will represent real progress in the dynamic transfer of specialized knowledge in the field of olive growing and olive oil production. Apart from delivering universal and free access to this information, the web application will welcome user suggestions for including new terms, new information and new reference languages, making it a collaborative tool that is also fed by its own users. With this tool we hope to respond to society's needs for multilingual communication in the area of olive oil and to help give a boost to economic activity in the olive sector.

In this work, in parallel to the presentation of the adaptive website, we will present a lexical repertoire integrated by new terms and expressions coined in this field (in the three working languages) in the last years. These neologisms reflect the most relevant innovations occurred in the olive oil sector over the last decade and, therefore, they must be compiled, sorted, systematized, and made accessible to the users in the web application we intend to develop.

Proceedings of the Globalex Workshop on Linked Lexicography, pages 62–68
Language Resources and Evaluation Conference (LREC 2020), Marseille, 11–16 May 2020
© European Language Resources Association (ELRA), licensed under CC-BY-NC

Building a domain-specific bilingual lexicon resource with Sketch Engine and Lexonomy: Taking Ownership of the Issues

Zaida Bartolomé-Díaz, Francesca Frontini

Universidad de Las Palmas de Gran Canaria
Calle Juan de Quesada, 30, 35001 Las Palmas de Gran Canaria, Las Palmas, Spain

Université Paul Valéry – Laboratoire Praxiling
Route de Mende, 34090 Montpellier - France

zaida.bartolome101@alu.ulpgc.es, francescafrontini@gmail.com

Abstract

Thanks to new technologies, the elaboration of specialized bilingual dictionaries can be made faster and more standardized, offering not only a dictionary of equivalents, but also the representation of a conceptual field.

Nevertheless, in view of these new tools and services, some of which are offered free of charge by European institutions, it is necessary to question the viability of their use by a lambda user and the previous knowledge required for such use, as well as the possible problems they may encounter.

In our communication we show a series of possible difficulties, as well as a methodological proposal and some solutions, by presenting an extract of a French-Spanish bilingual dictionary for the domain of architecture. The extract in question is a sample of about 30 terms created with the Lexonomy dictionary editor (Měchura 2017).

Keywords: bilingual lexicon, specialized lexicon, Lexonomy, architecture

1. Introduction

Due to the increasing process of globalization, professionals and specialized users need to communicate and use an appropriate terminology in each interlinguistic professional situation. Until now, the need to contrast terminological units adapted to each language pair and professional language required the simultaneous consultation of monolingual and bilingual dictionaries. Nowadays, as a result of the application of computational linguistics and corpus linguistics to language studies, it is undeniable that we are facing a new era of lexicography (Fuertes-Olivera 2012). Despite this, support for the creation of bilingual lexicographic resources dedicated to technical language is still insufficient.

With the emergence of online and born-digital dictionaries and resources and the new technologies that have emerged around the Lexicographic Linked Open Data cloud (LLOD), the horizon has broadened considerably, recently also due to initiatives such as the ELEXIS[1] project, which have been developed to provide lexicographers with services and tools to facilitate access to such services.

But it is essential to test specific cases and to verify the different existing technological tools in relation to the needs and knowledge of a lambda-user.

The objective of our paper is to present a practical case for the creation of a bilingual French-Spanish lexicon, specialized in the field of architecture, using the Lexonomy dictionary editor (Měchura 2017). Our goal is not only to create a dictionary of equivalents, but also to produce a resource that represents the linguistic and conceptual knowledge of our field and that we can, later, visualize on the Internet and connect to the Linked Data cloud, in order to promote the representation of lexicographic resources, which are currently still under-represented (Declerck 2018).

For the realization of this resource we started from a specialized corpus extracted from the Web using Sketch Engine[2]. Sketch Engine is a tool for building and exploring corpus. Through its algorithms it analyzes the different texts and is able to identify and extract specific terminology. It is also designed for text analysis or text mining applications.

After a domain-specific terminology extraction, we used the One-click Dictionary function of Sketch Engine to create a first draft of the dictionary, which we then customize and adapt to our needs and to the requirements of current language standards (a TEI serialization of LMF[3]) in the Lexonomy interface.

We intend to show the main problems encountered when a lexicographer or translator, not necessarily knowledgeable of programming or coding languages, manually refines and curates such a resource, and the solutions we have found to solve these problems, such as working off-line the XML file or sharing different sub-entries for avoiding repeat information. (Měchura 2018).

We will try to suggest a methodology applicable to any other technical domain for which there are no available resources or for under-represented language pairs.

2. Field of study

Studies and resources dedicated to the lexicographical treatment of architectural and technical terms in general language dictionaries are relatively scarce.

This field of architecture is perhaps one of the least analyzed specialized languages in the framework of the LSP, despite the importance of the current architectural

---

[1] https://elex.is/

[2] https://www.sketchengine.eu/

[3] Following the recently proposed ISO standard: https://www.iso.org/standard/75411.html.

historical heritage in both France and Spain and the variety of the subsets that make up its discourse.

Thus, through a quantitative and qualitative analysis of the existing dictionaries dedicated to architecture, whether on paper, electronic or born-digital, , we have remarked the evident lack of lexicographical material dedicated to this field of study, and even less when it comes to bilingual dictionaries combining French and Spanish.

Indeed, for this language pair, we have found very few dictionaries of this type, only four French-Spanish bilingual dictionaries specialized in architecture, published in 1967, 1968, 1969 and 2001, and only on paper.

This scarcity of studies in the field, as well as of lexical and terminological works, often poses serious problems for specialized users of a technical sector who are also often not sufficiently familiar with dictionaries, their usual contents and basic rules of management.

Once this lexicographic gap was identified, we thought it necessary to develop a resource dedicated to this field of study that would be easy to use and that would facilitate the development and transfer of knowledge, technologies, solutions and pilot projects to be carried out among French and Spanish speaking professionals in the field of architecture.

Moreover, from a lexicographical point of view, organized storage in a lexical database allows for better management and maintenance of information, and facilitates the detection and correction of errors. (Fernández-Pampillón Cesteros and Matesanz del Barrio 2006).

3.   Methodology

3.1   Selection of Corpus

Given that the construction of specialized dictionaries is generally carried out with corpus-based methodologies, the first difficulty we encounter is the lack of specialized corpora in our field of study. In our case we have not found a specific corpus in the field of architecture, neither monolingual, nor bilingual (neither parallel nor comparable.)

For this reason, we have decided to create our own corpus of study, specialized in architecture, starting from Web data.

In this sense, the Web today represents a huge corpus within the reach of linguists interested in specific studies, whose needs are not met by traditional and/or existing corpora.

The term "Web as corpus" was first introduced in 2001 by Kilgarriff and, two years later, developed by the article of the same title by Kilgarriff and Grefenstette (2003) in which arguments in favor of using the Web as a corpus were presented.

The Web is a good place for the discovery of neologisms (Hundt, Nesselhauf, and Biewer 2007), language use from a non-normative register (Lüdeling, Evert, and Baroni 2007), or obsolete language use not found in a traditional or existing corpus (Renouf and Kehoe 2006).

In order to conform our own comparable corpus, we have decided to use the Sketch Engine tool.

Sketch Engine has the option to create a parallel, bilingual or multilingual corpus for a specific field.

However, in our case our goal was to extract information about the specialized terminology for each of the two languages and not simply the terms or texts translated from each of them into the other.

So, we decided from the beginning to eliminate the idea of working with a parallel bilingual corpus and decided to form two specialized corpora separately in order to extract the specific terminology from each one of them.

Using the corpus creation tools offered by Sketch Engine, we have built our corpora from a specific search on the Web:

- For French we used a search query based on terms contained in *FrenceTerme* [4], related to the domaine: HABITAT ET CONSTRUCTION / Architecture (administrateur, -trice de bâti immobilier modélisé, agence d'architecture, bâti-immobilier-modélisé, bureau d'études techniques, calepinage, coupe, création architecturale, stylisme architectural, détail d'exécution, élévation, section, tirage).
Sketch Engine extracted a series of web pages and documents from the search. We then proceeded to analyze and clean up the different documents (removal of messages from forums, blogs, advertisements...). We finally formed a French corpus specialized in architecture, made up of 82 documents.

- In order to constitute the Spanish corpus, since an equivalent of FrenchTerme was unavailable, we used another function of Sketch Engine, and crawled the content of an online portal specialized in Spanish architecture (www.plataformaarquitectura.cl).
From this platform, which is the most read platform in Spanish dedicated to architecture according to the numbers of visits in 2019, a corpus composed of 65 documents was created.

3.2   Terminological extraction

Once our two specialized corpora were formed, we performed the standard procedure for terminology extraction proposed by Sketch Engine, comparing each of the corpuses with a general corpus in Spanish and French; as a result we obtained a series of representative architectural terms for each of the languages.

Since the objective of our work is to obtain a sample of a lexicon as well as the methodology for its creation, we will concentrate here only on the first 15 words of each language.

3.3   Draft dictionary

Since we worked with two separate comparable corpora, we could not directly form a single dictionary that would include both languages.

So, using the One-Click dictionary function of Sketch Engine, we first created a first draft dictionary for French,

---

[4] http://www.culture.fr/franceterme

from which, as indicated in the previous paragraph, we retain only the first 15 words of our terminology extraction.

Then, we manually added to this dictionary the words extracted from our Spanish corpus.

In this way we obtained a first small bilingual dictionary of 30 entries, unrelated to each other.

One of the problems that we found in this step, apart from the difficulty of adding one by one each of the 15 terms from the Spanish corpus, was the impossibility of relate our dictionary entries back to the both of the corpora. Indeed, Lexonomy offers the possibility to link the created dictionary with its original corpus available in Skechtengine. However, in our case, since we work from two comparable corpora, we can only link one of them to the bilingual dictionary.

3.4 Download the draft dictionary

At this point and after correctly understanding the operation of Lexonomy, we thought it is necessary to download the xml file and continue working on it using an xml editor (Oxygen).

From our point of view Lexonomy can be simple and easy to use to write some small entries, but if you really want to use the application for a more substantial work, with a greater number of terms and an in depth editing of the structure of each entry, working with off-line source files becomes more efficient.

At the same time the drawback is that it limits the options for several users to work on the same file online, which could be useful in the academic domain to carry out collaborative work with students, as well as being an impediment to the realization of more professional content.

3.5 Formatting the downloaded xml file off-line

The first problem we encounter when downloading the xml file from Lexonomy and open it in Oxygen is that each entry is organized independently.

The root element is minimal and does not contain information about the lexicon.

```xml
<?xml version="1.0"?>
<z8tq8vrq2>
<entry lxnm:entryID="1"
xmlns:lxnm="http://www.lexonomy.eu/">
    <headword
    xml:space="preserve">sujétion</headword>
    <partOfSpeech
    xml:space="preserve">an</partOfSpeech>
    <sense>
      <translation xml:space="preserve">sujeción
      </translation>
      <translation xml:space="preserve">fixación
      </translation>
      <example>
         <source><h>Sujétions</h><h>relatives</h>à
         l'ensemble des terrassements</source>
         <target> XXX </target>
      </example>
      </sense>
      <sense>
       <translation>limitación</translation>
       <example>
          <source>L'Entrepreneur fait son affaire auprès
          des services compétents de toutes démarches,
          autorisations ou
          <h>autres</h><h>sujétions</h>ayant trait au
          chantier, il fait établir notamment les
          branchements et canalisations pour la distribution
          de l'eau, de l'électricité et du téléphone
          correspondant aux besoins de chantier. </source>
          <target>XXX</target>
       </example>
    </sense>
</entry>

<entry lxnm:entryID="2"
xmlns:lxnm="http://www.lexonomy.eu/">
    <headword
    xml:space="preserve">coffrage</headword>
    <partOfSpeech
    xml:space="preserve">n</partOfSpeech>
    <sense>
      <translation xml:space="preserve">encofrado
      </translation>
      <example>
         <source xml:space="preserve">
         La partie haute du bâtiment également réalisée en
         coffrage inclinés est aussi d'une grande
         complexité, là encore des...</source>
         <target xml:space="preserve">XXX</target>
      </example>
    </sense>
</entry>
```

Figure 1. Extract of the XML file downloaded from Lexonomy

While the access via Lexonomy facilitates the task of creating an online version of the dictionary accessible to everyone, having an off line version of the dictionary with standard xml modeling is an important desiderata for the project, as it allows this resource to be used for more complex tasks, such as NLP and linking to other resources.

Since our intention is that eventually publish the final resource also following the aforementioned ISO LMF standard, an attempt was made to restructure our file using Oxygen and then try uploading it into Lexonomy again to verify compatibility.

In the previous Language resource management — Lexical markup framework (LMF), approved on 2008-03-21[5] we can find the Machine Readable Dictionary (MRD) extension which provides a metamodel package for representing data stored in machine readable dictionaries. This extension supports electronic machine-readable dictionary access for both human use and machine processing.

Since the MRD extension is based on the LMF core package and the morphological extension, it is designed to

---

[5] https://www.iso.org/standard/37327.html

interchange data with other LMF extensions where applicable.

Due to copyright reasons it is not possible to show here the MRD class Diagram here. It can be consulted by the corresponding ISO standard.

As indicated in this norm in a bilingual MRD, the Equivalent class represents the translation equivalent of the word form managed by the Lemma class. The Equivalent class has in a zero to many aggregate associations with the Sense class, which allows the lexicon developer to omit the Equivalent class from a monolingual dictionary.

While modeling our dictionary is possible, the standard is currently under revision as a multi part standard, with a part being dedicated to an xml serialization which uses the TEI dictionary model as a basis[6]. At the time of writing this module is being finalized, but not many examples exist of bilingual dictionaries in the new format, the proposed modeling we outline here was defined by consulting with an expert[7] , and is illustrated by the example in Figure 2:

```xml
<?xml version="1.0" encoding="UTF-8"?>
<TEI           xmlns="http://www.tei-c.org/ns/1.0"
type="lexicon">
  <teiHeader>
    <fileDesc>
      <titleStmt>
        <title>Lexique Bilingue Architecture</title>
      </titleStmt>
      <publicationStmt>
        <publisher>Zaida Bartolomé Diaz</publisher>
        <pubPlace>Montpellier</pubPlace>
        <date>2020</date>
        <availability><p>This is an open access work
        licensed under a Creative Commons Attribution 4.0
        International license.</p></availability>
        <ptr
        target="http://digitalcommons.unl.edu/zeabook/55
        "/>
      </publicationStmt>
      <sourceDesc><p>Born digital: no previous source
      exists.</p></sourceDesc>
    </fileDesc>
  </teiHeader>
<text>
  <body>
    <entry xml:lang="fr" xml:id="LA_1"
    xmlns:lxnm="http://www.lexonomy.eu/">
      <form type="lemma">
        <orth>sujétion</orth>
        <gramGrp>
          <pos>n.</pos>
        </gramGrp>
      </form>
      <sense n="1">
      <cit type="example">
          <quote><emph>Sujétions</emph>
```

```xml
          <emph>relatives</emph>à l'ensemble des
          terrassements
          </quote>
      </cit>
      <xr xml:lang="es" type="translation">
          <quote>sujeción</quote>
          <quote>fixación</quote></xr>
      </sense>
      <sense n="2">
      <cit type="example">
          <quote>L'Entrepreneur fait son affaire auprès
          des services compétents de toutes démarches,
          autorisations ou
          <emph>autres</emph><emph>sujétions</em
          ph>ayant trait au chantier, il fait établir
          notamment les branchements et canalisations
          pour la distribution de l'eau, de l'électricité et
          du téléphone correspondant aux besoins de
          chantier.</quote>
      </cit>
      <xr type="translationEquivalent">
      <ref xml:lang="es">limitación</ref></xr>
      </sense>
    </entry>
```

Figure 2. First version of TEI-LMF format of download xml file

As it can be observed this representation of the entry "sujetion" is included in a general <TEI> node of type lexicon; the <header> contains metadata information while lexical entries are included under <text><body>.

For each of the entries the section "Context" is represented by <cit type=example"><quote>…, in which we extract of the source corpus can be listed and linked by Sketch Engine. Each entry has one or more senses, and these in turn may have a <translationEquivalent>.

In view of this representation we have decided to make different modifications with which we believe we are advancing in our project to improve and provide a more professional and useful product.

First, to go further we wanted to add the **definition** section. To do this, rather than provide a definition of its own we wanted to collect a series of links to different dictionaries so that the user can go directly to a definition of the term in question provided by a monolingual technical dictionary.

Secondly, in addition, if we wish to create a dictionary of equivalents with cross entries between different entries, the term included in the <xr type: "translationEquivalent"> section should also be a separate entry, if it is not included in the extracted terms corresponding to the other language.

In that sense, our dictionary will also be enriched by new entries that will arise as a result of the translation of each term into the other language.

The following figure shows the resulting xml file after our modifications:

---

[6] See some examples in: https://github.com/DARIAH-ERIC/lexicalresources/tree/master/Schemas/LMFinTEI%20Specification

[7] Laurent Romary, currently co-leader of the new LMF Part 4 and expert of TEI.

```xml
<?xml version="1.0" encoding="UTF-8"?>
<TEI             xmlns="http://www.tei-c.org/ns/1.0"
type="lexicon">
  <teiHeader>
    <fileDesc>
      <titleStmt>
        <title>Lexique Bilingue Architecture</title>
      </titleStmt>
      <publicationStmt>
        <publisher>Zaida Bartolomé Diaz</publisher>
        <pubPlace>Montpellier</pubPlace>
        <date>2020</date>
        <availability><p>This is an open access work
licensed under a Creative Commons Attribution
4.0 International license.</p></availability>
        <ptr
target="http://digitalcommons.unl.edu/zeabook/5
5"/>
      </publicationStmt>
    <sourceDesc><p>Born digital: no previous source
exists.</p>
      </sourceDesc>
    </fileDesc>
  </teiHeader>
  <text>
    <body>
      <entry xml:lang="fr" xml:id="LA_1"
xmlns:lxnm="http://www.lexonomy.eu/">
        <form type="lemma">
          <orth>sujétion</orth>
          <gramGrp>
            <pos>n.</pos>
          </gramGrp>
        </form>
        <sense n="1">
          <xr xml:lang="es"
type="translationEquivalent">condición</xr>
          <def xml:lang="fr" type="CNRTL">
            <quote
type="https://www.cnrtl.fr/definition/suj%C3
%A9tion">Contrainte liée aux choses elles-
mêmes.</quote>
          </def>
          <cit type="example">
            -<quote><emph>Sujétions</emph>
            <emph>relatives</emph>à l'ensemble des
terrassements
            </quote>
          </cit>
        </sense>
        <sense n="2">
          <xr xml:lang="es"
type="translationEquivalent">limitación</xr>
          <def xml:lang="fr" type="Eyrolles">
            <quote type="https://www.editions-
eyrolles.com/Dico-
BTP/definition.html?id=8566"> Servitude
étant due. Dans un marché, les sujétions
représentent les travaux ou services à
effectuer.</quote>
          </def>
```

```xml
          <cit type="example">
            <quote>L'Entrepreneur fait son affaire auprès
des services compétents de toutes démarches,
autorisations ou
            <emph>autres</emph><emph>sujétions</emp
h>ayant trait au chantier, il fait établir
notamment les branchements et canalisations
pour la distribution de l'eau, de l'électricité et
du téléphone correspondant aux besoins de
chantier.</quote>
          </cit>
        </sense>
      </entry>
```

Figure 3. Entry "sujétion" re-defined

3.6   Importing this xml file to Lexonomy

As a next step we tried to import the file we have worked off-line into Lexonomy again and in order to test for compatibility.

When we tried to import the file back into Lexonomy the first problem was that the entries were not independent of each other. In order to work again on Lexonomy, each entry must be listed independently.

In view of this, we should ask ourselves how the metadata of a file should be defined in Lexonomy if we want this dictionary to be indexed and linked to the external resources and to the lexicographic cloud which projects such as ELEXIS are trying to build.

At this point and due to multiple problems, that prevent Lexonomy from a correctly recognizing of our file we have decided to recreate directly our scheme in our profile. Lexonomy doesn't recognize our file: it doesn't order the entries correctly and the structure is lost when we upload our document.

3.7   Recreating the TEI-LMF serialization directly in Lexonomy

As a result of our previous attempts, we decided to return to our first dictionary, which included all 15 French terms and all 15 Spanish terms.

The objective was to recreate the TEI-LMF serialization that we had previously developed off-line directly within in the Lexonomy interface. This of course required also an ad hoc a style sheet.

However, recreating this serialization in the Lexonomy interface poses several problems since the result is not exactly what we expected.

Nevertheless, a positive outcome if this operation is that through Lexonomy's interface we were able to create cross-reference between the different French and Spanish terms, which also allowed us to add terms (translations) that we had not initially foreseen.

We also decided to collect the collocates and thesauruses and make them sub-entries as recommended by Měchura (2018), so that the information could also be reused.

In this respect, it should be noted that Lexonomy requests that entries be re-indexed each time new sub-entries are created. Such indexing is very time consuming and often requires a restart of the application for the changes to be taken into account.

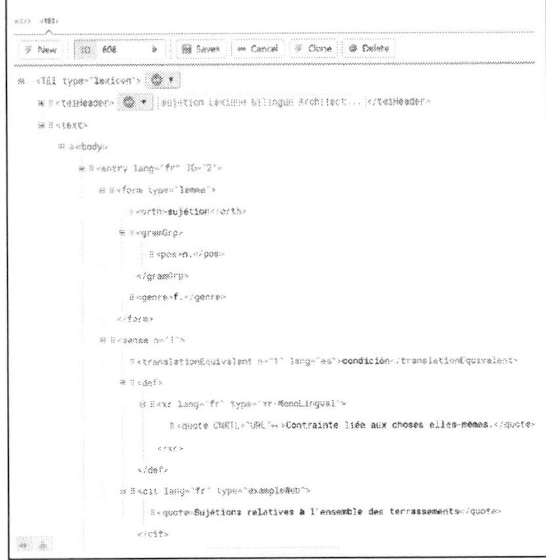

Figure 4. Recreating TEI-LMF serialization of an entry directly in Lexonomy

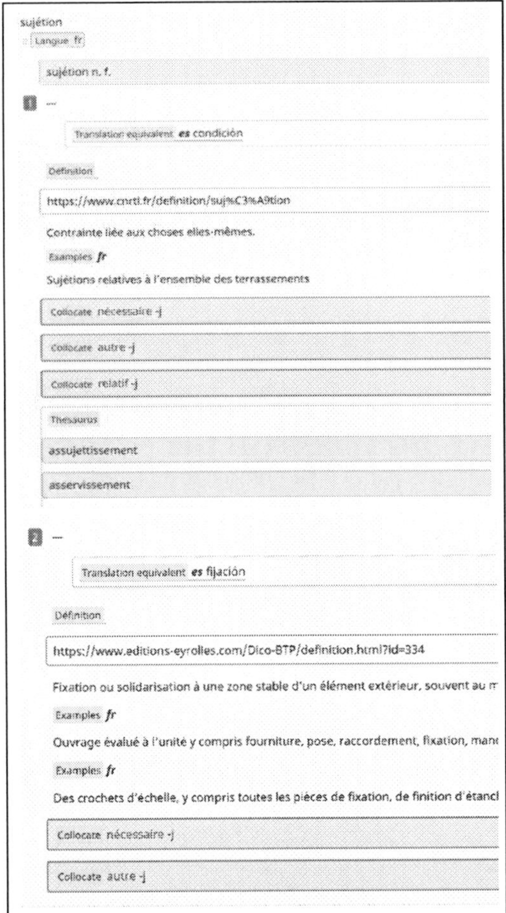

Figure 5. Style sheet of an entry defined directly in Lexonomy

4. Conclusions

After this first experience creating a dictionary of equivalents in a certain specialized field and for a couple of languages for which there are not yet enough resources, we can present several reservations:

- Regarding Sketch Engine we regret that there is no function or procedure to create a single, affordable corpus composed of different texts in different languages.

The fact that Sketch Engine only allows the creation of parallel corpus restricts its use, being limited to only possible use it when bilingual or multilingual parallel texts, or translations of a given corpus are available.

- Regarding to Lexonomy the first obstacle was, as expressed above, not being able to directly create a dictionary on Lexonomy through the one-click dictionary function from two different corpora, not even one that we can link ourselves subsequently.

We think that it could be interesting to contemplate the idea of creating a single dictionary in Lexonomy from two different corpora created in Sketch Engine.

This will also allow to improve the links to collocates or thesaurus items from these different corpora for different languages. As we can see in the example of the entry "sujétion" we have recovered from our French corpus linked the collocations and thesaurus items. However, when it comes to developing an entry in Spanish it will not be possible to link our corpus since only one is allowed.

As described in our methodology it was also impossible for us to make directly on Lexonomy a dictionary that will contemplate the TEI-LMF serialization, mainly due to the fact that it is not possible to form a root that gathers all the metadata and all the entries from a same lexicon.

As we have observed when we have downloaded our file from Lexonomy and opened it in an XML editor these metadata are non-existent and if we try to do the opposite, the Lexonomy editor does not recognize a common root for all the entries since each one of them must be independent.

In view of this, we must ask ourselves how the metadata of a Lexonomy dictionary will be recorded.

We believe that if we don't contemplate this common root that collects metadata and all the entries of a dictionary it will be complicated, if not impossible, that a dictionary created and stored in Lexonomy can be tracked, found and shared with other users.

Regarding the display of our dictionary in Lexonomy we can point out mainly the fact that external references cannot be directly displayed with a hyperlink.

Until now (possibly in June when the new version will be implemented) Lexonomy does not allow to directly include hyperlinks to external pages. It is therefore necessary to collect and display the full link.

Finally, we regret the fact that the sub-entries do not work properly, and it is often necessary to restart the application in order to reindex them.

In spite of our objections, we believe that the idea of creating this database- interface in which to store and visualize lexicographical data is really interesting and since it is relatively recent we believe that it needs to continue evolving until it becomes fully operational.

We believe that experiences like the one presented above mostly serve to have a real awareness of the existing problems and to be able to take into account the feedbacks of the users' experiences.

5. Bibliographical References

Declerck, T. 2018. 'Towards a Linked Lexical Data Cloud Based on Ontolex-Lemon.P'. In *Proceedings of the LREC 2018 Workshop "6th Workshop on Linked Data in Linguistic (LDL-2018)"*, 91. Miyazaki, Japan: In John P. McCrae, et al., editors.

Fernández-Pampillón Cesteros, A., and M. Matesanz del Barrio. 2006. 'Los Diccionarios Electrónicos: Hacia Un Nuevo Concepto de Diccionario'. *Estudios de Lingüística Del Español* 24 (Nuevos géneros discursivos: los textos electrónicos). http://elies.rediris.es/elies24/pampillon_cap1.htm.

Fuertes-Olivera, P. 2012. 'Lexicography and the Internet as a (Re-)Source'. *Lexicographica* 28. https://doi.org/10.1515/lexi.2012-0005.

Hundt, M., N. Nesselhauf, and C. Biewer. 2007. 'Corpus Linguistics and the Web'. In *Corpus Linguistics and the Web*, In M. Hundt, N. Nesselhauf, C. Biewer (Eds.), 1–5. Amsterdam – New York: Rodopi.

Kilgarriff, A., and G. Grefenstette. 2003. 'Introduction to the Special Issue on the Web as Corpus'. *Computational Linguistics* 29 (September): 333–47. https://doi.org/10.1162/089120103322711569.

Lüdeling, Anke, Stefan Evert, and Marco Baroni. 2007. 'Using Web Data for Linguistic Purposes'. In *Corpus Linguistics and the Web*, edited by Marianne Hundt, Nadja Nesselhauf, and Carolin Biewer. Brill | Rodopi. https://doi.org/10.1163/9789401203791_003.

Měchura, M. 2017. 'Introducing Lexonomy: An Open-Source Dictionary Writing and Publishing System'. In *Electronic Lexicography in the 21st Century: Proceedings of ELex 2017 Conference*, 662–79, 18 pp. Leiden: In I. Kosem, C. Tiberius, M. Jakubíček, J. Kallas, S. Krek, V. Baisa.

Měchura, M. 2018. 'Shareable Subentries in Lexonomy as a Solution to the Problem of Multiword Item Placement'. In *The XVIII EURALEX International Congress: Lexicography in Global Contexts*, 223–32, 10 pp. Ljubljana, Slovenia: In. Jaka Čibej, Vojko Gorjanc, Iztok Kosem and Simon Krek.

Renouf, A., and A. Kehoe. 2006. . '. Introduction: The Changing Face of Corpus Linguistics'. In *The Changing Face of Corpus Linguistics*, In A. Renouf & A. Kehoe (Eds.). Amsterdam – New YorK: Rodopi.

Proceedings of the Globalex Workshop on Linked Lexicography, pages 69–75
Language Resources and Evaluation Conference (LREC 2020), Marseille, 11–16 May 2020

MWSA Task at GlobaLex 2020: RACAI's Word Sense Alignment System using a Similarity Measurement of Dictionary Definitions

Vasile Păiș, Dan Tufiș, Radu Ion
Research Institute for Artificial Intelligence "Mihai Drăgănescu", Romanian Academy
CASA ACADEMIEI, 13 "Calea 13 Septembrie", Bucharest 050711, ROMANIA
{vasile, tufis, radu}@racai.ro

Abstract

This paper describes RACAI's word sense alignment system, which participated in the Monolingual Word Sense Alignment shared task organized at GlobaLex 2020 workshop. We discuss the system architecture, some of the challenges that we faced as well as present our results on several of the languages available for the task.

Keywords: word sense alignment, semantic similarity, BERT, gloss similarity

1. Introduction

The "Monolingual Word Sense Alignment" (MWSA) task aimed at identifying a degree of similarity between word definitions across multiple dictionaries, in the same language. For this purpose, a corpus (Ahmadi et al., 2020) was provided for multiple languages. For each language, word senses from two distinct dictionaries were extracted and participating systems had to classify the relationship between the senses in one of five categories: "exact", "broader", "narrower", "related" or "none".

Each provided entry in the evaluation set contains the following information: the lemma associated with the two definitions (the definiendum), the part of speech, two fields corresponding to the first and second dictionary entries (the definientia). Additionally, in the training set the relationship label is also provided.

Given this information, the task can be seen either as a word sense disambiguation problem, considering the sense of the definiendum in each of the definitions, or as a sentence similarity problem, considering the relatedness of the two definitions if they were sentences.

Word sense disambiguation (WSD) is the ability to identify the meaning of words in context in a computational manner (Navigli, 2009). This is an extremely hard problem, previously described as an AI-complete problem (Mallery, 1988), equivalent to solving central problems of artificial intelligence. This happens because difficult disambiguation issues can be resolved only based on knowledge. For the purpose of the MWSA task, a WSD approach will consider at each step the definiendum and its two contexts as expressed by the dictionary definitions.

Sentence similarity aims at computing a similarity measure between two sentences based on meanings and semantic content. For this purpose, the two definitions are treated like sentences and their meaning is compared. In this case the definiendum is not directly used, only the meaning expressed by the definiens being considered.

The present paper presents our system developed in the context of the MWSA shared task. We start by presenting related research, then continue with the implementation of our system and finally present concluding remarks.

2. Related Work

Word sense disambiguation is a very old task in natural language processing. Already in 1940s it is viewed as a fundamental task of machine translation (Weaver, 1949). Early systems employed manually created lists of disambiguation rules (Rivest, 1987). The power of these systems was demonstrated in the first Senseval competition (Kilgarriff, 2000), where decision lists were the most successful techniques employed (Yarowsky, 2000).

One of the earliest attempts at using additional digital resources in the form of machine-readable dictionaries is known as the Lesk algorithm, after its author (Lesk, 1986). In this case, the dictionary sense of a word having the highest overlap with its context (the most words in common) is considered to be the correct one. A Lesk-based similarity measure can also be computed for entire sentences. A survey of different semantic text similarity methods is given in Islam and Inkpen (2008).

With the introduction of the unsupervised distributional representation of words, new sentence similarity measures have become available. These representations are also known as "word embeddings" and include GloVe (Pennington et al., 2014), Skip-gram and CBOW (Bengio et al., 2003) and further refinements such as those described in Bojanowski et al. (2016). In all of these variants, a unique representation is computed for each word based on all the contexts it appears in. This is not directly usable for WSD since the representation remains the same regardless of the word context. However, short text or sentence similarity measures can be computed by using the word embeddings representation of each word (Kenter and Rijke, 2015). One of the advantages of using word embeddings representations is the availability of such pre-computed vectors for many languages (Grave et al., 2018), trained on a mixture of Wikipedia and Common Crawl data. Additionally, on certain languages there are pre-computed vectors available computed on more language representative corpora, such as (Păiș and Tufiș, 2018).

A more recent representation of words is represented by their contextual embeddings. Well-known models of this type are ELMo (Peters et al., 2018) and BERT (Devlin et al., 2019). They provide a word representation in context. Therefore, as opposed to previous embedding models, the word representation is not fixed, but determined based on the actual context the word appears in at runtime.

Currently such pre-trained representations are not yet available for all languages, but multilingual models do exist, covering multiple languages in the same model, such as (Artetxe and Schwenk, 2019). Recent studies have confirmed that BERT multilingual models seem to create good representations usable in a large number of experiments, even though concerns have been expressed regarding certain language pairs (Pires et al., 2019).

Sentence-BERT (Reimers and Gurevych, 2019) is a system for determining sentence embeddings. These are representations of entire sentences that can be used to assess sentence similarity.

3. Dataset and Basic Processing

The dataset proposed for the MWSA task is comprised of training and test data for 15 languages. For each of the languages, a tab separated file is available for evaluation containing 4 columns (lemma, part-of-speech, first definition, second definition) with one additional column in the training data (the relatedness of the two definitions). The definitions come from two distinct sources and are related to the word presented in the first column.

As mentioned in the introduction, the definition similarity issue can be considered a sentence similarity problem. However, definitions are usually not regular sentences. Considering the "English_nuig" portion of the dataset, which consists of definitions taken from the Princeton English WordNet (Miller, 1995) and the Webster's 1913 dictionary, the following types of definitions can be identified:

- A list of synonyms (example: "a pennant; a flag or streamer", "a wing; a pinion")
- One or more expressions detailing the word (example: "not having a material body", "wild or intractable; disposed to break away from duty; untamed")
- Entire sentences (example: "a tower built by Noah's descendants (probably in Babylon) who intended it to reach up to heaven; God foiled them by confusing their language so they could no longer understand one another").

Other characteristics of definitions include:

- Further clarifications given in parentheses (example: "(Genesis 11:1-11)", "(probably in Babylon)", "(approximately)")
- Definitions tend to use a simpler language, out of more common words (usually explaining a less common word by means of common words)
- There can be additional clarifications or examples at the end of the definitions starting with "--" (example: "-- usually used of people, especially women;", "-- contrary to")
- For things like proper names or historical events there can be years or periods given in parentheses (example: "(1805)", "(1909-1984)").

For other languages in the dataset similar observations can be made. Nevertheless, some specifics can also be identified. For example, in the Dutch part of the corpus first definitions usually start with a number (example: "1.a/|\Van personen", "II.6.c/|\(Onz.) Zonder nadere bep.").

Given these corpus characteristics, a first phase before any actual algorithm implementation must consist in cleaning the definitions and pre-processing towards obtaining actual definientia. Since in most cases a single definition text actually groups together multiple simpler definitions our goal for pre-processing is to actually split them into individual ones (will also reference to them as "sub-definitions"). A first step is to split the definition text by ";" characters. However, since some of the sub-definitions may still be complex, we followed some of the approaches for sentence decomposition described in Haussmann (2011). We paid special attention to cases where multiple alternatives were given in the definition text, usually by means of coordinating conjunctions.

Taking an example definition "of plain or coarse features; uncomely; ugly; -- usually used of people, especially women" this would be expanded into 4 sub-definitions: "of plain features", "of coarse features", "uncomely" and "ugly". The final part, after the "--" is removed during the cleaning phase. Even though this final part could provide some information, it appears only in one of the definition pairs and therefore it was deemed not useful for the analysis algorithms.Further primary processing operations include lemmatization and part-of-speech tagging. Given the observations presented previously and the examples shown, we considered that a regular annotation pipeline would not produce good results, since these are usually trained on regular text, containing complete sentences. Therefore, we decided to employ a statistical based annotation, considering the most frequent lemma and part-of-speech that appears in a large enough corpus. For this purpose, we used the Open American National Corpus (Ide and Macleod, 2001) for the English language, the Spoken Dutch Corpus (Corpus Gesproken Nederlands – CGN) (Hoekstra et al., 2000) for the Dutch language, the PAISA corpus (Lyding et al., 2014) for the Italian language and the available Universal Dependencies treebanks for the Spanish language.

The choice of the aforementioned resources for lemmas and part-of-speech was justified by their public availability online as well as the relatively short timeframe allocated for the purpose of the MWSA task.

Dataset structure for the languages in which our system participated is presented in Tables 1-4 for the training part and in Table 5 for the test part. The part of speech is associated with the defined word and the relation categories "exact", "narrower", "broader", "related" and "none" are presented as they appear in the training set.

POS	Exact	Narr.	Broad.	Rel.	None	Total
Noun	409	143	11	16	2115	2694
Verb	230	100	19	25	4381	4755
Adj	149	58	7	8	588	810
Adv	12	9	2	2	53	78

Table 1. Dataset structure for the English training set

POS	Exact	Narr.	Broad.	Rel.	None	Total
Noun	264	14	40	24	8616	8958
Verb	77	9	7	7	4664	4766
Adj	93	5	4	3	4013	4118
Adv	10	1	0	4	1363	1378

Table 2. Dataset structure for the Dutch training set

POS	Exact	Narr.	Broad.	Rel.	None	*Total*
Noun	161	43	22	23	773	*1022*
Verb	120	66	11	54	695	*946*

Table 3. Dataset structure for the Italian training set

POS	Exact	Narr.	Broad.	Rel.	None	*Total*
Noun	350	72	50	38	1718	*2228*
Verb	129	24	22	10	865	*1051*
Adj	160	29	19	16	767	*991*
Adv	20	0	0	1	50	*71*
Conj.	2	1	0	3	22	*28*
Adp.	4	0	0	1	44	*49*
Affix	5	1	0	1	27	*34*
Interj.	1	0	0	0	0	*1*

Table 4. Dataset structure for the Spanish training set

	Noun	Verb	Adjective	Adverb	Total
English	177	262	100	5	544
Dutch	834	0	90	0	924
Italian	136	69	0	0	205
Spanish	171	119	150	4	444

Table 5. Dataset structure for test sets

Some common observations can be extracted from the above tables. In all the analyzed languages the predominant parts-of-speech associated with the entries are nouns and verbs, in both training and test sets. Additional part of speech words present are usually adjectives and adverbs. For the Italian dataset only nouns and verbs are provided while the Spanish data set also has a few entries (a total of 112) with other part of speech tags, present only in the training set: conjunction, adposition, affix, interjection.

Considering the English dataset alone, the nouns and verbs together total 7449 entries while the rest account for only 888 entries. From this point of view, it is expected that any system trained on the training set and making use of part-of-speech information will probably work better on nouns and verbs.

With regard to relationship classes, for all datasets it seems the "none" class is the most used, followed by the "exact" class. For the English dataset, the "none" class accounts for 7137 entries, the "exact" class has 800 entries and all the other classes account for 400 entries. Given this huge difference between the available examples associated with each class, it is expected that a system trained on this dataset will perform better on "none" and "exact" and less on the other classes.

4. System Architecture

The overall system is constructed as a series of modules that can be turned on or off depending on what resources are available for a certain language. Each module produces one or more features that can be finally fed into a decision tree or random forest classifier, thus producing the final result. The overall system diagram is presented in Figure 1.

The first two modules "Cleanup" and "Definition decomposition" were already presented in the previous section. Their functionality is about obtaining clean sub-definitions. The following modules usually make use of these sub-definitions, but there are also features computed on the entire definition directly after the cleanup pre-

processing. Modules using sub-definitions, as detailed below, will compute a score for each sub-definition pair. Finally, the scores are combined by selecting the maximum score between all sub-definition pairs.

The first series of features is based on variants of the Lesk algorithm. We use three types of algorithms based on complete words, lemmas and stems. For each sub-definition pair (the first taken from the first definition and the second from the second definition) we compute a score based on the common indicators between the two. Finally, the algorithm keeps the maximum number of words in common as well as the maximum and minimum number of words in the sub-definitions corresponding to the first and second definition. For stemming we used a Porter stemmer algorithm (Rijsbergen, 1980; Porter, 1980).

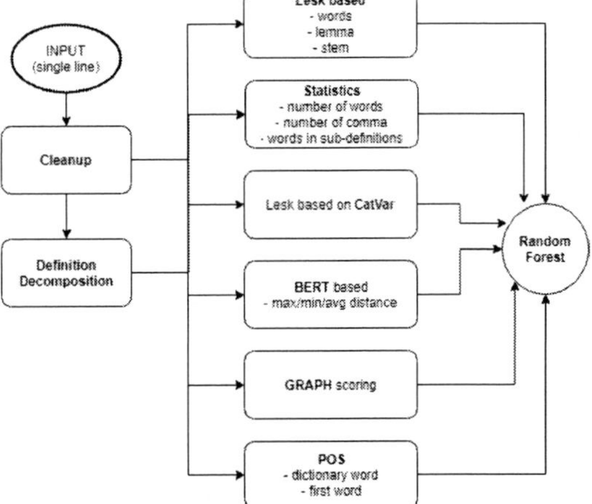

Figure 1. System architecture

An additional enhancement was realized by implementing a Lesk algorithm variant by incorporating the cluster information from the Categorial Variation Database (Catvar) (Habash and Dorr, 2003). Catvar is a database of clusters of uninflected words (lexemes) and their categorial (i.e. part-of-speech) variants.

As mentioned in the "Related work" section, BERT is a word embeddings model allowing for word representation in context and this representation was used in Sentence-BERT (Reimers and Gurevych, 2019) for obtaining sentence-level representations. We exploited this by incorporating a series Sentence-BERT based features. Thus, for each sub-definition pair we computed the Sentence-BERT representation and obtained the cosine distance between those. Finally, the minimum, maximum and average distances were computed and used as features. Also, a complete embedding was computed on the entire definition and the cosine distance between the two definitions was used as another feature.

A novel algorithm was implemented using a graph representation. For each sub-definition pair, the component words were added to the graph. Then, the lemmas of the words were added. Finally, synonyms and related words (see below) were added as well. These were extracted from WordNet. The extraction process involves a further sense disambiguation in order to detect relevant synsets. This was achieved using a basic Lesk-based disambiguation algorithm between the synset definition available in WordNet and the input sub-definition. In order to exploit the word order within the sub-definitions and allow for missing words, additional edges were added between adjacent words in the sub-definitions. An example is given in Figure 2 for the sub-definitions "refuse to accept" and "refuse to receive". This is a very simple example in which a word appears in both sub-definitions and the remaining words are actually detected as being synonyms.

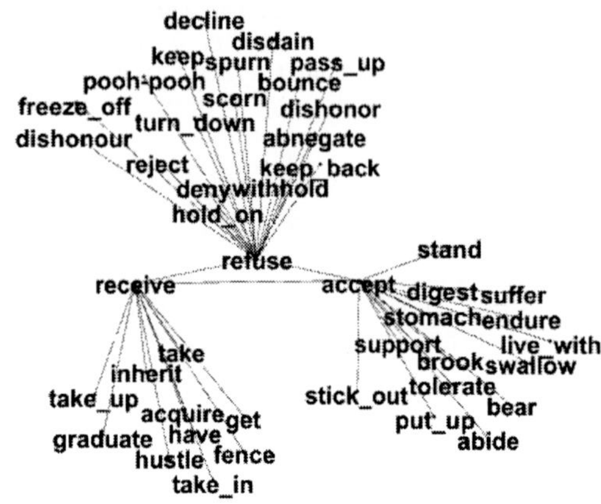

Figure 2. Example graph-based representation for "refuse to accept" and "refuse to receive"

Finally, a score was computed based on the distance between words belonging to the two sub-definitions.

Since all these algorithms make use of statistics or pre-trained word vectors without further optimization on the training corpus, we present results from each algorithm alone in Table 6.

Algorithm	Accuracy 5-class
Lesk words	0.8502
Lesk lemma	0.8501
Lesk stem	0.8496
Lesk Catvar	0.8221
Graph	0.8539
BERT avg. sub-definitions	0.8676

Table 6. Accuracy results from different algorithms on the English training set

From Table 6 it can be seen that the BERT average calculation on the sub-definitions seems to produce the best accuracy score. However, by comparing the different algorithms it seems that each algorithm produces good results in different contexts (considering the observations from section 3, above). Therefore, the final classification module becomes very important, especially combined with other features that could allow a decision between different scores.

Statistical features which were computed included the total number of words, minimum and maximum number of words in sub-definitions, number of comma characters.

Furthermore, from several manual investigations on the training data it was deemed useful to have a comparison

between the first words of sub-definitions having the same part of speech as the defined word. This comparison is realized by means of synonyms and is further used as a feature. For example, let's consider the sub-definitions associated with the word "holograph" which has the indicated part of speech "noun": "handwritten book" and "a document". In this case we are interested in comparing "book" and "document" since these have the same part of speech ("noun") as the defined word.

Furthermore, considering the observations regarding definition structure from section 3, an additional feature was created with 3 possible values: 0, if both sub-definitions are single word (not considering stop words); 1, if one of the sub-definitions is a single word and the other is a more complex expression; 2, if both sub-definitions are complex expressions.

A total of 17 features were finally used in a Random Forest Classifier (Ho, 1995). The classifier hyperparameters were trained and optimized using a grid search approach with cross validation on the training set.

The final cross validation measurement of mean accuracy on the training set indicated a value of 0.881 with a variation of +/- 0.02. This is above the score obtained on the test set, thus indicating some potentially significant variations in the data used. Nevertheless, our system obtained a final score of 0.798 on the 5-class accuracy evaluation, thus positioning the system on the first place for the English language competition.

For the other languages in which we participated (Dutch, Italian and Spanish) we deactivated the modules using WordNet based synonyms. We acknowledge the existence of wordnets for the aforementioned languages, however due to the short amount of time available for the task we were not able to technically integrate these resources into our system. Nevertheless, this was an exercise proving the modularity of the developed system and the possibility to adapt to different available resources. Furthermore, even with this disadvantage, the system was able to be on the first place for the Dutch language and on second place for Italian and Spanish.

5. System Evaluation

Once the test set annotations were released, we were able to evaluate our system, including all the other algorithms on the final data. Table 5, above, already contains an analysis of the test dataset part-of-speech structure. Distribution of available gold annotations in the test dataset are presented in tables 7-10 for the English, Dutch, Italian and Spanish languages.

POS	Exact	Narr.	Broad.	Rel.	None	Total
Noun	39	18	0	2	118	177
Verb	31	11	1	10	209	262
Adj	14	0	2	4	80	100
Adv	1	0	0	0	4	5

Table 7. Dataset structure for the English test set

POS	Exact	Narr.	Broad.	Rel.	None	Total
Noun	40	1	10	1	782	834
Adj	3	0	3	0	84	90

Table 8. Dataset structure for the Dutch test set

POS	Exact	Narr.	Broad.	Rel.	None	*Total*
Noun	23	6	2	8	97	*136*
Verb	5	9	3	1	51	*69*

Table 9. Dataset structure for the Italian test set

POS	Exact	Narr.	Broad.	Rel.	None	*Total*
Noun	29	8	4	1	129	*171*
Verb	17	5	0	0	97	*119*
Adj	24	12	5	3	106	*150*
Adv	2	0	0	0	2	*4*

Table 10. Dataset structure for the Spanish test set

Test dataset similarity tags follow a distribution like that of the training set. However, the distinction between "exact" and "none" classes is emphasized even more. In the English, Dutch and Spanish datasets there are cases where the number of "narrower", "broader" or "related" tags is equal to zero for certain parts of speech. By looking at the total numbers of tags in each category in the English data set, it can be observed that there are only three of type "broader". Similarly, for the other languages analyzed there are tags for which the total number is equal to or less than 5.

The official evaluation was performed using the CodaLab website[1]. Results on the test datasets for our system are presented in Table 11. This evaluation contains 4 indicators: accuracy (the percentage of scores for which the predicted label matches the reference label, considering all five classes), precision, recall and F-measure (taking into account accuracy in predicting the link but not the type of the link, thus considering only 2 classes: none and non-none).

	5-Class Accuracy	2-Class Precision	2-Class Recall	2-Class F-measure
English	0.798	0.746	0.353	0.480
Dutch	0.944	0.846	0.190	0.310
Italian	0.761	0.760	0.333	0.463
Spanish	0.786	0.667	0.655	0.661

Table 11. System evaluation on the test dataset

Our system obtained first place for the English and Dutch accuracy score (considering all 5 classes) and second place for the Italian and Spanish accuracy. Probably the lower score for Italian and Spanish is due to the fewer language resources that we used and thus to the fewer modules of the system that were involved, as described in section 4.

Looking at the 2-class measures, our system reached high precision and was on the first place for English and Dutch and on the second place for Italian and Spanish. Compared to other systems our recall was lower resulting in a F-measure that situated our system on second and third place with regard to this metric.

Similar to the individual algorithm evaluation provided in Table 6 on the training set, we provide accuracies on the test set for the English language in Table 12.

As mentioned in section 4, these algorithms are not dependent on the training set, being statistical in nature, therefore we would expect seeing similar scores. However, a slightly lower score than the one on the training set could be attributed to a potential difference between the two sets. Tables 1 and 7 provide comparison between the training and test sets for the English language and one of the possible differences is the high number of nouns in the training set as compared to the more balanced number of nouns and verbs in the test set. Another difference is the reduced number of "narrower", "broader" and "related" definitions.

Algorithm	Accuracy 5-class
Lesk words	0.6985
Lesk lemma	0.6912
Lesk stem	0.6930
Lesk Catvar	0.6415
Graph	0.7445
BERT avg. sub-definitions	0.7096

Table 12. Accuracy results from different algorithms on the English test set

The addition of a Random Forest classifier combining all the available features improved the overall accuracy from 0.744 (in the case of the Graph-based algorithm, which obtained the highest individual score) to 0.798, which was the final score achieved by our system on the English language.

6. Conclusions and Future Work

This paper presented our system proposal[2] for the Monolingual Word Sense Alignment 2020 shared task. The system is composed of multiple modules which can be enabled or not depending on the linguistic resources available for a particular language. Finally, a random forest classifier is trained on the provided training dataset using the features produced by the different modules. The system was able to achieve state-of-the-art performance for the English language, by using all the implemented modules, as described in section 4 above. Furthermore, with a reduced set of modules, due to the resources available to us in the short amount of time for this competition, we were able to achieve first place in the Dutch language competition and second place in the Italian and Spanish competitions.

The overall system contains both language independent modules (like some of the Lesk based approaches and purely statistical features) and modules requiring the presence of language resources. In the second case, these range from basic resources (synonyms, stemming algorithms) to more advanced resources (WordNet, lemmatization, part of speech tagging) and even the presence of a BERT model (either multilingual or language specific).

Having a modular architecture means the system can be used on any language and it can adapt itself (also its results) to the available resources. As always, having more language resources available translates into a better system performance. Of course, integrating resources for additional languages requires manual intervention on the system to allow it to process the new resources in their respective formats. This also explains our limited participation in the task's languages since we had to integrate different resources (with different formats) available for the different languages.

---

[1] https://competitions.codalab.org/competitions/22163

[2] https://github.com/racai-ai/MWSA2020

Implemented modules can be used individually, even without a training set. This set was needed in the last stage when training the final classifier together with additional statistical features. Therefore, it is our hope that this implementation can be adapted for Romanian language as well. Currently a large annotated Reference Corpus of Contemporary Romanian Language (CoRoLa) (Mititelu et al., 2018) is available for our research together with the Romanian WordNet (Tufiș et al, 2008). Currently, as far as we know, there is no monolingual BERT model available for Romanian language. However, multilingual models, similar to the one used for the purpose of the MWSA task, are available. Finally, we envisage to further include such a system in the RELATE platform (Păiș et al., 2019) dedicated to processing Romanian language.

7. Acknowledgements

Part of this work was conducted in the context of the ReTeRom project. Part of this work was conducted in the context of the Marcell project.

8. Bibliographical References

Ahmadi, S., McCrae, P.J., Nimb, S., Troelsgård, T., Olsen, S., Pedersen, S.B., Declerck, T., Wissik, T., Monachini, M., Bellandi, A., Khan, F., Pisani, I., Krek, S., Lipp, V., Váradi, T., Simon, L., Győrffy, A., Tiberius, C., Schoonheim, T., Moshe, B.Y., Rudich, M., Ahmad, A.R., Lonke, D., Kovalenko, K., Langemets, M., Kallas, J., Dereza, O., Fransen, T., Cillessen, D., Lindemann, D., Alonso, M., Salgado, A., Sancho, L.J., Ureña-Ruiz, R., Simov, K., Osenova, P., Kancheva, Z., Radev, I., Stanković, R., Krstev, C., Lazić, B., Marković, A., Perdih, A. and Gabrovšek, D. (2020). A Multilingual Evaluation Dataset for Monolingual Word Sense Alignment. Proceedings of the 12th Language Resource and Evaluation Conference (LREC 2020).

Artetxe, M. and Schwenk, H. (2019). Massively Multilingual Sentence Embeddings for Zero-Shot Cross-Lingual Transfer and Beyond. Transactions of the Association for Computational Linguistics. 7. 597-610. 10.1162/tacl_a_00288.

Bengio, Y., Ducharme, R., Vincent, P. (2003). A neural probabilistic language model, Journal of Machine Learning Research, 3, pp.1137–1155.

Bojanowski, P., Grave, E., Joulin, A., Mikolov, T. (2016). Enriching Word Vectors with Subword Information, arXiv:1607.04606.

Grave, E., Bojanowski, P., Gupta, P., Joulin, A. and Mikolov, T. (2018). Learning Word Vectors for 157 Languages. In *Proceedings of the International Conference on Language Resources and Evaluation (LREC 2018)*, arXiv:1802.06893.

Devlin J., Chang, M.W., Lee, K. and Toutanova K. (2018). BERT: Pre-training of Deep Bidirectional Transformers for Language Understanding. In *Proceedings of NAACL-HLT 2019*, pages 4171–4186.

Habash, N. and Dorr, B. (2003). A Categorial Variation Database for English. In *Proceedings of the North American Association for Computational Linguistics*, Edmonton, Canada, pp. 96 -102.

Haussmann, E. (2011). Contextual sentence decomposition with applications to semantic full-text search. Master's thesis, University of Freiburg.

Ho, T. K. (1995). Random Decision Forests. In *Proceedings of the 3rd International Conference on Document Analysis and Recognition*, Montreal, QC, 14–16 August 1995. pp. 278-282.

Hoekstra, H., M. Moortgat, I. Schuurman & T. van der Wouden (2000). Syntactic Annotation for the Spoken Dutch Corpus Project (CGN). In W. Daelemans, K. Sima'an, J. Veenstra & J. Zavrel (Eds.), Computational Linguistics in the Netherlands 2000. 73-87. Amsterdam: Rodopi.

Ide, N., Macleod, C. (2001). The American National Corpus: A Standardized Resource of American English. Proceedings of Corpus Linguistics 2001, Lancaster UK.

Islam, A. and Inkpen, D. (2008). Semantic text similarity using corpus-based word similarity and string similarity. ACM Trans. Knowl. Discov. Data. 2, 2, Article 10 (July 2008), 25 pages.

Kenter, T. and Rijke, M. (2015). Short text similarity with word embeddings. In *Proceedings of the 24th ACM international on conference on information and knowledge management*, pp 1411-1420.

Kilgarriff, A., Palmer, M. (eds., 2000): Senseval98: Evaluating Word Sense Disambiguation Systems, vol. 34 (1–2). Kluwer, Dordrecht, the Netherlands.

Lesk, M. (1986). Automatic sense disambiguation using machine readable dictionaries: How to tell a pine cone from an ice cream cone. In *Proceedings of the 5th SIGDOC* (New York, NY). 24–26.

Lyding, V., Stemle, E., Borghetti, C., Brunello, M., Castagnoli, S., Dell'Orletta, F., Dittmann, H., Lenci, A., Pirrelli, V. (2014): "The PAISÀ Corpus of Italian Web Texts" In *Proceedings of the 9th Web as Corpus Workshop (WaC-9)*, Association for Computational Linguistics, Gothenburg, Sweden, April 2014. pp. 36-43.

Mallery, J. C. (1988). Thinking about foreign policy: Finding an appropriate role for artificial intelligence computers. Ph.D. dissertation. MIT Political Science Department, Cambridge, MA.

Miller, G.A. (1995). WordNet: A Lexical Database for English. Communications of the ACM Vol. 38, No. 11: 39-4.

Mititelu, B.V., Tufiș, D. and Irimia, E. (2018). The Reference Corpus of Contemporary Romanian Language (CoRoLa). In Proceedings of the 11th Language Resources and Evaluation Conference – LREC'18, Miyazaki, Japan, European Language Resources Association (ELRA).

Navigli, R. (2009). Word Sense Disambiguation: A Survey. ACM Computing Surveys. Vol. 41, No. 2.

Păiș, V., Tufiș, D. (2018). Computing distributed representations of words using the COROLA corpus. In Proceedings of the Romanian Academy, Series A, Volume 19, Number 2/2018, pp. 403–409.

Păiș, V., Tufiș, D. and Ion, R. (2019). Integration of Romanian NLP tools into the RELATE platform. In Proceedings of the International Conference on Linguistic Resources and Tools for Processing Romanian Language – CONSILR 2019, pages 181-192.

Pennington, J., Socher, R. and Manning C.D. (2014). GloVe: Global Vectors for Word Representation. In *Proceedings of Empirical Methods in Natural Language Processing (EMNLP)*, pp 1532-1543.

Peters, M.E., Neumann, M., Iyyer, M., Gardner, M., Clark, C., Lee, K. and Zettlemoyer, L. (2018). Deep contextualized word representations. In *Proceedings of the 2018 Conference of the North American Chapter of the Association for Computational Linguistics: Human Language Technologies*, Volume 1, pp. 2227-2237.

Pires, T., Schlinger, E. and Garette, D. (2019). How multilingual is Multilingual BERT? arXiv:1906.01502.

Porter, M.F. (1980). An algorithm for suffix stripping, Program, 14(3) pp 130−137.

Reimers, N. and Gurevych, I. (2019). Sentence-BERT: Sentence Embeddings using Siamese BERT-Networks. In *Proceedings of the 2019 Conference on Empirical Methods in Natural Language Processing*, pp 3982-3992.

Rijsbergen, C.J., Robertson, S.E. and Porter, M.F. (1980). New models in probabilistic information retrieval. London: British Library. British Library Research and Development Report, no. 5587.

Rivest, R. L. (1987). Learning decision lists. Mach. Learn. 2, 3, 229−246.

Tufiş, D., Ion, R., Bozianu, L. Ceauşu, A. and Ştefănescu, D. (2008). Romanian Wordnet: Current State, New Applications and Prospects. In *Proceedings of the 4th Global WordNet Conference, GWC-2008*, pp. 441-452.

Weaver, W. (1949). Translation. In Machine Translation of Languages: Fourteen Essays (written in 1949, published in 1955), W. N. Locke and A. D. Booth, Eds. Technology Press of MIT, Cambridge, MA, and John Wiley & Sons, New York, NY, 15−23.

Yarowsky, D. (2000). Hierarchical decision lists for word sense disambiguation. Comput. Human. 34, 1-2, 179−186.

Proceedings of the Globalex Workshop on Linked Lexicography, pages 76–83
Language Resources and Evaluation Conference (LREC 2020), Marseille, 11–16 May 2020
© European Language Resources Association (ELRA), licensed under CC-BY-NC

UNIOR NLP at MWSA Task - GlobaLex 2020:
Siamese LSTM with Attention for Word Sense Alignment

Raffaele Manna, Giulia Speranza, Maria Pia di Buono, Johanna Monti
UNIOR NLP Research Group
University of Naples "L'Orientale" - Naples, Italy
{rmanna, gsperanza, mpdibuono, jmonti}@unior.it

Abstract

In this paper we describe the system submitted to the ELEXIS Monolingual Word Sense Alignment Task. We test different systems, which are two types of LSTMs and a system based on a pretrained Bidirectional Encoder Representations from Transformers (BERT) model, to solve the task. LSTM models use fastText pre-trained word vectors features with different settings. For training the models, we did not combine external data with the dataset provided for the task. We select a sub-set of languages among the proposed ones, namely a set of Romance languages, i.e., Italian, Spanish, Portuguese, together with English and Dutch. The Siamese LSTM with attention and PoS tagging (LSTM-A) performed better than the other two systems, achieving a 5-Class Accuracy score of 0.844 in the Overall Results, ranking the first position among five teams.

Keywords: Word Sense Alignment, Siamese LSTM, BERT, Text Similarity, Semantic Text Similarity, Semantic Classification

1. Introduction

As the number of lexical resources has been increased widely in the last decade, the need of integrating complementary information from several sources and knowledge bases is growing. The integration of such different information requires a process capable of aligning both monolingual and multilingual lexical resources preserving the granularity of semantic relations among senses.

The alignment of sense descriptions of lexical resources represents a crucial task for many Natural Language Processing (NLP) and Machine Translation (MT) applications. Indeed, it has been shown that aligned lexical-semantic resources can lead to better performance in NLP and MT applications than using the resources individually (Matuschek and Gurevych, 2013).

To the aim of improving large-scale and interlinked lexical-semantic resources, covering different information types and languages, many research efforts in Word Sense Alignment (WSA) area have been carried out. According to Matuschek and Gurevych (2013), WSA is the identification of pairs of senses from two lexical-semantic resources which denote the same meaning. WSA improves semantic interoperability among resources in that it allows sense matching and disambiguation, supporting an enhanced semantic processing and contributing to the creation and development of lexical-semantic resources. WSA can be performed both on multilingual data (Carpuat et al., 2006), in order to align senses among languages, and monolingual data for merging different resources (Caselli et al., 2013).

Some WSA-related shared tasks have been organized as different application scenarios. Among those, the one proposed within HLT/NAACL 2003 Workshop on Building and Using Parallel Text (Mihalcea and Pedersen, 2003) which focused on word alignment to find correspondences between words and phrases in parallel texts. Starting from a sentence aligned in a bilingual corpus in languages L1 and L2, this task aims at indicating which word token in the corpus of language L1 corresponds to which word token in the corpus of language L2.

The 1st "Monolingual Word Sense Alignment" Shared Task has been organised by the ELEXIS Project[1], as part of the GLOBALEX (Global Alliance for Lexicography)[2] - Linked Lexicography workshop at the 12th Language Resources and Evaluation Conference (LREC 2020).

The task consists of developing a system capable of predicting the semantic relation between two monolingual senses extracted from two different sources. Five types of relations among the two senses are considered: *exact* if the two entries express the same sense, *broader* if the sense of the first entry is more generic and includes the second entry's sense, *narrower* if the first entry conveys a more specific sense than the second one, *related* if the two senses are somehow connected to one-another for some aspects and *none* if the two entries express two totally different senses, so that no match is to be found.

We test different systems, namely a system based on a pretrained Bidirectional Encoder Representations from Transformers (BERT) model and two types of LSTMs, to solve the task. LSTM models use pretrained fastText features with different settings. For training the models, we did not combine external data and adjust the class distribution of the provided data set neither. We select a sub-set of languages among the proposed ones, namely Romance languages, i.e., Italian, Spanish, Portuguese, together with English and Dutch. The Siamese LSTM with attention and PoS tagging (LSTM-A) performed better than the other two systems, achieving a 5-Class Accuracy score of 0.844 in the Overall Results. The system ranked the first position among five teams in the Overall Results and ranked different positions for each language we selected.

The remainder of the paper is organized as follows: first, we introduce some related work (Section 2), then, in Section 3, we describe the dataset provided by the task organisers and subsequently discuss the implemented systems (Section 4).

---

[1] https://elex.is/
[2] https://globalex.link/

Finally, we comment system results and present our conclusion and future work, respectively in Section 5 and 6.

2. Related Works

Previous works related to WSA mainly adopt two approaches: similarity-based and graph-based or a combination of both.

Niemann and Gurevych (2011) use a two-step approach to align WordNet noun synsets and Wikipedia articles using the Personalized PageRank (PPR) algorithm (Agirre and Soroa, 2009) and a word overlap measure, reporting a performance of 0.78 F1-Measure and 94.5% accuracy.

Meyer and Gurevych (2011) align Wiktionary and WordNet using similarity of glosses, cosine (COS) or personalized page rank (PPR) similarity, reaching a F1 of 0.661 with the COS & PPR method.

In order to semi-automatically align GermaNet with sense definitions from Wiktionary, Henrich et al. (2011) use an approach based on bag of words and word overlap.

Laparra et al. (2010) make use of a shortest path algorithm (SSI-Dijkstra+) to align FrameNet lexical units with WordNet synsets.

The graph-based approach is applied in Matuschek and Gurevych (2014) who use Dijkstra-WSA algorithm (Matuschek and Gurevych, 2013) to calculate a distance-based similarity measure between word senses for aligning WordNet and OmegaWiki, WordNet and Wiktionary, Wiktionary and Wikipedia (English) and Wiktionary-Wikipedia (German), modelling different aspects of sense similarity by applying machine learning, outperforming the state of the art. Recently, Ahmadi et al. (2019) proposes a textual and semantic similarity method with a weighted bipartite b-matching algorithm (WBbM) to align WordNet and Wiktionary.

In a way, the task of the word sense alignment can be compared to the task of defining and computing the similarity between two texts and, in particular, between two sentences. Among different construction methods and selection of the learning features and algorithms used, one of the best performing state of the art models is a Siamese adaptation of the Long Short-Term Memory (LSTM) network.

The Siamese network (Bromley et al., 1994) is an architecture for non-linear metric learning with similarity information. The Siamese network learns representations that incorporate the invariance and selectivity purposes through explicit information about similarity and dissimilarity between pairs of objects. One of the first research to adopt a Siamese LSTM architecture for labeled textual pairs of variable-length sequences is presented by Mueller and Thyagarajan (2016). In this work, a LSTM model with Siamese architecture is applied to assess semantic similarity between sentences. They provide word-vectors supplemented with synonymic information to the LSTMs, which use a fixed size vector to encode the underlying meaning expressed in a sentence.

Neculoiu et al. (2016) show that the bidirectional LSTM with a Siamese architecture achieves good results in learning a similarity metric on variable length character sequences in the task of job title normalization. The model projects variable length strings into a fixed-dimensional embedding space by using only information about the similarity between pairs of strings.

3. Dataset

For the ELEXIS monolingual WSA task, training data from different dictionaries and linguistic resources are available in several languages: Basque, Bulgarian, Danish, Dutch, English[3], Estonian, German, Hungarian, Irish, Italian, Portuguese, Russian, Serbian, Slovene and Spanish.

For each language, the organisers have provided a definitive training set containing the lemma shared between the two entries of the dictionaries, the PoS of the entries, the definition (gloss) of the sense of the first entry, the definition (gloss) of the sense of the second entry and the label indicating the relation between the two senses (*exact*, *broader*, *narrower*, *related* or *none*). A test dataset without the labels of the relation upon which to test the model is also provided (Ahmadi et al., 2020).

The following examples, extracted from the English_nuig training dataset, show data pairs for some of the relation types[4] between the glosses for the lemma *follow*, PoS-tagged as *verb*.

SOURCE: Princeton English WordNet (a) - Webster's 1913 Dictionary (b).

1. Type of relation: *exact*

   (a) *to be the product or result*

   (b) *to result from, as an effect from a cause, or an inference from a premise*

2. Type of relation: *narrower*

   (a) *choose and follow; as of theories, ideas, policies, strategies or plans*

   (b) *to copy after; to take as an example*

3. Type of relation: *related*

   (a) *travel along a certain course*

   (b) *to walk in, as a road or course; to attend upon closely, as a profession or calling*

4. Type of relation: *none*

   (a) *imitate in behavior; take as a model*

   (b) *to succeed in order of time, rank, or office*

In Table 1 we report the information about the training data composition provided for the languages (Dutch, English[5], Italian, Portuguese and Spanish) we chose to train our system on (section 4). The datasets in the different languages are not homogeneous in their respective sizes nor in the lemmas' PoS coverage.

---

[3]For the English language two datasets have been provided: the English_nuig containing glosses taken from the Princeton English WordNet and the Webster's 1913 dictionary, and the English_kd, which contains glosses from the Password and Global dictionary series provided by K Dictionaries through Lexicala.

[4]For the verb *follow*, taken as example, no *broader* relation is found in the dataset.

[5]We chose to use the English_nuig dataset.

For each language we provide the number of Aligned and Different senses according to the PoS of the lemma (e.g., (V), (N)). The Aligned Sense refers to the several combinations derived from the alignment between the first gloss (sense) coming from the first source and the second gloss (sense) from the second source; whereas the Different Sense is the total number of unaligned glosses coming from both dictionaries.

Some languages do not present some of the possible PoS, e.g., Italian which includes only verbs and nouns and no lemmas belonging to other categories.

Indeed, the dataset analysis reveals that some PoS are much more frequent in some languages than in others. The most frequent PoS attributed to lemmas in the English, Italian and Spanish datasets is *verb*, whereas in Portuguese and Dutch there is a conspicuous number of lemmas Pos-tagged as *noun*. Furthermore, with the exception of the Italian dataset, where no *adjective* or *adverb* occurrences are to be found (N/A), in the other languages' datasets adjectives are more present than adverbs. Other types of PoS (e.g., adposition, affix, conjunction) are only found in the Spanish and Portuguese datasets. As far as the size of training data is concerned, the Dutch language dataset appears to be larger compared to other languages, followed by English, Spanish, Italian and Portuguese, as it is shown in the Total column in Table 1. In addition, it is worth stressing that even though the training data are imbalanced, as reported in Table 2, we did not apply any technique to adjust the class distribution of a data set. For all the languages investigated, the datasets show a predominance of *none* and *exact* relations if compared to the other semantic relations types selected as possible candidates in the shared task.

With reference to the combination of relation and PoS, we notice that the number of aligned *exact* senses whose lemma was PoS-tagged as *noun* is higher in all the languages, whereas the label *none* is more frequently associated to the PoS *verb* in the English dataset and to the PoS *noun* in the Italian, Spanish, Portuguese and Dutch datasets. The total number of each relation type as well as the total number of relations in each training set are also reported.

4. System Description

To address the problem of WSA, we build three different models. We first investigate the capabilities of BERT, one of the most recent language representation models, released by Google in 2018. Then, we build two models based on Siamese LSTM (LSTM and LSTM-A), which has been recently applied to solve short text similarity tasks for multiple domains and languages (de Souza et al., 2020). Those two systems use two different types of lexical-semantic information as features and different settings.

The first LSTM takes gloss pairs as input with only few preprocessing steps. Gloss pairs are represented as word vectors trained on WSA datasets and intersected with pre-trained word vectors. We use this vector addition or intersection to find a set A containing n words closer to the words vectors set trained on the gloss pairs in the training data. This was useful for possibly incorporating similar or related words not present in gloss pairs (Gagliano et al., 2016). The attention mechanism is not included in the pa-

rameters of this model.

The second LSTM (LSTM-A) includes more lexical-semantic information about the glosses with respect to the one described above. Indeed, such an LSTM model gives attention only to the words in sense descriptions which present the same PoS category assigned to the lemma they refer to. In other words, given a lemma labelled as noun, e.g., *dealer* and the following two glosses which refer to the target lemma:

1. *a <u>seller</u> of illicit goods*

2. *one who deals; one who has to do, or has concern, with others; esp., a <u>trader</u>, a <u>trafficker</u>, a <u>shopkeeper</u>, a <u>broker</u>, or a <u>merchant</u>;*

The model only process the words underlined in the pair of senses, which present the same lemma PoS. Then, in this model, the attention mechanism is used.

BERT   Given the novelty and popularity of BERT model in the NLP field, we decide to use and implement with no fine-tuning efforts a semantic relations classification system based on this model. For this, we have used English-BERT[6] (Eng-BERT) to predict the relations of English senses and Multilingual BERT[7] (M-BERT) to predict the relations in the other languages involved in the experiments (i.e., Dutch, Italian, Portuguese and Spanish).

English BERT (Devlin et al., 2018) is a bi-directional model based on the transformer architecture. The transformer architecture is an architecture based solely on attention mechanism.

In the context of WSA shared task, we use the uncased large version of Eng-BERT to deal with the alignment of the English senses. This version has 24 layers and 16 attention heads and generates 1024 dimension vector for each word. We use 1024 dimension vector of the Extract layer as the representation of the glosses. Our classification layer consists of a single Dense layer. The dense layer consists of 3 units and the *softmax* activation function was used. The loss function used is *binary crossentropy*. The Adam optimizer is used for training the model for 15 epochs.

Whereas, for Romance languages and Dutch, Multilingual BERT is used, it is trained on monolingual Wikipedia articles of 104 different languages. It is intended to enable Multilingual BERT fine-tuned in one language to make predictions for another language. In our research, we use the M-BERT model having 12 layers and 12 heads. This model generates 768 dimension vector for each word. We used the 768 dimension vector of the Extract layer as the representation of the glosses and a single Dense layer is used as a classification relations model. The hyperparameters used for training the model is the same as mentioned above.

LSTM   Since word sense alignment is viewed as a supervised learning problem in this shared task, the model takes as input two gloss pairs having different sequence length and a label for the pair which describes the underlying similarity or semantic relation between gloss pairs.

---

[6]Available at: https://github.com/google-research/bert

[7]Available at: https://huggingface.co/models?filter=multilingual

Languages	Senses	V	N	ADJ	ADV	Other PoS	Total
Dutch	Aligned	4766	8958	4118	1378	N/A	19220
	Different	**514**	**1730**	**602**	**119**	**N/A**	**2965**
English_nuig	Aligned	4755	2694	810	78	N/A	8337
	Different	**1109**	**1690**	**571**	**63**	**N/A**	**3433**
Italian	Aligned	946	1022	N/A	N/A	N/A	1968
	Different	**514**	**605**	**N/A**	**N/A**	**N/A**	**1119**
Spanish	Aligned	1051	2228	991	72	112	2342
	Different	**406**	**1127**	**504**	**47**	**31**	**2084**
Portuguese	Aligned	405	807	189	9	1	1411
	Different	**111**	**361**	**144**	**12**	**1**	**629**

Table 1: Number of Different and Aligned Senses in the Training Data

Languages	Relations	V	N	ADJ	ADV	Other PoS	Total
Dutch	Exact	77	264	93	10	N/A	444
	Broader	7	40	N/A	4	N/A	51
	Narrower	9	14	5	1	N/A	29
	Related	9	24	3	4	N/A	40
	None	4664	8616	4013	1363	N/A	18656
							19220
English_nuig	Exact	230	409	149	12	N/A	800
	Broader	19	11	7	2	N/A	39
	Narrower	100	143	58	9	N/A	310
	Related	25	16	8	2	N/A	51
	None	4381	2115	588	53	N/A	7137
							8337
Italian	Exact	120	161	N/A	N/A	N/A	281
	Broader	11	22	N/A	N/A	N/A	33
	Narrower	66	43	N/A	N/A	N/A	109
	Related	54	23	N/A	N/A	N/A	77
	None	695	773	N/A	N/A	N/A	1468
							1968
Portuguese	Exact	29	103	43	2	1	178
	Broader	N/A	2	1	N/A	N/A	3
	Narrower	3	18	10	1	N/A	32
	Related	5	7	10	N/A	N/A	22
	None	368	677	125	6	N/A	1176
							1411
Spanish	Exact	129	350	160	20	12	671
	Broader	23	50	19	N/A	N/A	92
	Narrower	24	72	29	N/A	2	127
	Related	10	38	16	1	5	70
	None	865	1718	797	50	93	3523
							4483

Table 2: Type of Relations and PoS in the Training Data

In our approach, we adopt a Siamese LSTM architecture for two of our models, namely LSTM and LSTM-A. Such an architecture is based on two identical sub-networks for each LSTM model. Indeed, it has been shown that Siamese LSTM produces a mapping from a general space f variable length sequences into an interpretable representation with fixed dimensionality vector space (Mueller and Thyagarajan, 2016). Thus, each sub-network reads a gloss and generates a fixed representation. In addition, as we previously stated, for one of the LSTM models (LSTM-A) we build a model based on word vectors which represent each preprocessed input gloss, keeping only words that belong to the same PoS of the lemma whose senses must be aligned. Then, this model employs its final hidden state as a vector representation for each gloss. Afterwards, the similarity and the semantic relation brought by the labels between these representations are used as a predictor of words senses similarity.

4.1. Preprocessing

For preprocessing the glosses we perform the following steps: tokenization, gloss lowercasing, gloss cleaning and word tagging with PoS tags using tools provided by spaCy package[8].

Tokenizer First we tokenize the glosses to identify all the expressions such as dates, time, currencies, acronyms. We use a Tokenizer[9] with the default settings for the languages involved. To this, we add some custom rules (regular expressions) to match all the expressions mentioned above. In this way, we keep all these expressions as one token, so later we can normalize them reducing the vocabulary size.

Gloss Cleaning As second step, we remove the punctuation and some particular elements that appear in the glosses. In fact, in several glosses, some markers are frequent, and are used to denote the different uses of a given sense (e.g., the domain) *(Anat.)*, figurative use *(Fig.)* and more.In addition to these, several specific notations related to the lexical resources associated with glosses such as numbered lists of the word sense and any residual HTML tags have been found and removed.

PoS Tagging As a final step, for the Romance languages considered in the experiments, we tag each word/token in the glosses with PoS information. Also Dutch and English glosses are involved in this PoS tagging step.To perform this step, we use the core model packages provided by the *spaCy*. For each language involved in this task, a gloss tagging was performed.

To accomplish this and build the linguistic features to be passed to the model, the PoS category belonging to each of the lemma items present in the data is taken into consideration. Then, only tokens tagged with the same PoS information as the target lemma have been kept in the glosses.

This procedure aims at isolating, keeping and processing only semantically related words, such as synonyms, hyperonyms and more.

4.2. Siamese LSTM

Word embeddings are dense vector representations of words (Mikolov et al., 2013), capturing their semantic and syntactic information. Like many top performing semantic similarity systems, our LSTMs take as input word-vectors which have been pre-trained on an external corpus intersecting these with our own word embeddings, using fast-Text. Thus, the word embeddings are used for initializing the weights of the first layer (embedding layer) of our network. We use the 300-dimensional fastText word embeddings (Bojanowski et al., 2017) trained on Common Crawl and Wikipedia[10].

In the model, there are two identical LSTM networks, $LSTM_a$ and $LSTM_b$ each of which process one of the pre-processed glosses in a given pair. Both subnetworks share the same weights, in order to project both glosses to the same vector space and thus be able to make a meaningful comparison between them. So, we just focus on siamese architectures with tied weights such that $LSTM_a = LSTM_b$. The LSTM model learns a mapping from the space of variable length sequences of d_{in}-dimensional vectors into $R^{d_{rep}}$ ($d_{in} = 300$, $d_{rep} = 50$). Sense similarities in the representation space are subsequently used to infer the glosses underlying semantic similarity. More concretely, each gloss (represented as a sequence of word vectors belonging to the same PoS as the lemma) $x_1,...,x_T$, is passed to the LSTM, which updates its hidden state at each sequence-index.

In some cases, especially in long sequences, RNN architectures, such as LSTM, might not be able to hold all the important information in its final hidden state. In order to intensify the important elements (e.g., words) in the final representation, we use an attention mechanism (Chi and Zhang, 2018), that combines all the intermediate hidden states using their relative importance.

The final representation of each gloss is encoded by $h_T \in R^{d_{rep}}$, the last hidden state of the model. For a given pair of glosses, our approach applies a pre-defined similarity function $g : R^{d_{rep}} \times R^{d_{rep}} \to R$ to their LSTM-representations. Then, given the LSTM gloss representations, these are use to infer the glosses' underlying semantic similarity applying a simple Manhattan similarity function.

4.3. Regularization

The parameters of the model are optimized using the Nadam method (Ruder, 2016). We use the simple but effective technique of dropout (Srivastava et al., 2014) on the recurrent units (with probability 0.15) and between layers (with probability 0.25) to prevent overfitting. Dropout prevents co-adaptation of neurons and can also be thought as a form of ensemble learning, in that for each training item a subpart of the whole network is trained. Moreover, we apply dropout to the recurrent connections of both LSTMs (Gal and Ghahramani, 2016) to avoid overfitting. Finally, we stop the training of the network, after the validation loss stops decreasing (i.e., early-stopping).

5. Results and Evaluation

The official evaluation was performed using the CodaLab platform[11]. The official evaluation metrics for the ELEXIS Monolingual Word Sense Alignment shared task are: Accuracy, Precision, Recall and F-Measure.

The organizers provided the script for evaluation, which is performed for each chosen language. Besides this language-based evaluation, an average of the scores achieved for each language is added and ranked.

In the context of the MWSA shared task, the accuracy is calculated on the basis of the matches between predicted label and the reference label on the five classes. Instead, Precision, Recall and F-Measure are considered as the accuracy in predicting the type of relations according to a binary classification. In other words, predicting a sense pair as *related*, *narrower* or *broader* when the gold standard is *exact* is considered correct. On the contrary, it is considered incorrect to predict a "positive" relation when *none* is present in the gold standard or vice versa.

---

[8] https://spacy.io/

[9] https://keras.io/preprocessing/text/

[10] Publicly available at: https://fasttext.cc/docs/en/pretrained-vectors.html

[11] https://competitions.codalab.org/competitions/22163

Our team UNIOR NLP ranked 1st out of five teams in the Overall Results of the scores among the selected languages[12]. These results were achieved submitting the results obtained from LSTM with attention mechanism and with augmented lexical-semantic information related to the lemma PoS category (LSTM-A).

As previously stated, the LSTM-A system is the only one we submitted officially, nevertheless we evaluated all the models. Table 3 shows the results obtained for each language by each one of our three systems and the overall results. Our best performing system in predicting the type of semantic relations between the senses is the Siamese LSTM with attention and PoS information (LSTM-A).

In fact, as shown in table 3, our model reaches a 5-Class Accuracy score of 0.844 and a 2-Class F-Measure score of 0.594 in the overall results.

Our system performs quite well for Italian and Spanish sense pairs. In both languages, we ranked 1st among four teams with a 5-Class Accuracy score of 0.766 and a 2-Class F-Measure score of 0.741 for Italian, while correspondingly 0.829 and 0.810 for Spanish.

Whereas for Portuguese our model ranked as 2nd among four teams with a 5-Class Accuracy score of 0.933 and a a 2-Class F-Measure score of 0.641.

We chose to train our system mainly on Romance languages such as Italian, Spanish and Portuguese due to their common linguistic root which makes their lexico-grammar features very similar and comparable.

In addition, we chose to include the English and Dutch languages in order to compare the system also on totally, morpho-syntatically different languages to test and compare the results. In these two languages, our system performs and predicts slightly less well than the predictions related to the group of Romance languages, at least comparing them with the predictions made by the other teams. In fact, on the English data set, our system ranked as 4th among six teams with a 5-Class Accuracy score of 0.759 and a 2-Class F-Measure score of 0.634. In Dutch, instead, our system ranked last among six teams with a 5-Class Accuracy score of 0.931 and a 2-Class F-Measure score of 0.145.

Hence, as the results in Table 3 show, LSTM-A which also holds PoS information outperforms the semantic relations classifier based on BERT and the LSTM system fed only with word vectors.

As for the other two systems, as shown in the overall results in Table 3, LSTM predicts better than the BERT based classifier. In some cases, however, the two systems almost achieve the same promising results at least for the 5-Class Accuracy. It means that the two systems are able to predict one of the five correct relations in large datasets such as the English, Portuguese and Dutch ones.

In addition to this last explanation, we propose some ideas to clarify the BERT based results in relation to the training and testing data imbalances. Looking at the performances of the BERT based model in the table 3, we can surprisingly observe a divergence of results between English and Portuguese according to the 5-Class Accuracy. In fact, one could expect higher results for a language with more resources available as in the English case.

Instead, for Portuguese language, the BERT model is able to achieve a high accuracy performance compared to the results for English, despite English language benefiting from more data.

A possible reason could lie in the imbalance of the labels distribution between the train and test data. Considering the train data statistics shown in table 2 above and bearing in mind the different sizes of the data, we can see that the most represented label is *none*, followed by *exact* in both English and Portuguese as well as other languages. Whereas in the test sets, the *none* proportion is equal to 75.6% for English and 93.6% (almost the whole test set) for the Portuguese language.

Therefore, the BERT model is capable to manage and learn better the predominant class-label *none* in the train data and predicts more often that class-label. Thus, given the aforementioned predominance of *none* relations in the test data, the model seems to achieve higher performance for Portuguese than English. Also, if we consider the 2-class Precision for these two languages in Table 3, we can notice that the BERT model tries to generalize and predict the label *exact* and those related to that. In this, the BERT model appears to be less effective given the greater attention paid to the *none* label. Despite this, it manages to get a higher score for English than for Portuguese.

As mentioned earlier, it is worth stressing that we use a Bert based classifier without fine-tuning efforts for the context of the WSA task. This means that, tuning different parameters to tackle a word sense-alignment task, a BERT based model could achieve different results. Here, we note that our BERT based semantic relations classifier does not perform very well compared to the two LSTM models with a Siamese architecture.

6. Conclusion

We use BERT based classifier and two Siamese LSTM systems to predict semantic relations between pairs of glosses in English, Dutch, Italian, Portuguese and Spanish. Our LSTM-A[13] enriched with PoS information performs remarkably well in predicting semantic relations on the test set and ranked 1st in the official overall results. Equally, it ranked 1st in the Italian and Spanish languages. Therefore, the information provided by the PoS category of the target lemma was incisive in correctly predicting the relations for each combination of monolingual senses coming from two different lexical resources.

The results obtained in this MWSA shared task have been achieved by a system with a very widespread architecture in the state of the art related to the lexicon-semantic similarity of sentences. In the future, we plan to investigate the possibilities of applying and test BERT based systems in word sense alignment tasks.

For future work, we also intend to test our model for bilingual or multilingual word sense alignment on different re-

---

[12]https://competitions.codalab.org/competitions/22163#results

[13]https://github.com/unior-nlp-research-group/MWSA20

Languages	Models	5-Class A	2-Class P	2-Class R	2-Class F1
Dutch	M-BERT	0.827	0.131	0.293	0.181
	LSTM	0.847	0.181	0.344	0.238
	LSTM-A	0.931	0.455	0.086	0.145
English	Eng-BERT	0.593	0.314	0.375	0.342
	LSTM	0.658	0.473	0.593	0.526
	LSTM-A	0.759	0.586	0.692	0.634
Italian	M-BERT	0.575	0.285	0.245	0.264
	LSTM	0.726	0.633	0.789	0.703
	LSTM-A	0.766	0.729	0.754	0.741
Portuguese	M-BERT	0.803	0.122	0.309	0.175
	LSTM	0.812	0.180	0.523	0.268
	LSTM-A	0.933	0.541	0.786	0.641
Spanish	M-BERT	0.457	0.262	0.481	0.339
	LSTM	0.722	0.545	0.709	0.616
	LSTM-A	0.829	0.742	0.891	0.810
Overall Results	BERT	0.651	0.223	0.341	0.260
	LSTM	0.753	0.402	0.591	0.470
	LSTM-A	**0.844**	**0.611**	**0.642**	**0.594**

Table 3: Model Results

sources. In addition, we would also integrate other Romance languages such as Catalan, French and Romanian.

7. Acknowledgements

This work has been partially supported by Programma Operativo Nazionale Ricerca e Innovazione 2014-2020 - Fondo Sociale Europeo, Azione I.2 "Attrazione e Mobilità Internazionale dei Ricercatori" Avviso D.D. n 407 del 27/02/2018 and by POR Campania FSE 2014-2020 "Dottorati di Ricerca a Caratterizzazione Industriale".
Authorship contribution is as follows: Raffaele Manna is author of Section 4, Giulia Speranza is author of Section 2 and 3, Maria Pia di Buono is author of Section 1 and 6, Johanna Monti is author of Section 5.

8. Bibliographical References

Agirre, E. and Soroa, A. (2009). Personalizing pagerank for word sense disambiguation. In *Proceedings of the 12th Conference of the European Chapter of the ACL (EACL 2009)*, pages 33–41.

Ahmadi, S., Arcan, M., and McCrae, J. (2019). Lexical sense alignment using weighted bipartite b-matching. In *2nd Conference on Language, Data and Knowledge (LDK 2019)*. NUI Galway.

Ahmadi, S., McCrae, J. P., Nimb, S., Khan, F., Monachini, M., Pedersen, B. S., Declerck, T., Wissik, T., Bellandi, A., Pisani, I., Troelsgård, T., Olsen, S., Krek, S., Lipp, V., Váradi, T., Simon, L., Győrffy, A., Tiberius, C., Schoonheim, T., Ben Moshe, Y., Rudich, M., Abu Ahmad, R., Lonke, D., Kovalenko, K., Langemets, M., Kallas, J., Dereza, O., Fransen, T., Cillessen, D., Lindemann, D., Alonso, M., Salgado, A., Sancho, J. L., Ureña-Ruiz, R.-J., Simov, K., Osenova, P., Kancheva, Z., Radev, I., Stanković, R., Perdih, A., and Gabrovšek, D. (2020). A Multilingual Evaluation Dataset for Monolingual Word Sense Alignment. In *Proceedings of the 12th Language Resource and Evaluation Conference (LREC 2020)*, Marseille, France.

Bojanowski, P., Grave, E., Joulin, A., and Mikolov, T. (2017). Enriching word vectors with subword information. *Transactions of the Association for Computational Linguistics*, 5:135–146.

Bromley, J., Guyon, I., LeCun, Y., Säckinger, E., and Shah, R. (1994). Signature verification using a" siamese" time delay neural network. In *Advances in neural information processing systems*, pages 737–744.

Carpuat, M., Fung, P., and Ngai, G. (2006). Aligning word senses using bilingual corpora. *ACM Transactions on Asian Language Information Processing (TALIP)*, 5(2):89–120.

Caselli, T., Vieu, L., Strapparava, C., and Vetere, G. (2013). Aligning verb senses in two italian lexical semantic resources.

Chi, Z. and Zhang, B. (2018). A sentence similarity estimation method based on improved siamese network. *Journal of Intelligent Learning Systems and Applications*, 10(4):121–134.

de Souza, J. V. A., Oliveira, L. E. S. E., Gumiel, Y. B., Carvalho, D. R., and Moro, C. M. C. (2020). Exploiting siamese neural networks on short text similarity tasks for multiple domains and languages. In *International Conference on Computational Processing of the Portuguese Language*, pages 357–367. Springer.

Devlin, J., Chang, M.-W., Lee, K., and Toutanova, K. (2018). Bert: Pre-training of deep bidirectional transformers for language understanding. *arXiv preprint arXiv:1810.04805*.

Gagliano, A., Paul, E., Booten, K., and Hearst, M. A. (2016). Intersecting word vectors to take figurative language to new heights. In *Proceedings of the Fifth Workshop on Computational Linguistics for Literature*, pages 20–31.

Gal, Y. and Ghahramani, Z. (2016). A theoretically grounded application of dropout in recurrent neural networks. In *Advances in neural information processing systems*, pages 1019–1027.

Gurevych, I. and Niemann, E. (2011). The people's web meets linguistic knowledge: automatic sense alignment of wikipedia and wordnet.

Henrich, V., Hinrichs, E., and Vodolazova, T. (2011). Semi-automatic extension of germanet with sense definitions from wiktionary. In *Proceedings of the 5th Language and Technology Conference (LTC 2011)*, pages 126–130.

Laparra, E., Rigau, G., and Cuadros, M. (2010). Exploring the integration of wordnet and framenet. In *Proceedings of the 5th Global WordNet Conference (GWC 2010), Mumbai, India*.

Matuschek, M. and Gurevych, I. (2013). Dijkstra-wsa: A graph-based approach to word sense alignment. *Transactions of the Association for Computational Linguistics*, 1:151–164.

Matuschek, M. and Gurevych, I. (2014). High performance word sense alignment by joint modeling of sense distance and gloss similarity. In *Proceedings of COLING 2014, the 25th International Conference on Computational Linguistics: Technical Papers*, pages 245–256.

Meyer, C. M. and Gurevych, I. (2011). What psycholinguists know about chemistry: Aligning wiktionary and wordnet for increased domain coverage. In *Proceedings of 5th International Joint Conference on Natural Language Processing*, pages 883–892.

Mihalcea, R. and Pedersen, T. (2003). An evaluation exercise for word alignment. In *Proceedings of the HLT-NAACL 2003 Workshop on Building and using parallel texts: data driven machine translation and beyond*, pages 1–10.

Mikolov, T., Chen, K., Corrado, G., and Dean, J. (2013). Efficient estimation of word representations in vector space. *arXiv preprint arXiv:1301.3781*.

Mueller, J. and Thyagarajan, A. (2016). Siamese recurrent architectures for learning sentence similarity. In *thirtieth AAAI conference on artificial intelligence*.

Neculoiu, P., Versteegh, M., and Rotaru, M. (2016). Learning text similarity with siamese recurrent networks. In *Proceedings of the 1st Workshop on Representation Learning for NLP*, pages 148–157.

Ruder, S. (2016). An overview of gradient descent optimization algorithms. *arXiv preprint arXiv:1609.04747*.

Srivastava, N., Hinton, G., Krizhevsky, A., Sutskever, I., and Salakhutdinov, R. (2014). Dropout: a simple way to prevent neural networks from overfitting. *The journal of machine learning research*, 15(1):1929–1958.

Proceedings of the Globalex Workshop on Linked Lexicography, pages 84–91
Language Resources and Evaluation Conference (LREC 2020), Marseille, 11–16 May 2020
© European Language Resources Association (ELRA), licensed under CC-BY-NC

Implementation of Supervised Training Approaches for Monolingual Word Sense Alignment:
ACDH-CH System Description for the MWSA Shared Task at GlobaLex 2020

Bajčetić Lenka, Yim Seung-Bin
Austrian Centre for Digital Humanities and Cultural Heritage
Vienna
{lenka.bajcetic, seung-bin.yim}@oeaw.ac.at

Abstract
This paper describes our system for monolingual sense alignment across dictionaries. The task of monolingual word sense alignment is presented as a task of predicting the relationship between two senses. We will present two solutions, one based on supervised machine learning, and the other based on pre-trained neural network language model, specifically BERT. Our models perform competitively for binary classification, reporting high scores for almost all languages.

Keywords: Monolingual Word Sense Alignment, Lexicography, BERT, Gloss Similarity

1. Introduction

This paper presents our submission for the shared task on monolingual word sense alignment across dictionaries as part of the GLOBALEX 2020 – Linked Lexicography workshop at the 12th Language Resources and Evaluation Conference (LREC). Monolingual word sense alignment (MWSA) is the task of aligning word senses across resources in the same language.

Lexical-semantic resources (LSR) such as dictionaries form valuable foundation of numerous natural language processing (NLP) tasks. Since they are created manually by experts, dictionaries can be considered among the resources of highest quality and importance. However, the existing LSRs in machine readable form are small in scope or missing altogether. Thus, it would be extremely beneficial if the existing lexical resources could be connected and expanded.

Lexical resources display considerable variation in the number of word senses that lexicographers assign to a given entry in a dictionary. This is because the identification and differentiation of word senses is one of the harder tasks that lexicographers face. Hence, the task of combining dictionaries from different sources is difficult, especially for the case of mapping the senses of entries, which often differ significantly in granularity and coverage. (Ahmadi et al., 2020)

There are three different angles from which the problem of word sense alignment can be addressed: approaches based on the similarity of textual descriptions of word senses, approaches based on structural properties of lexical-semantic resources, and a combination of both. (Matuschek, 2014)

In this paper we focus on the similarity of textual descriptions. This is a common approach as the majority of previous work used some notion of similarity between senses, mostly gloss overlap or semantic relatedness based on glosses. This makes sense, as glosses are a prerequisite for humans to recognize the meaning of an encoded sense, and thus also an intuitive way of judging the similarity of senses. (Matuschek, 2014)

The paper is structured as follows: we provide a brief overview of related work in Section 2, and a description of the corpus in Section 3. In Section 4 we explain all important aspects of our model implementation, while the results are presented in Section 5. Finally, we end the paper with the discussion in Section 6 and conclusion in Section 7.

2. Related Work

Similar work in monolingual word sense alignment has previously been done mostly for one language in mind, for example (Henrich et al., 2014), (Sultan et al., 2015) and (Caselli et al., 2014).

Researchers avoid modeling features according to a specific resource pair, but aim to combine generic features which are applicable to a variety of resources. One example is the work of (Matuschek and Gurevych, 2014) on alignment between Wiktionary and Wikipedia using distances calculated with Dijkstra-WSA, an algorithm which works on graph representations of resources, as well as gloss similarity values.

Recent work in monolingual corpora linking includes (McCrae and Buitelaar, 2018) which utilizes state-of-the-art methods from the NLP task of semantic textual similarity and combines them with structural similarity of ontology alignment.

Since our work is focusing on similarity of textual descriptions, it is worth mentioning that there have been lots of advances in natural language processing with pre-trained contextualized language representations relying on large corpora (Devlin et al., 2018), which have been delivering improvements in a variety of related downstream tasks, such as word sense disambiguation (Scarlini et al., 2020) and question answering (Yang et al., 2019). However, we could not find any related work leveraging the newest advances with neural network language models (NNLM) for monolingual word sense alignment. For this reason we have chosen to implement our classifiers based on two approaches: one which is feature-based, and the other one using pre-trained NNLMs.

3. Dataset

The dataset used to train and test our models was compiled specifically with this purpose in mind (Ahmadi et al., 2020). The complete corpus for the shared task consists of sixteen datasets from fifteen European languages.[1] The gold standard was obtained by manually classifying the level of semantic similarity between two definitions from two resources for the same lemma.

The data was given in four columns: lemma, part-of-speech (POS) tag and two definitions for the lemma. The fifth column which the system aims to predict contains the semantic relationship between definitions. This falls in one of the five following categories: EXACT, BROADER, NARROWER, RELATED, NONE.

The data was collected as follows: a subset of entries with the same lemma is chosen from the two dictionaries and a spreadsheet is created containing all the possible combinations of definitions from the entries. Experts are then asked to go through the list and choose the level of semantic similarity between each pair. This has created a huge number of pairs which have no relation, and thus the dataset is heavily imbalanced in favor of NONE class. Two challenges caused by the skewness of data were identified. Firstly, the models should be able to deal with underrepresented semantic relations. Secondly, evaluation metrics should consider the imbalanced distribution.

Table 1 displays the distribution of relations between two word definitions and the imbalance of the labels in the training data. We have implemented several ways to battle this, such as undersampling and oversampling, as well as doubling the broader, narrower, exact and related class by relying on their property of symmetry, or applying ensemble learning methods, such as random forest.

4. System Implementation

We aimed to explore the advantages of two different approaches, so we created two different versions of our system. One is the more standard, feature-based approach, and the other is a more novel approach with pre-trained neural language models, specifically BERT (Devlin et al., 2018). The novel approach was used for English and German dataset, in addition to the feature based approach.

4.1. Feature-based models

4.1.1. Preprocessing

Firstly, we loaded the datasets and mitigated imbalanced distribution of relation labels by swapping the two definitions and thus doubling the data samples for related labels, i.e. BROADER, NARROWER, EXACT, RELATED. For example, one English data sample for English head word *follow* has the definition pair *"keep to"* and *"to copy after; to take as an example"* and the relation *"narrower"*. We swap the order of definition pair and change the relation to *"broader"*. An outcome of this swapping process is the generalisation of the dataset. Since two definitions are from different dictionaries, features derived by comparing the two sets of definitions is dependent on the dictionaries.

By swapping the definitions, more general features can be calculated, since the columns contain definitions of two dictionaries, instead of one. This aspect could make the trained feature-based models more robust against new dictionaries. After doubling the data samples, we applied upsampling to match the number of samples of NONE category.

For linguistic preprocessing, the definitions were tokenized using Spacy[2] for English and German, and NLTK[3] for other languages. For languages other than English and German, stopwords were removed from the definitions, in order to create word embedding models. Word vectors included in Spacy language models were used for English and German. We have compiled stopword lists for all languages using several resources found on the Web.[4]

4.1.2. Feature Extraction

Since many of the languages in the dataset have very few open-source resources and tools, and of uncertain quality, the features used are mostly based on word embeddings. The word embeddings were trained using the sets of definitions provided and the Word2Vec(Mikolov et al., 2013) model from *gensim(Řehůřek and Sojka, 2010)* Python library. To calculate the vector of a definition we used the average of word embeddings of consisting tokens. Sentence similarity was calculated with different similarity measures, namely cosine distance, Jaccard similarity, and word mover distance (WMD). For English and German, we used Spacy's built-in language models for word embeddings. The English language model used, *en_core_web_lg* has 685k unique vectors over 300 dimensions, while the German model, *de_core_news_md* has 20k unique vectors over 300 dimensions. Additionally, similarity calculation based on contextualized word representation ELMo (Peters et al., 2018) was used for English to model semantic differences depending on the context.

We selected a different set of features for each classification model from the features described below. Complete list of features used by each classification model is shown in Table 4.

Overall, we used the following features:

- Statistical features: Difference in length of definitions was added as a feature.

- Similarity measures based features: In addition to the word embedding comparisons between the word definition pair, we calculated similarity of the most similar word to the headword by calculating cosine similarity for list of word embeddings of tokens of definitions excluding stopwords and headword word embedding.

- Part-of-speech based features: We included one-hot encoded POS of the headword, as well as difference in POS count of two definitions as features. The POS count was not done for most languages as we were not certain in the quality of existing POS-taggers.

---

[1]The dataset is still growing, and the current version can be found here: https://github.com/elexis-eu/MWSA

[2]https://spacy.io/

[3]https://www.nltk.org/

[4]https://github.com/Xangis/extra-stopwords   and
https://www.rdocumentation.org/packages/stopwords/versions/0.1.0

Language	Broader	Narrower	Exact	Related	None	Total	None %
Basque	82	124	359	170	2496	3231	77%
Bulgarian	153	151	522	275	2256	3357	67%
Danish	172	302	1007	32	14271	15784	90%
Dutch	51	29	444	40	18656	19220	97%
English	39	310	800	51	7137	8337	85%
Estonian	92	105	921	6	1077	2201	49%
German	381	281	321	106	3322	4411	75%
Irish	62	40	664	117	1729	2612	66%
Italian	33	109	281	77	1468	1968	75%
Portuguese	3	32	178	22	1176	1411	83%
Russian	107	11	265	61	2757	3201	86%
Serbian	101	56	413	173	5052	5795	87%
Slovene	176	433	408	105	5595	6717	83%

Table 1: Label distribution of training datasets

- Lexico-syntactic features: One feature exploiting the structure of definitions was to compare the first token of definitions for equality. We also counted matching lemma in the pair of sentences and normalized by the combined length of sentences. Normalization was applied, because we wanted how much overlap exists between two definitions with respect to the length. Without normalization, longer definitions might tend to have higher number of matching lemma. Depth of dependency tree was calculated to add information about structural complexity of definitions. Occurrences of semicolons were also added, since lots of definitions were comprised of multiple short definitions concatenated by semicolon. Additionally, Root word of dependency trees were compared for each definition pair.

- Word sense based features: WordNet[5] was used to count the number of synsets of headwords. Average count of synsets were also added as feature. It was calculated by simply counting synsets for each token of definitions in wordnet and taking the average. These features were used for English only, due to the availability of its primary resource, WordNet.

Standardization was applied for some features,*length difference, pos count difference, and cosine simlarities* prior to training some machine learning models in order to bring the features to similar scale to the other features. Standardization was done by applying Scikit-learn Standard-scaler, which calculates the standardized value of feature by taking the difference of the feature value to the mean value and dividing it by standard deviation.

4.1.3. Classification Models

We tried several machine learning models, mostly from *scikit learn*[6] library for Python: logistic regression, support vector machine, random forest classifier, and decision tree. Classification models were trained by tuning hyperparameters with grid search over 5-fold cross-validation. The hyperparameters used for the submitted models are listed in Table 6. Due to imbalanced nature of the datasets, we have used balanced accuracy and weighted f1-measure for model evaluation. For languages other than English and German, we have ultimately settled for the random forest classifier as it has consistently given the best results.

4.2. Fine-tuning of Pre-trained Neural Network Language Models

For English and German, we additionally fine-tuned pre-trained neural network language models(NNLM), BERT(Devlin et al., 2018) and RoBERTa(Liu et al., 2019) in particular, using simpletransformers [7] on top of pre-trained models provided by transformers python[8] libraries on Google Cloud Platform [9].

In general, applications of pre-trained language models to downstream tasks can be categorized into feature-based and fine-tuning based approaches. Recently, BERT (Devlin et al., 2018), which stands for Bidirectional Encoder Representations from Transformers, have been proven to be beneficial for improving different downstream NLP tasks. BERT is designed to pre-train deep bidirectional representations from unlabeled text by jointly conditioning on both left and right context in all layers and is trained on masked word prediction and next sentence prediction tasks. As a result, the pre-trained BERT model can be fine-tuned with just one additional output layer to create state-of-the-art models for a wide range of tasks (Devlin et al., 2018). Sun et al. (2020) present different approaches to fine-tune BERT for downstream tasks, including pre-training on in-domain data, multi-task fine-tuning and different layers and learning rates.

MWSA task can be ultimately regarded as sentence pair classification task and BERT can be easily fine-tuned for it, since its use of self-attention mechanism(Vaswani et al., 2017) to encode concatenated text pair effectively includes bidirectional cross attention between two sentences. We follow the fine-tuning approach presented in the original paper (Devlin et al., 2018), and adapt our definition pairs as input sequence $[CLS], x_1, ..., x_n[SEP]y_1, ..., y_n[EOS]$ and use [CLS] representation for classification layer.

---

[5]https://wordnet.princeton.edu/
[6]https://scikit-learn.org/stable/

[7]https://github.com/ThilinaRajapakse/simpletransformers
[8]https://huggingface.co/transformers/index.html
[9]https://cloud.google.com/

Language	5-class Accuracy	2-class Precision	2-class Recall	2-class F-Measure
Baseline	**0.789**	0.211	0.050	0.081
Basque	0.407	**0.223**	**0.738**	**0.342**
Baseline	**0.728**	0.250	0.011	0.020
Bulgarian	0.395	**0.331**	**0.842**	**0.475**
Baseline	**0.817**	**0.300**	0.023	0.043
Danish	0.522	0.253	**0.756**	**0.379**
Baseline	0.936	0.000	0.000	0.000
Dutch	**0.940**	**0.636**	**0.241**	**0.350**
Baseline	0.752	0.000	0.000	0.000
English	**0.766**	0.612	0.533	0.570
English BERT Large	0.654	0.467	**0.850**	0.602
English RoBERTa	0.763	**0.619**	0.782	**0.691**
Baseline	0.482	0.545	0.093	0.159
Estonian	**0.565**	**0.707**	**0.806**	**0.754**
Baseline	0.777	0.000	0.000	0.000
German	0.777	0.709	0.448	0.549
German BERT	**0.798**	**0.738**	**0.608**	**0.667**
Basline	**0.583**	**0.680**	0.185	0.291
Irish	0.549	0.631	**0.891**	**0.739**
Baseline	**0.693**	0.000	0.000	0.000
Italian	0.537	**0.418**	**0.719**	**0.529**
Baseline	**0.921**	0.083	0.024	0.037
Portuguese	0.870	**0.311**	**0.762**	**0.441**
Baseline	**0.754**	**0.438**	0.179	0.255
Russian	0.606	0.372	**0.821**	**0.512**
Baseline	**0.853**	0.000	0.000	0.000
Serbian	0.599	**0.190**	**0.464**	**0.269**
Baseline	**0.834**	0.100	0.009	0.017
Slovene	0.442	**0.173**	**0.587**	**0.268**
Average	0.615	0.413	0.694	0.414

Table 2: Comparison of evaluation Results of MWSA from the final evaluation

We have experimented with different pre-trained models, such as BERT Base, BERT Large and RoBERTa for English, which claims to have improved original BERT models by tweaking different aspects of pre-training, such as bigger data and batches, omitting of next sentence prediction, training on longer sequences and changing the masking pattern (Liu et al., 2019). For German, we used the models published by deepset.ai[10] and Bavarian State Library [11]. The training was done on NVIDIA Tesla P100 GPU, different parameter settings have been tried out to find the best performing model for each NNLM. Due to the size of the pre-trained language models and limitations in computation powers, we were only able to explore hyperparameter combinations selectively. Different pre-trained language models were used and were evaluated in the early phase of the experiments, to limit the parameter exploration space. Evaluation of the models were done by comparing Matthews Correlation Coefficient, accuracy and cross entropy. We monitored the three metrics also during training to determine when the model starts to overfit and adjusted hyperparameters for further tuning. It quickly turned out that bigger pre-trained models deliver better results. The tendency that bigger pre-trained models perform better on MWSA is in line with observations made by the original BERT paper authors by comparing BERT Base and Large for different downstream tasks(Devlin et al., 2018), or RoBERTa performing better than original BERT on selected downstream tasks(Liu et al., 2019). For this reason, we have conducted more hyperparameter test combinations for those models(RoBERTa Large for English, and DBMDZ for German). When using bigger models, such as RoBERTa or BERT Large, smaller train-batch-size was selected due to resource limitation. Original BERT models were trained with 512 sequence length, but since the MWSA datasets mostly have short sentence pairs, we experimented with shorter sequence length of 128 and 256 to save memory usage and be more flexible with respect to batch size. Complete list of parameter values tested and the values of the submitted models are shown in Table 5.

$$w_c = \frac{total\ \#\ of\ samples}{\#\ labels \times \#\ datasamples\ of\ c} \tag{1}$$

With appropriate hyperparameters, English and German classifiers based on BERT (German) and RoBERTa (English) showed convergence with repsect to the Cross-

[10]https://deepset.ai/german-bert

[11]https://github.com/dbmdz/berts

entropy loss function. Classes were weighted according to the distribution for loss calculation. The weight for label class C, w_c is determined inversely proportional to label frequencies shown in equation 1. The values used for training is listed in Table 5

5. Results

Results of our MWSA models are presented in Table 2, including baseline models for each language provided by the organizers. In this section we explain the evaluation measures proposed by the organizers for model evaluation and review the results of the two approaches we have explored, feature-based MWSA and fine-tuning NNLM.

5.1. Evaluation Measures

The final submission was evaluated in terms of five class prediction accuracy, as well as binary classification scored with precision, recall, and F-measure. Binary evaluation metrics are calculated by considering relation labels BROADER, NARROWER, RELATED and EXACT as one class of label and NONE classified pairs as the other class. In addition, the organizers provide an average grade over all languages participated in. Our system participated for all languages excluding Hungarian and Spanish, and the results can be seen in Table 1. We argue that due to the imbalanced datasets, 5-class accuracy without balancing cannot adequately represent the model qualities and should only be interpreted holistically together with binary evaluation measures. For example, English baseline model has 5-class accuracy of 0.752, but 2-class F1-measure of 0.0 which indicates that the model is classifying the most of the definition pairs as none-related. The ratio of none related pairs in English training dataset(85%) supports this interpretation. While our both English models show similar 5-class accuracy with respect to the base classifier, they have higher 2-class f1-score, thus higher 2-class precision and recall. Table 3 additionally shows the result of our feature-based English model and RoBERTa based model in comparison with NONE classifier, which classifies all pairs as NONE. It shows that all three models have similar (5-class) accuracy with 0.76, 0.77 and 0.76. Thus, the measure is not sufficient to represent the difference in quality of the models, which can be assumed to exist when looking into the precision and recall for each label. Macro averaged or weighted averaged metrics show that our models perform better. We argue that for future work of MWSA weighted f1-measure or balanced accuracy should be used for adequate evaluation of imbalanced 5-class datasets.

5.2. Result Interpretation and Model Comparison

Our interpretation of the evaluation metrics indicates that our monolingual word sense alignment models show best overall performance for majority of languages. English and German pre-trained NNLM based models perform particularly well, while feature-based models delivered competitive overall results.

Feature-based models showed good results especially in terms of binary recall and f1-measure. However, they perform poorly when it comes to binary precision and the results vary for five-class accuracy. Aside from the peculiar

aspect of 5-class accuracy for this task described above, there are several reasons for this variety in results. All the models are dependent on the quality and size of their corresponding datasets. Also our sampling strategies to deal with imbalanced data may have caused the models to overfit certain patterns of definitions pairs having some kind of relations(BROADER, NARROWER, EXACT, RELATED) and classified some of NONE-related pairs as being related, which could explain high recall and low precision. Another important aspect is the availability and quality of tools for semantic parsing and lexical resources for all the languages. To investigate the results in more detail we present precision, recall, f1-measure for label predictions of English model in Table 3. We can see that the model fails in detecting BROADER, NARROWER, and RELATED class, while performing moderately in detecting EXACT relations.

The BERT based models for English and German performed well in all binary evaluation measures, with English RoBERTa model placing first out of five teams in all three binary evaluation measures. There was no submission from other teams for German, thus no detailed analysis was possible. Nevertheless the German BERT based model outperformed the base model and achieved relatively high scores in binary precision and f-measure. For both languages the neural language model based approaches outperformed feature-based classifiers in all binary evaluation metrics. The English RoBERTa model is on par with the random forest classifier in terms of 5-class accuracy and precision, but outperforms it when it comes to binary recall and binary 2-class f-measure by significant margins. Different to the feature-based classifier, the NNLM based model manages to classify some of the NARROWER relations correctly(Table 3, but precision and recall are still very low. Confusion matrix showed that the model tends to classify NARROWER relations as EXACT. In contrast to English random forest model, German feature-based classifier cannot compete with the neural language model in all evaluation metrics, lack of more sophisticated features used by English feature-based classifier, such as ELMo sentence embedding or wordnet based features are possible reasons. However, the pre-trained German language model is pre-trained on smaller dataset (16GB of data) than English (RoBERTa: 160GB), thus it is to assume there might be room for improvement of both approaches.

For English models, which we have investigated more in detail, we can clearly see the correlation between number of data samples in each category and the performance of the models on those categories. BROADER and RELATED relations were only trained on 10 and 20 samples respectively, which we believe is too little to model pattern variety of complex natural language expressions.

6. Discussion

As previously mentioned, an important property of the provided datasets is the extreme imbalance in the favor of NONE class. For future work, it would be useful to acquire more examples of the classes less represented in the dataset. Since classifiers are prone to overfitting, it would be useful to expand the datasets with definitions extracted from more dictionaries. This way it would be easier to get a more gen-

	NONE classifier			Features-based			RoBERTa-based			
	Prec.	Rec.	F1	Prec.	Rec.	F1	Prec.	Rec.	F1	Support
BROADER	0.00	0.00	0.00	0.00	0.00	0.00	0.00	0.00	0.00	3
NARROWER	0.00	0.00	0.00	0.00	0.00	0.00	0.14	0.17	0.16	29
EXACT	0.00	0.00	0.00	0.44	0.60	0.51	0.47	0.74	0.58	85
RELATED	0.00	0.00	0.00	0.00	0.00	0.00	0.00	0.00	0.00	16
NONE	0.76	1.00	0.86	0.86	0.89	0.87	0.92	0.84	0.88	411
accuracy			0.76			0.77			0.76	
macro avg.	0.15	0.20	0.17	0.26	0.30	0.28	0.31	0.35	0.32	
weighted avg.	0.57	0.76	0.65	0.71	0.77	0.74	0.78	0.76	0.76	

Table 3: Evaluation results of test set prediction by English models. NONE classifier predicts all labels to NONE

eral and robust classifier. Our feature-based models showed that differentiating exact semantic relation is a difficult task, especially NARROWER and EXACT relations get mixed up by the English model, more work on methodologies to distinguish these relations will help to improve 5-class accuracy. A different idea to consider would be to opt for specific classifiers for each pairing of two dictionaries, where features used could be dictionary-dependant and possibly more precise, e.g. numbers of semicolons or other formatting aspects which are dictionary-specific.

Another possible issue we identified for this task is that dictionary definitions have different or atypical language usage in terms of structure of sentences, term occurrences, additional information expressed with symbols, such as semicolons, hyphens. For this reason, we think that building language models based on multiple dictionaries might help to further increase accuracy of the models.

For German and English we demonstrated that fine-tuning neural network language models outperform the feature-based approaches. Considering that the pre-trained models were trained on more general corpora, further studies involving pre-training on dictionary data and further fine-tuning different aspects described in (Sun et al., 2020) might lead to improvements of the models.

7. Conclusion

In this paper we describe our system submission for the Monolingual Word Sense Alignment shared task at Globalex 2020. Our solution consists of a separate random forest classifier trained for each language, while a BERT-based solution is implemented for English and German. The feature-based classifiers perform competitively for binary classification and employing fine-tuning of pre-trained BERT models for monolingual word sense alignment is showing promising results and should be investigated further.

8. Acknowledgements

This work was supported by funding from the European Union's Horizon 2020 research and innovation programme under grant agreement No 731015.

9. References

Ahmadi, S., McCrae, J. P., Nimb, S., Troelsgard, T., Olsen, S., Pedersen, B. S., Declerck, T., Wissik, T., Monachini, M., Bellandi, A., Khan, F., Pisani, I., Krek, S., Lipp, V., Varadi, T., Simon, L., Gyorffy, A., Tiberius, C., Schoonheim, T., Moshe, Y. B., Rudich, M., Ahmad, R. A., Lonke, D., Kovalenko, K., Langemets, M., Kallas, J., Dereza, O., Fransen, T., Cillessen, D., Lindemann, D., Alonso, M., Salgado, A., Sancho, J. L., Urena-Ruiz, R.-J., Simov, K., Osenova, P., Kancheva, Z., Radev, I., Stankovic, R., Krstev, C., Lazic, B., Markovic, A., Perdih, A., and Gabrovsek, D. (2020). A Multilingual Evaluation Dataset for Monolingual Word Sense Alignment. In *Proceedings of the 12th Language Resource and Evaluation Conference (LREC 2020)*.

Caselli, T., Strapparava, C., Vieu, L., and Vetere, G. (2014). Aligning an italian wordnet with a lexicographic dictionary: Coping with limited data.

Devlin, J., Chang, M.-W., Lee, K., and Toutanova, K. (2018). Bert: Pre-training of deep bidirectional transformers for language understanding.

Henrich, V., Hinrichs, E., and Barkey, R. (2014). Aligning word senses in germanet and the dwds dictionary of the german language.

Liu, Y., Ott, M., Goyal, N., Du, J., Joshi, M., Chen, D., Levy, O., Lewis, M., Zettlemoyer, L., and Stoyanov, V. (2019). Roberta: A robustly optimized BERT pretraining approach. *CoRR, abs/1907.11692*.

Matuschek, M. and Gurevych, I. (2014). High performance word sense alignment by joint modeling of sense distance and gloss similarity. In *Proceedings of COLING 2014, the 25th International Conference on Computational Linguistics: Technical Papers*.

Matuschek, M. (2014). *Word Sense Alignment of Lexical Resources*. Ph.D. thesis, Technischen Universitat Darmstadt.

McCrae, J. P. and Buitelaar, P. (2018). Linking datasets using semantic textual similarity. *Cybernetics and information technologies*, 18.

Mikolov, T., Sutskever, I., Chen, K., Corrado, G. S., and Dean, J. (2013). Distributed representations of words and phrases and their compositionality. In C. J. C. Burges, et al., editors, *Advances in Neural Information Processing Systems 26*, pages 3111–3119. Curran Associates, Inc.

Peters, M. E., Neumann, M., Iyyer, M., Gardner, M., Clark, C., Lee, K., and Zettlemoyer, L. (2018). Deep contextualized word representations. In *Proc. of NAACL*.

Řehůřek, R. and Sojka, P. (2010). Software Framework for Topic Modelling with Large Corpora. In

Proceedings of the LREC 2010 Workshop on New Challenges for NLP Frameworks, pages 45–50, Valletta, Malta, May. ELRA. `http://is.muni.cz/publication/884893/en`.

Scarlini, B., Pasini, T., and Navigli, R. (2020). SensEm-BERT: Context-Enhanced Sense Embeddings for Multilingual Word Sense Disambiguation.

Sultan, M. A., Bethard, S., and Sumner, T. (2015). Feature-rich two-stage logistic regression for monolingual alignment. In *Proceedings of the 2015 Conference on Empirical Methods in Natural Language Processing*.

Sun, C., Qiu, X., Xu, Y., and Huang, X. (2020). How to Fine-Tune BERT for Text Classification? *arXiv:1905.05583 [cs]*, February. arXiv: 1905.05583.

Vaswani, A., Shazeer, N., Parmar, N., Uszkoreit, J., Jones, L., Gomez, A. N., Kaiser, L., and Polosukhin, I. (2017). Attention Is All You Need. *arXiv:1706.03762 [cs]*, December. arXiv: 1706.03762.

Yang, W., Xie, Y., Lin, A., Li, X., Tan, L., Xiong, K., Li, M., and Lin, J. (2019). End-to-End Open-Domain Question Answering with BERTserini. *Proceedings of the 2019 Conference of the North*, pages 72–77. arXiv: 1902.01718.

Feature	EU	BG	DA	NL	EN	ET	DE	GA	IT	PT	RU	SR	SL
cosine sim	O		O	O		O	O	O		O		O	
jaccard sim	O		O	O		O	O	O		O		O	
tfidf similarity	O	O	O	O		O	O	O	O	O	O	O	O
elmo similarity					O								
similarity diff to target					O								
first word same	O	O	O	O		O	O	O	O	O	O	O	O
root word same	O	O	O	O		O	O	O	O	O	O	O	O
length difference	O	O	O	O	O	O	O	O	O	O	O	O	O
pos count difference				O	O		O						
target pos		O	O	O	O	O	O	O	O	O	O	O	O
lemma match count	O	O	O	O	O	O	O	O	O	O	O	O	O
pos count				O	O		O						
dep. tree depth					O								
target word synset count					O								
average synset count					O								
semicolon count					O								

Table 4: Features used for each classifier, with language codes according to ISO 639-1

Parameter	value set	English	German
used model	BERT English(Large) German BERT(deepset.ai, DBMDZ cased)	RoBERTa(Large)	DBMDZ German BERT
label weights		NONE: 0.23 EXACT: 2.08 BROADER: 42.05 NARROWER:5.37 RELATED:32.69	NONE: 0.27 EXACT: 2.74 BROADER: 2.31 NARROWER:3.13 RELATED:8.32
max-seq-length	64, 128, 256, 512	256	256
train-batch-size	8, 16, 32	16	32
num-train-epochs	2,3,5,7,10,15	2	7
weight-decay	0.3, 0.5	0.3	0.3
learning-rate	1e-6, 8e-6, 9e-6, 1e-5, 3e-5, 4e-5,5e-5	9e-6	3e-5

Table 5: Language model and Hyperparameters used for fine-tuning NNLM to MWSA

Parameter	EU	BG	DA	NL	EN	ET	DE	GA	IT	PT	RU	SR	SL
max-features	3	3	3	auto	log2	2	auto	3	3	3	3	3	3
max-depth	10	10	10	30	10	10	30	10	10	7	10	10	10
min-samples-leaf	3	3	5	5	2	3	3	4	3	3	3	3	3
min-samples-split	10	2	10	8	5	2	8	2	8	5	2	5	8
n-estimators	100	100	100	500	300	50	500	100	200	50	50	100	100

Table 6: Hyperparameters used for Random Forest Classifier

Proceedings of the Globalex Workshop on Linked Lexicography, pages 92–97
Language Resources and Evaluation Conference (LREC 2020), Marseille, 11–16 May 2020
© European Language Resources Association (ELRA), licensed under CC-BY-NC

NUIG at TIAD: Combining Unsupervised NLP and Graph Metrics for Translation Inference

John P. McCrae and Mihael Arcan

Data Science Institute, Insight Centre for Data Analytics
National University of Ireland Galway
john@mccr.ae, mihael.arcan@insight-centre.org

Abstract

In this paper, we present the NUIG system at the TIAD shard task. This system includes graph-based metrics calculated using novel algorithms, with an unsupervised document embedding tool called ONETA and an unsupervised multi-way neural machine translation method. The results are an improvement over our previous system and produce the highest precision among all systems in the task as well as very competitive F-Measure results. Incorporating features from other systems should be easy in the framework we describe in this paper, suggesting this could very easily be extended to an even stronger result.

Keywords: translation inference, machine translation, multiway translation, document embeddings

1. Introduction

Translation inference is the task of inferring new translations between a pair of languages, based on existing translations to one or more pivot language. In the particular context of the TIAD task (Gracia et al., 2019), there is a graph of translations shown in Figure 1 available from the Apertium project (Forcada et al., 2011) and the goal is to use this graph of translations to infer missing links (shown with dotted lines), in particular between English, French and Portuguese. This year, we combined two systems that had participated in a previous task (Arcan et al., 2019; McCrae, 2019) and show that this combination can improve the results. This combination consists of an unsupervised cross-lingual document embeddings system called Orthonormal Explicit Topic Analysis (McCrae et al., 2013, ONETA) and the results of unsupervised machine translation using the multi-way neural machine translation (NMT) approach (Ha et al., 2016). We also further extended this system by developing a new methodology of analysing the graph to find candidates and we show that most of the candidates (74.5%) that are likely to be correct are at a graph distance of 2, that is they are discoverable using only a single pivot translation, while quite a large amount of translations cannot be inferred using the graph (23.1%). This shows that the use of more sophisticated graph metrics is unlikely to gain more improvement in this task and that attention should instead be directed to unsupervised NLP techniques. We also analyzed the provided reference data and found that the data seems to diverge quite distinctly from the training data, suggesting that there may be a need to look for more robust methods of evaluation for future editions of this task.

2. Methodology

2.1. Graph Extraction

One of the principal challenges of working with the TIAD data is that there are a very large number of entities and it is difficult to predict which ones are likely to be good candidates for translation inference. Following, the intuition that translations should be connected in the graph, we wish to find for a pair of languages l_1, l_2 all the entities that are

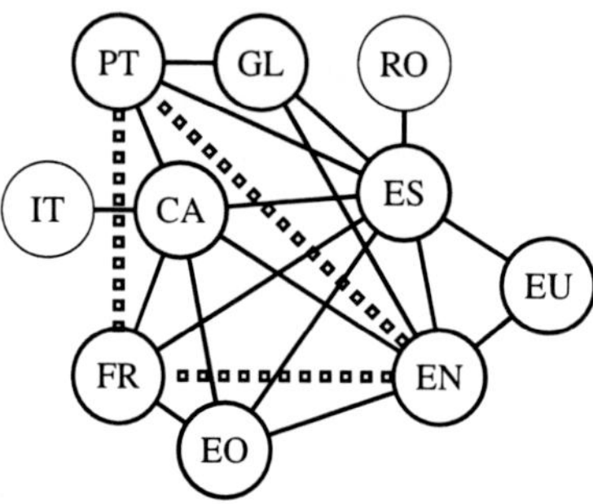

Figure 1: Languages available in the Apertium training data (solid lines) and language pairs to be inferred in the translation graph (dotted lines)

connected. As the graph of all TIAD connections contains 1,053,203 nodes connected with 531,053 edges, calculating all the possible connections between the edges of the graph can be quite challenging when approached naively.

We developed the following approach to constructing the set of distances between all nodes in two languages, based on a set of translations T_{l_i,l_j} by language and a lexicon of words W_i for language l_i as shown in Algorithm 1.

The first step of this algorithm is to initialize two distance lists $dist_1$ and $dist_2$ that measure the distance between terms in l_1 or l_2 respectively and all terms in languages other than l_1 or l_2. The next step is then to iterate through all translations between languages other than l_1 and l_2 and connect the distance metrics $dist_1$ and $dist_2$. In this way, the first value of $dist_1$ contains only terms in l_1 and so they can easily be implemented as an array of associative arrays and hence kept quite sparse. Finally, we iterate through the words of l_1 and l_2 and calculate the distance between each word. This relies on the *keys* function which returns the list of terms in a third language, which have a non-infinite distance in $dist_1$ and $dist_2$. In practice, this is implemented by taking the smaller of the associative arrays associated with $dist_1$ or $dist_2$ and filtering the results according to the presence in the larger associative array. As such, while the worst-case performance of the algorithm is

Graph Distance	Correct	Total	Precision	Recall
2	30,988	40,321	0.7685	0.7452
3	838	19,820	0.0423	0.0202
4	102	24,113	0.0042	0.0025
5	38	36,848	0.0010	0.0001
6	4	37,178	0.0001	0.0000
7	5	47,686	0.0001	0.0000
8	1	42,378	0.0000	0.0000
9	0	47,739	0.0000	0.0000
10	0	39,261	0.0000	0.0000
11	1	39,246	0.0000	0.0000
12	0	29,902	0.0000	0.0000
13	0	26,441	0.0000	0.0000
14	0	19,531	0.0000	0.0000
15	0	15,484	0.0000	0.0000
16	0	10,799	0.0000	0.0000
17	0	7,549	0.0000	0.0000
18	0	4,792	0.0000	0.0000
19	0	3,163	0.0000	0.0000
20	0	2,201	0.0000	0.0000
21	0	1,134	0.0000	0.0000
22	0	528	0.0000	0.0000
23	0	258	0.0000	0.0000
24	0	52	0.0000	0.0000
25	0	3	0.0000	0.0000
Unconnected	9,606	1.3×10^9	0.0000	0.2310

Table 1: Evaluation of English-Spanish Apertium dataset based on graph distance

---

Algorithm 1: Distance calculation algorithm

Result: The distances between in l_1 and l_2: $dist$

for $l \in L, l \neq l_1, l \neq l_2$ **do**
    for $(s,t) \in T_{l_1,l}$ **do**
        $dist_1(s,t) \leftarrow 1$
    end
    for $(s,t) \in T_{l_2,l}$ **do**
        $dist_2(s,t) \leftarrow 1$
    end
end
for $l_i \in L, l_j \in L, l_i \neq l_1, l_i \neq l_2, l_i \neq l_1, l_j \neq l_2$ **do**
    for $(s,t) \in T_{l_i,l_j}$ **do**
        for $u \in W_1$ **do**
            $dist_1(u,t) \leftarrow$
            $\min(dist_1(u,t), dist_1(u,s)+1)$
        end
        for $u \in W_2$ **do**
            $dist_2(u,t) \leftarrow$
            $\min(dist_2(u,t), dist_2(u,s)+1)$
        end
    end
end
for $s \in W_1$ **do**
    for $t \in W_2$ **do**
        $dist(s,t) \leftarrow$
        $\min_{u \in \text{keys}(s,t)} dist_1(s,u) + dist_2(u,t)$
    end
end

---

still $\mathcal{O}(|W_1| \times |W_2| \times |W'_{1,2}|)$ where $W'_{1,2}$ is the words in all languages other than l_1 and l_2, in fact the calculation of *keys* is

$$\mathcal{O}[\min(|X_1(s)|, |X_2(t)|) \times \log \max(|X_1(s)|, |X_2(t)|)]$$

Where:

$$X_i(s) = \{u : dist_i(s,u) < \infty\}$$

In order to analyze the results of this analysis, we considered the provided Apertium training data holding out the translations for one language pair, namely English-Spanish, and the results are presented in Table 1. We see that there are 46,004 terms in the English data and 28,615 terms in the Spanish data meaning there are potentially 1.3 billion translations that can be inferred. Our algorithm found that only 496,427 of these term pairs are connected in the Apertium graph, which overlaps quite well with the correct translations in the Apertium data. In fact, 23.1% of translations from the gold standard are not connected whereas 76.9% are connected at graph distance 2, that is inferred by a single pivot translation. For this reason, we used this method as the basis for generating candidate translations, in particular, we only considered translations that were at graph distance 2 or 3, and in addition, we extracted the size of the *keys* set for each translation as it was a useful and readily available statistic.

2.2. ONETA

The OrthoNormal Explicit Topic Analysis (ONETA) methodology used in the system was not much changed from how it was applied previously (McCrae, 2019), only this time instead of just using a single language for finding potential pivots, the results of the graph distance method were used to select all translations at distance 2 or 3. For the purpose of completeness, we will briefly recap the methodology here. ONETA aims to find a vector to represent a term satisfying

$$\phi_{\text{ONETA}}(d_i)^{\mathsf{T}} \phi_{\text{TF-IDF}}(d_j) = \delta_{ij}$$

It does this by constructing the TF-IDF vectors for each of the words and organizing them in a matrix $\mathbf{X}$ and then the vector for ONETA can be obtained as[1]:

$$\phi_{\text{ONETA}}(d_i) = \mathbf{X}^{+} \phi_{\text{TF-IDF}}(d_j)$$

Where:

$$x_{ij} = \phi_{\text{TF-IDF}}(d_i)^{\mathsf{T}} \phi_{\text{TF-IDF}}(d_j)$$

It was shown (McCrae et al., 2013) that this can be efficiently approximated by organizing the matrix $\mathbf{X}$ into the form

$$\mathbf{X} \simeq \begin{pmatrix} \mathbf{A} & \mathbf{B} \\ \mathbf{0} & \mathbf{C} \end{pmatrix}$$

And using the following form of the projection:

$$\phi_{\text{ONETA}}(d_i) = \begin{pmatrix} \mathbf{A}^{+} & -\mathbf{A}^{+}\mathbf{B}\mathbf{C}^{+} \\ \mathbf{0} & \mathbf{C}^{+} \end{pmatrix} \phi_{\text{TF-IDF}}(d_j).$$

2.3. Multi-way Neural Machine

To perform experiments on neural machine translation (NMT) models with a minimal set of parallel data, i.e. for less-resourced languages, we trained a multi-source and multi-target NMT model (Ha et al., 2016) with well-resourced language pairs. In our work, we have chosen parallel corpora in the Romance language family, i.e. Spanish, Italian, French, Portuguese, Romanian, as well as English. To train the multi-way NMT system, we used all possible language combinations within the targeted Romance language family, but excluded the English-Spanish, English-French, English-Portuguese and Portuguese-French language pair.

Neural Machine Translation Setup We used Open-NMT (Klein et al., 2017), a generic deep learning framework mainly specialised in sequence-to-sequence models covering a variety of tasks such as machine translation, summarisation, speech processing and question answering as NMT framework. Due to computational complexity, the vocabulary in NMT models had to be limited. To overcome this limitation, we used byte pair encoding (BPE) to generate subword units (Sennrich et al., 2016). BPE is a data compression technique that iteratively replaces the most frequent pair of bytes in a sequence with a single, unused byte. We used the following default neural network training parameters: two hidden layers, 500 hidden LSTM (long short term memory) units per layer, input feeding enabled, 13 epochs, batch size of 64, 0.3 dropout probability, dynamic learning rate decay, 500 dimension embeddings.

---

[1]$\mathbf{X}^{+}$ denotes the Moore-Penrose pseudo-inverse

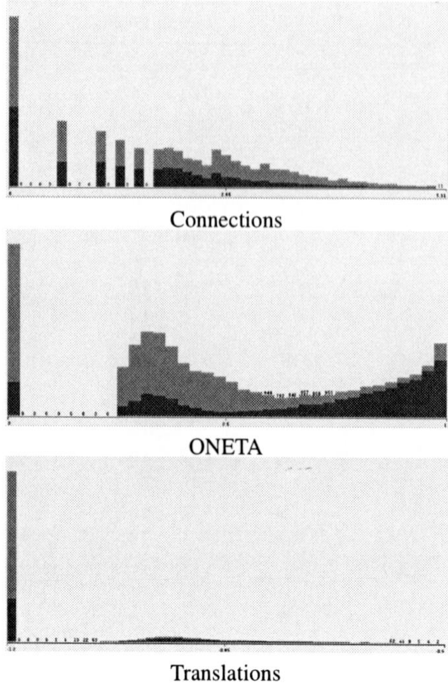

Figure 2: Distribution of the features relative to correct (blue) translations and incorrect (red) translations

Dataset for NMT training To train the multi-way model, we used the DGT (Directorate General for Translation) corpus (Steinberger et al., 2012), a publicly accessible resource provided by the European Commission to support multilingualism and the re-use of European Commission information available in 24 different European languages. The English, Spanish, French, Romanian, Italian and Portuguese languages were selected to train the multi-way NMT system, from which we extracted 200,000 translated sentences present in all six languages within the DGT corpus (Table 2).

3. Results

3.1. Results on Apertium

In order to develop and train our system, we used the available Apertium data as a gold standard. In this case, we held out the English-Spanish translation data and tried to predict the values in this dataset. From our methods, we had the following features

Distance The graph distance, either 2 or 3.

Connections The size of the *keys* set used in calculating the graph distance. To improve the result, we scaled this logarithmically.

ONETA The score coming out of ONETA. We scaled this geometrically to obtain a roughly even distribution of values.

Translation & Inverse Translation The perplexity of the translation. As the translation methodology is not

Multi-Way	Source		Target		
	# Subwords	# Uniq. Subwords	# Subwords	# Uniq. Subwords	# Lines
train	131,146,463	32,180	121,544,872	32,161	4,400,000
validation	656,154	29,380	608,006	29,408	22,000

Table 2: Dataset statistics for the DGT corpus the combined multi-way dataset used to train the translation system

symmetric we obtained two scores for English $\rightarrow$ Spanish and Spanish $\rightarrow$ English. As the perplexity naturally decreases for longer outputs, we divided it by the number of tokens in the output score.

An analysis of these features using 10-fold cross-validation compared is shown in Table 3. Note that due to the limitation of using only those translations that have a graph distance of 2 or 3, the highest recall we could achieve is 0.76 and the highest F-Measure is 0.870.

Method	Precision	Recall	F-Measure
ONETA	0.772	0.501	0.607
Connections	0.568	0.678	0.618
Translations	0.767	0.453	0.570
Random Tree	0.758	0.565	0.647
Random Forest	0.774	0.602	0.677
J48	0.822	0.599	0.693
Naïve Bayes	0.821	0.518	0.635
Logistic Regression	0.821	0.591	0.687
SVM	0.820	0.583	0.681

Table 3: Performance of our system on predicting English-Spanish Apertium data

3.2. Task Results

The official results from the organizers are reproduced in Table 4. We can see from this that in all evaluations, the system described in this paper (labelled 'NUIG'), produced the highest precision in its results. However, as we saw in the Apertium analysis we had a significant drop in recall compared to the baselines and these overall meant that the system was 2nd or 3rd in terms of F-Measure. We also note that the systems to beat ours were those based on one-time inverse consultation (Tanaka and Umemura, 1994), and it should be relatively easy to combine these results into our architecture, suggesting that we could easily obtain a much stronger result.

3.3. Discussion

The organizers of the TIAD task released a small part of the evaluation dataset, and it appears that this dataset has significant differences to the translations that form Apertium. For example, in Table 5, the translation for chestnuts are given [2], and we see that the gold standard gives 'châtaigne' as does our system but also gives two more terms 'châtaignier' and 'marronnier', which our system

does not. These terms refer to chestnut as a tree and our system correctly predicts that this is a translation of 'chestnuttree' and fails to generate a translation for these terms, principally because they only occur in a single translation language pair (French-Esperanto) and so are not connected in any way to the English. More concerningly, the term 'marron' is missed in the gold standard, as well as by our system, even though this is the translation preferred by several online sources. In Figure 3, we see a relative plot of the correct terms in the released gold standard versus the graph distance calculated according to the training data. The distribution is quite different from the training data, with much less of the data being connected by a single pivot translation (that is at graph distance 1) and much more distant connections. It is especially surprising that some of the translations are at a distance of 4 or 5, which for English-Portuguese and French-Portuguese represents about 9% of the data but in the training set, while the precision of such distant links was less than 1% in the training set.

4. Conclusion

We have presented the results of our system for the TIAD task that combined unsupervised document embedding, unsupervised machine translation and graph analysis to produce a very high precision result. We have seen that the graph metrics are a good initial filtering, but that the main improvement can be achieved by incorporating metrics related to unsupervised multilingual NLP and the one-time inverse consultation method. This leads us to some obvious paths that can improve our results for future evaluations.

Acknowledgements

This publication has emanated from research supported in part by a research grant from Science Foundation Ireland (SFI) under Grant Number SFI/12/RC/2289_P2, co-funded by the European Regional Development Fund, as well as by the H2020 project Prêt-à-LLOD under Grant Agreement number 825182.

Bibliographical References

Arcan, M., Torregrosa, D., Ahmadi, S., and McCrae, J. P. (2019). Inferring translation candidates for multilingual dictionary generation. In *Proceedings of the 2nd Translation Inference Across Dictionaries (TIAD) Shared Task.*

Forcada, M. L., Ginestí-Rosell, M., Nordfalk, J., O'Regan, J., Ortiz-Rojas, S., Pérez-Ortiz, J. A., Sánchez-Martínez, F., Ramírez-Sánchez, G., and Tyers, F. M. (2011). Apertium: a free/open-source platform for rule-based machine translation. *Machine translation*, 25(2):127–144.

---

[2]This is the second example given by the organizer for this language pair

System	EN-FR			EN-PT			FR-PT		
	P	R	F	P	R	F	P	R	F
Baseline OTIC	0.67	**0.44**	**0.53**	0.64	0.38	0.48	0.74	0.54	**0.62**
Baseline word2vec	0.37	0.41	0.39	0.23	**0.39**	0.29	0.27	0.34	0.30
NUIG	**0.80**	0.35	0.49	**0.68**	0.31	0.43	**0.84**	0.40	0.54
ACOLI Baseline	0.57	0.30	0.39	0.48	0.24	0.32	0.63	0.27	0.38
ACOLI WordNet	0.59	0.18	0.28	0.54	0.13	0.21	0.62	0.15	0.24
CL - Embeddings	-	-	-	0.52	0.35	0.42	0.55	0.34	0.42
Ciclos - OTIC	-	-	-	0.57	0.44	**0.50**	0.67	**0.55**	0.60
Multi-Strategy	-	-	-	0.52	0.34	0.41	0.58	0.34	0.43

Table 4: The performance of systems in the TIAD-2020 benchmark from the organizers in terms of **P**recision, **R**ecall and **F**-Measure

English	French	Gold Standard	Our System	Graph Distance
chestnut	châtaigne	Yes	Yes	2
chestnut	châtaignier	Yes	No	∞
chestnut	marronnier	Yes	No	∞
chestnut	marron	No	No	2
chestnuttree	châtaignier	?	Yes	2

Table 5: Translations in the released gold standard and our system

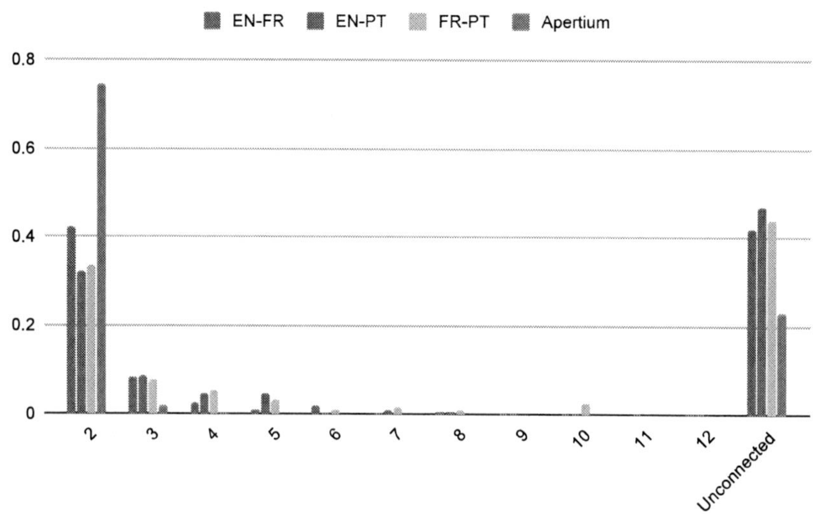

Figure 3: Distribution of translations relative to distance in training data

Gracia, J., Kabashi, B., Kernerman, I., Lanau-Coronas, M., and Lonke, D. (2019). Results of the translation inference across dictionaries 2019 shared task. pages 1–12.

Ha, T., Niehues, J., and Waibel, A. H. (2016). Toward multilingual neural machine translation with universal encoder and decoder. *CoRR*, abs/1611.04798.

Klein, G., Kim, Y., Deng, Y., Senellart, J., and Rush, A. M. (2017). OpenNMT: Open-Source Toolkit for Neural Machine Translation. In *Proceedings of the 55th Annual Meeting of the Association for Computational Linguistics*, pages 67–72.

McCrae, J., Cimiano, P., and Klinger, R. (2013). Orthonormal explicit topic analysis for cross-lingual document matching. In *Proceedings of the 2013 Conference on Empirical Methods in Natural Language Processing*, pages 1732–1742.

McCrae, J. P. (2019). TIAD Shared Task 2019: Orthonormal Explicit Topic Analysis for Translation Inference across Dictionaries. In *Proceedings of the 2nd Translation Inference Across Dictionaries (TIAD) Shared Task*.

Sennrich, R., Haddow, B., and Birch, A. (2016). Neural Machine Translation of Rare Words with Subword Units. *Proceedings of the 54th Annual Meeting of the Associa-*

tion for Computational Linguistics, abs/1508.07909.

Steinberger, R., Eisele, A., Klocek, S., Pilos, S., and Schlüter, P. (2012). DGT-TM: A freely available Translation Memory in 22 languages. In *Proceedings of the 8th International Conference on Language Resources and Evaluation (LREC12)*, pages 454–459, Istanbul, Turkey.

Tanaka, K. and Umemura, K. (1994). Construction of a bilingual dictionary intermediated by a third language. In *Proceedings of the 15th conference on Computational linguistics-Volume 1*, pages 297–303. Association for Computational Linguistics.

Proceedings of the Globalex Workshop on Linked Lexicography, pages 98–105
Language Resources and Evaluation Conference (LREC 2020), Marseille, 11–16 May 2020
© European Language Resources Association (ELRA), licensed under CC-BY-NC

Translation Inference by Concept Propagation

Christian Chiarcos, Niko Schenk, Christian Fäth
Applied Computational Linguistics (ACoLi)
Goethe University Frankfurt, Germany
{chiarcos, n.schenk, faeth}@em.uni-frankfurt.de

Abstract

This paper describes our contribution to the Third Shared Task on Translation Inference across Dictionaries (TIAD-2020). We describe an approach on translation inference based on symbolic methods, the propagation of concepts over a graph of interconnected dictionaries: Given a mapping from source language words to lexical concepts (e.g., synsets) as a seed, we use bilingual dictionaries to extrapolate a mapping of pivot and target language words to these lexical concepts. Translation inference is then performed by looking up the lexical concept(s) of a source language word and returning the target language word(s) for which these lexical concepts have the respective highest score. We present two instantiations of this system: One using WordNet synsets as concepts, and one using lexical entries (translations) as concepts. With a threshold of 0, the latter configuration is the second among participant systems in terms of F1 score. We also describe additional evaluation experiments on Apertium data, a comparison with an earlier approach based on embedding projection, and an approach for constrained projection that outperforms the TIAD-2020 vanilla system by a large margin.

Keywords: Translation Inference, Bilingual Dictionaries, Auto-Generating Dictionaries

1. Background

The Third Shared Task on Translation Inference across Dictionaries[1] (TIAD-2020) has been conducted in conjunction with the GlobaLex workshop at the 12th Language Resources and Evaluation Conference (LREC-2020, Marseille, France). As in previous editions, the objective is to automatically obtain new bilingual dictionaries based on existing ones. The evaluation is performed against a blind test set provided by a commercial partner (KDictionaries, Tel Aviv), so that a particular challenge is to optimize against data with unknown characteristics. For this edition, participants were provided with a test data excerpt to study its characteristics before the submission of final results.

Our system from TIAD-2019 (Donandt and Chiarcos, 2019) was based on translation inference over bilingual dictionaries by means of *embedding propagation*: Given word embeddings[2] for a particular pivot (seed) language, we extrapolated the embeddings of all languages with translations into (or from) the pivot language (first generation languages) by adding the corresponding English language scores. Where translations into (or from) the seed language are missing, translations into (or from) first generation languages are used to deduce embeddings in the same manner for second generation languages, etc. In this way, word embeddings are propagated through the entire dictionary graph. For predicting translations, we then use cosine similarity between source and target language vectors, constrained by a similarity threshold.

This approach is both simple and knowledge-poor; it uses no other multilingual resources than the ones provided by the task organizers, and it is particularly well-suited to address under-resourced languages as addressed in language documentation (i.e., languages for which no substantial corpora [neither monolingual, nor parallel] are available, but the majority of published language data is represented in

secondary resources such as word lists and grammars). The objective for developing this system was to facilitate language contact studies (esp., cognate detection) for the Caucasus, and to address semantic similarity for low-resource language varieties for which only word lists are provided and where no basis for inducing native word or parallel embeddings exists. Despite its simplicity and the highly specialized domain of application it was designed for, our system performed well among participant systems, being a high precision system with top F1 score (precision 0.64, recall 0.22, F1 0.32; the closest competitor system had the scores: precision 0.36, recall 0.31, F1 0.32). At the same time, none of the participant systems outperformed the organizer's baselines, and we suspected the following reasons:

- The characteristics of the training data (Apertium dictionaries were designed for machine translation, i.e., to give the most *common* translation) and the evaluation data (KDictionaries dictionaries were designed for language learning, i.e., to give the most *precise* translation) may be so different that optimization against external resources (or the provided training data) does not improve performance over the evaluation data.

- Participant systems, in particular those based on word embeddings (by embedding projection or other techniques), are probably effective at capturing the main sense of a word, but they lose on secondary senses because these are under-represented in the corpora used to derive the original embeddings but over-represented in the evaluation data.

Whereas TIAD-2019 was reductionist in that every lexical entry was represented by a single vector (capturing its main sense, resp. a weighted average of all its senses), our current TIAD-2020 contribution is tailored towards the second aspect: we aim to preserve the diversity of translations provided in the training data by *propagating lexical concepts* rather than embeddings.

---

[1] https://tiad2020.unizar.es/

[2] We used 50-dimensional GloVe embeddings (Pennington et al., 2014) for English.

2. Approach

We assume that a key weakness of the neural approach implemented for TIAD-2019 was that it produces one single representation for a lexical entry, and that translations are identified by their distance from that representation. While this is a robust and reliable strategy for the most frequent sense of a particular word, we expect it to be less effective for polysemous or homonymous words, and to fail for rare and specialized senses. Indeed, identifying and classifying such senses, e.g., the use of a term in a particular domain of science, is a core tasks of lexicography, and part of the motivation for manual labor. We expect that KDictionary data is substantially richer in that regard that Apertium data.

Hence, instead of projecting embeddings for lexical entries, we project lexical concepts as identified in monolingual lexical resources. The most prominent, and widely used family of resources for this regard are word nets. Our approach on concept projection is based on WordNet synsets (Fellbaum, 1998). If source language and target language use the same synset identifiers (concepts), the target language translations of a particular source language word can be extrapolated from concepts by returning the most representative target language words for the concept associated with the source language. The challenge here is to develop metrics that express and maintain confidence of the association between a word and a concept. Based on these metrics, thresholds can be used to limit the set of possible concepts for a lexeme and possible lexicalizations of a concept. We employ the following core metrics:

- $P(concept|lexeme)$: probability of a concept for a given lexeme (source or target word)

- $P(lexeme|concept)$: lexicalization probability of a lexeme (source or target word) for a given concept

- $P(target|source)$: translation probability of a target word for a particular source word

- $P(source|target)$: translation probability of a source word for a particular target word

To initialize these metrics, we do not employ external resources to estimate them, but rather derive them from the branching factor within a WordNet, resp. a bilingual dictionary:

- $P(concept|lexeme) := \frac{1}{concepts(lexeme)}$, where $concepts(lexeme)$ is the number of concepts for a particular lexeme.

- $P(lexeme|concept) := \frac{1}{lexemes(concepts)}$, where $lexemes(concept)$ is the number of lexemes for a particular concept.

- $P(target|source) := \frac{1}{targets(source)}$, where $targets(source)$ is the number of target language words that the source word can be translated to (for a particular pair of source and target languages).

- $P(source|target) := \frac{1}{sources(targets)}$, where $sources(targets)$ is the number of source language words that the target word can be used for as translation (for a particular pair of source and target languages).

1. Initialization: For every (seed language) word that has a WordNet entry, assign its synset IDs as concepts as well as $P(concept|lexeme)$ and $P(lexeme|concept)$ scores.

2. First generation projection: For every *source* word without associated concepts that does have a translation relation to one or more *target* words (with associated concepts), calculate the *concept* probabilities as follows:

$$P(source|concept) :=$$
$$\sum_{target} P(source|target)\, P(target|concept)$$

$$P(concept|source) :=$$
$$\sum_{target} P(concept|target)\, P(target|source)$$

3. Iterate projection (second generation projection), until no more source words with translation relations to target words with associated concepts can be found.

In second and later generations, this procedure leads to a large number of low-probability associations between lexemes and concepts. To explore whether this has a negative effect, we also implemented a constrained variant (parameter `-constrained`): During projection, only those links between a lexeme and a concept are preserved that have maximum score (s=*source*, c=*concept*):

$$P(s|c) \mapsto \begin{cases} 0 & \exists k. P(s|c) < P(s|k) \\ P(s|c) & \text{otherwise} \end{cases}$$

$$P(c|s) \text{ analogously}$$

Using concept and lexicalization probability, translation inference (i.e., prediction *pred* of a target language word for a given source language word *source*) basically boils down to the following selection procedure:

$$pred = \operatorname*{argmax}_{target} \sum_{concept} P(target|concept) P(concept|source)$$

We deviate from this trivial model as we aim to produce one prediction per concept, for a number of concepts with high values for $P(concept|source)$. In many cases, we found plain probabilities as extrapolated from the graph (we use no external resources except for concept inventories) to be indistinctive, so we coupled concept probability and lexicalization probability:

$$pred = \operatorname*{argmax}_{target} \sum_{concept} \frac{P(target|concept) P(concept|target)}{P(concept|source)\, P(source|concept)}$$

The intuition behind this term is that we return translation pairs that are optimal for every concept in both translation directions (from source to target language and vice versa). Algorithmically, we did not return the maximum value, but multiple translations, so we work directly with score metrics for a particular source word *source*:

$$score(concept) = P(concept|source)P(source|concept)$$

Accordingly, the score for a translation candidate *target* is:

$$score(target) = \sum_{concept} \frac{P(target|concept)P(concept|target)}{P(concept|source)\ P(source|concept)}$$

For translation prediction, we adopt the following selection procedure:

1. For translating the word *source*, retrieve the list of candidate concepts $C = \{concept|P(concept|source) > 0\}$ and the list of candidate translations $T = \{target|\exists concept \in C.P(target|concept) > 0\}$.

2. Sort C for decreasing $score(concept)$, sort T for decreasing $score(target)$

3. Optional: Restrict C to the first m elements (parameter -maxConcepts)

4. Optional: Enforce minimum concept score κ (parameter -minConcScore), i.e., eliminate all concepts from C with $score(concept) < \kappa$. The first element of C is maintained.

5. Initialize the result set R with the maximum lexicalization(s), i.e., lexicalizations with scores identical to that of the first element in T: $R = \{target|score(target) = score(t_1)\}$

6. For every element c_i in C, and those lexicalizations of c_i that are not R, add the lexicalization *target* with maximum $P(target|concept)$ score to R. For candidates with identical $P(target|concept)$, return the target with maximum $score(target)$, i.e., maximum $P(concept|target)$, the highest degree of specificity.

7. Optional: Enforce minimum lexicalization score τ (parameter -minLexScore), i.e., eliminate all predictions *target* from R with $score(target) < \min(\tau, score(t_1))$

8. Iterate in step 6 until no more lexicalizations are being added. Optional: limit iterations to n (parameter -maxLexPerConcept)

This procedure has a considerable number of parameters:

- The concept inventory being used

- unrestricted or constrained (-constrained) projection

- m (-maxConcepts): maximum number of concepts considered for translation inference

- n (-maxLexPerConcept): maximum number of lexicalizations per concept

- κ (-minConcScore): minimum $score(concept)$ for concepts considered during translation

- τ (-minLexScore): minimum $score(target)$ for possible translations

For every translation *target*, we return $score(target)$. For the official evaluation, the task organizers applied an additional threshold of 0.5 onto these values. As the aggregate diagram in Figure 1 does, however, show, our systems perform best (in terms of F1) without this additional threshold. For our TIAD submission, this feature space was partially explored only, and it is likely that the KDictionary dictionaries used for evaluation require a different setting from the Apertium dictionaries that we take as input. As mentioned above, the Apertium dictionaries are designed for machine translation, so they are optimized for capturing the most frequent translation(s), whereas KDictionaries are designed for educational purposes, so they are optimized for capturing the most precise definition of words. In consequence, it is possible that a larger m and a lower κ score lead to better results on KDictionary data than they do on Apertium data. Our primary goal was thus not to fine-tune our systems to the Apertium data, but instead, to assess the contribution of concept inventories on translation inference across dictionaries.

3. Data & Preprocessing

We use the tab-separated value (TSV) edition of the dictionaries provided by the task organizers. Whereas we only use the languages and language pairs provided in these dictionaries, it would be possible to add more language pairs to be processed by our approach, as long as they are available in the TIAD-TSV format. We provide such data for more than 1,500 language pairs as part of the ACoLi dictionary graph (Chiarcos et al., 2020),[3] but this has not been considered in this experiment.

As for concept inventories, we use WordNet data, and we expect it to come as TSV data in accordance to the Open Multilingual WordNet specifications (Bond and Foster, 2013, OMW),[4] i.e., a three-column table containing synset ID in the first column, the string 'lemma' (or other relation identifiers) in the second column, and the word form in the third column. As for the word form, we differ from the OMW format by requiring that it is a Turtle string with a language tag, e.g., `"able"@en` instead if `able` in the English OMW WordNet. For OMW data, we provide a script that adds quotes and BCP47 language tags. We also provide a converter that produces OMW TSV from the RDF edition of Princeton WordNet 3.1.

A key advantage of OMW data is that it provides cross-linguistically uniform synset identifiers, so that multiple

---

[3] `https://github.com/acoli-repo/acoli-dicts`

[4] `http://compling.hss.ntu.edu.sg/omw/`

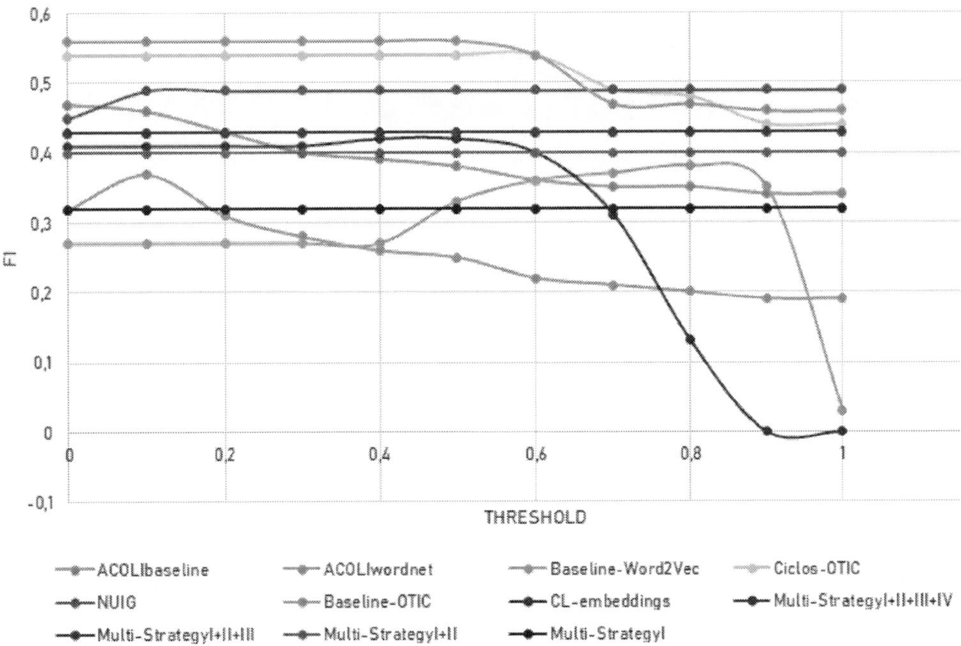

Figure 1: Official systems results (F1) per threshold.

WordNets can be combined for concept induction,[5] and our experiments included concept projection from multiple languages. The submitted system was based on the respective target language edition of OMW dictionaries (e.g., French for predicting English translations for French), as our internal experiments (see Tab. 3 below) indicated that combining multiple OMW dictionaries can produce worse results. Aside from projecting WordNet synsets, we also provide a baseline system that uses target language expressions instead of concepts (i.e., it is initialized with every target language expression being mapped to itself as a concept). The objective for doing so is to provide and to evaluate a knowledge-poor approach and also to evaluate the potential benefits that WordNet synsets might entail for this task.

4. Evaluation and Extensions

4.1. TIAD-2020 results

Based on the internal parameter optimization, we submitted results for the configurations summarized in Table 1, with the full Apertium graph as training data. Aiming for a typical number of translations per pair, we limited our predictions to the five highest-scoring translations. For achieving the reported results on precision (P), recall (R), F1 (F) and coverage (C), the task organizers applied an additional threshold of 0.5. Aside from the formal evaluation, they also provide the average results for variable thresholds, indicating that our systems perform better without an additional threshold (Table 2).

Both in our internal evaluation and in the official results, we found that using WordNet synsets for translation inference leads to a substantial decrease of translation quality in comparison to our baseline system that just projects translations. In terms of F1 measure, and without an additional threshold, this baseline system performs second among participant systems, whereas the WordNet-based system (in all configurations tested by the task organizers) ranks among the last three.

This may not be the last word on the usefulness of WordNet for translation inference across dictionaries, but it indicates that WordNet synsets are probably too coarse-grained for this task, so that relevant lexical distinctions are lost.[6] This may be compensated by corpus information about concept and lexicalization frequency, or, alternatively, by distributional methods to assess the prototypicality of a lexeme for a synset, e.g., the cosine similarity between word embeddings and synset embeddings as produced by (Rothe and Schütze, 2017). This approach can be a road to be explored in the future. For the moment, the intermediate summary is that projection-based translation inference performs better when translations are directly projected. It is conceivable to have better performance when word senses are projected, rather than synsets, but then, elaborate statistics about word sense frequencies would be necessary to select among projected word senses – that we do not possess at the moment.

---

[5]In principle, OMW synset identifiers can be used to generate translations *without any additional dictionary data*, for our TIAD-2020 contribution, we excluded the respective target language WordNet from projection experiments.

[6]As the high coverage of the ACoLi WordNet with threshold 0.0 (Tab. 2) shows, the drop in recall in comparison to the ACoLi baseline configuration is not the result of insufficient lexical coverage in the respective WordNets.

source	pt	pt	en	en	fr	fr
target	en	fr	fr	pt	en	pt
ACoLi WordNet, unconstrained, threshold 0.5						
WordNet	OMW Portuguese		OMW English		OMW French	
m	0.0	0.0	0.0	0.0	0.0	0.0
n	0.0	0.0	0.0	0.0	0.0	0.0
κ	∞	∞	∞	∞	∞	∞
τ	∞	∞	∞	∞	∞	∞
P	0.67	0.6	0.54	0.59	0.66	0.62
R	0.16	0.12	0.13	0.18	0.2	0.15
F	0.25	0.2	0.21	0.28	0.31	0.24
C	0.34	0.17	0.28	0.34	0.31	0.23
ACoLi Baseline, unconstrained, threshold 0.5						
m	0.0	0.0	0.0	0.0	0.0	0.0
n	0.0	0.0	0.0	0.0	0.0	0.0
κ	∞	∞	∞	∞	∞	∞
τ	∞	∞	∞	∞	∞	∞
P	0.66	0.64	0.48	0.57	0.63	0.63
R	0.26	0.26	0.24	0.3	0.32	0.27
F	0.38	0.37	0.32	0.39	0.42	0.38
C	0.54	0.36	0.51	0.55	0.48	0.42
best-performing participant system per language						
	Ciclos-OTIC	ACoLi Baseline	Ciclos-OTIC	NUIG	ACoLi Baseline	Ciclos-OTIC
F	0.53	0.37	0.5	0.49	0.42	0.6
C	0.79	0.36	0.74	0.55	0.48	0.74
baseline	OTIC	OTIC	OTIC	OTIC	OTIC	OTIC
F	0.51	0.72	0.48	0.53	0.48	0.62
C	0.76	0.8	0.68	0.71	0.54	0.72

Table 1: Official TIAD-2020 results per language

system	P	R	F	C
better-performing participant systems (wrt. F1 score)				
Ciclos-OTIC	0.64	0.47	0.54	0.76
NUIG	0.77	0.35	0.49	0.54
ACoLi baseline, unconstrained (best threshold and official threshold)				
0.0	0.37	0.64	0.47	0.96
0.5	0.60	0.28	0.38	0.48
ACoLi WordNet, unconstrained (best thresholds and official threshold)				
0.0	0.22	0.64	0.32	0.96
0.1	0.52	0.28	0.37	0.48
0.5	0.61	0.16	0.25	0.28
baselines (with thresholds)				
W2V (0.8)	0.48	0.32	0.38	0.59
W2V (0.5)	0.30	0.37	0.33	0.68
OTIC (0.5)	0.69	0.48	0.56	0.71

Table 2: TIAD-2020 evaluation results: Averaged scores for systems with variable threshold

4.2. Constrained concept projection

For the official TIAD evaluation, we submitted systems with unconstrained concept projection only. In a follow-up experiment, we also evaluated constrained projection as a promising direction to counter the weakness of WordNet-based concept projection. This may indeed be the case, as we could confirm that constrained projection systematically outperforms unconstrained projection of WordNet synsets. For this evaluation, we replicated the TIAD evaluation setting by aiming to predict an Esperanto-English dictionary (and excluding it from the training data). Our evaluation setup differs from TIAD evaluation in that we do not exclude out-of-vocabulary words (that cannot be predicted from other dictionaries). Table 3 summarizes the overall results, but even in this configuration, direct projection of translation outperformed concept-based translation inference. As a side-observation, we found that using multilingual WordNets can have a negative impact on precision, possibly because of imprecisions in the alignment between multilingual synsets. We also found that concept projection from *selected* dictionaries (here Esperanto-Spanish and Spanish-English only) may lead to slightly better F1 scores than projection over the *full* set of dictionaries. However, it is not clear whether this represents a factual improvement, as it is naturally accompanied with a lower degree of coverage (not reported in the table).

4.3. Comparison with embedding projection

Our second objective was to evaluate concept-based translation inference in comparison with the embedding projection we provided to TIAD-2019. Unfortunately, the results are not directly comparable, so that they can be evaluated only for the internal evaluation setup also applied for constrained concept projection.

Our TIAD-2019 system employed a simple technique for projecting word embeddings from a seed language (or, if multilingual embeddings are available, from multiple seed languages) over the translation graph. For a given word in the source language, with embedding $\vec{s}$, its translations are predicted from the cosine similarity between $\vec{s}$ and the vectors of translation candidates $\vec{t_{1..n}}$ in the target languages. Aside from seed languages and the original word embeddings, its main parameters are the number of translation candidates returned (-maxMatches) and a minimum similarity threshold applied to the predictions (-minScore). We used English as a seed language, with the same vectors (50-dimensional GloVe embeddings) as in our TIAD-2019 submission.

The results are summarized in Tab. 4: We report the best-performing configurations for -minSimilarity=0.0 (-maxMatches $\in$ $\{1,...,5\}$), -maxMatches=5 (-minSimilarity $\in$ $\{0.0, 0.1, ..., 1.0\}$) and -minSimilarity=0.9 (-maxMatches $\in \{1,...,5\}$). One important observation here is that the best-performing configuration is one that limits the number of predicted translations to 1, indicating that the neural model performs best for predicting the translations based on the *main* sense. In other words, the Apertium dictionaries seem to avoid additional synonyms for synonymous target language translations of a given source word, but to provide alternative translations to express target language translations that relate to different source language senses (and are not synonymous in the target language).

The question is now whether WordNet concepts can be used in a meaningful manner to provide translations for secondary senses. In line with the findings of the TIAD-2020 evaluation, the unconstrained WordNet systems basically fail and are outperformed by direct translation projection ('ACoLi baseline') by a large margin. However, this is not the case for *constrained* WordNet systems that reach (or,

depending on configuration, beat) the neural baseline. This indicates that our approach is indeed capable of preserving lexicographically relevant sense distinctions. The overall best-performing system is, however, not based on WordNet concepts, but on direct translation projection.

Furthermore, we find that projection is an effective approach only if it is limited. Constrained projection generally produces better results, in particular for WordNet concepts, and the additional filters that κ, τ, n and m provide can be employed to reach further, substantial, improvements over the vanilla systems we submitted to TIAD-2020. Although we cannot evaluate on TIAD task data directly, we see our approach as a promising direction for future participation in future tasks. In particular, we substantially outperform the best-performing TIAD-2020 system, the OTIC baseline provided by the task organizers.[7]

5. Discussion & Conclusion

In this paper, we described the vanilla implementation we provided for the Third Shared Task on Translation Inference Across Dictionaries, as well as a number of subsequently developed improvements to this system.

We developed our system in an attempt to address a likely source of shortcomings of our earlier TIAD-2019 system. We did not resubmit our TIAD-2019 system, however, because we expected the evaluation data to be identical. This is not the case, and the data may have different characteristics than the 2019 data, as the substantial boost in performance of the organizer baseline system systems indicate. Instead, we performed a comparative evaluation for our 2019 and 2020 systems on the EO-EN Apertium dictionary.

We assume that our 2019 system, based on the projection of embeddings for lexical entries over the translation graph, performs relatively well on capturing the most frequent sense, but that it fails for translation relations of secondary senses. We thus explored the possibility of projecting WordNet synsets over the translation graph, and using these for translation inference. In order to evaluate the effectiveness of synsets for this purpose, we also performed a baseline experiment where we projected translations instead of concepts. To our surprise, This baseline outperformed WordNet-based translation inference in all configurations.

This is also confirmed by the TIAD evaluation, albeit our baseline fares relatively well among the first three systems (with variable threshold) – the WordNet system does not.

In the internal evaluation, we also compared our 2019 system. In its vanilla configuration (with unrestricted projec-

---

[7] As for the comparably poor performance of the OTIC baseline in our setting in comparison to the TIAD-2020 blind evaluation, this seems to be due to a coverage issue. We ran the evaluation over the entire Esperanto vocabulary in the Apertium graph. However, when out-of-vocabulary words are excluded from the evaluation, i.e., words for which no pivot language translation can be found, OTIC (pivot Spanish, threshold 0.5) yields precision 0.67, recall 0.62, and F1 0.65, roughly corresponding to the TIAD-2020 scores of the OTIC system. Another difference in our evaluation was that we did not distinguish homonyms with different part of speech tags.

constrained	κ	τ	n	m	WordNet	dictionaries	P	R	F
no	0	0	∞	∞	none	all	0.26	0.32	0.29
yes	0	0	∞	∞	none	all	0.52	0.25	0.33
no	0	0	∞	∞	none	EO-ES-EN	0.63	0.22	0.33
yes	0	0	∞	∞	none	EO-ES-EN	0.68	0.18	0.28
no	0	0	∞	∞	en	EO-ES-EN	0.10	0.24	0.14
yes	0	0	∞	∞	en	EO-ES-EN	0.48	0.19	0.27
no	0	0	∞	∞	en	all	0.03	0.36	0.05
yes	0	0	∞	∞	en	all	0.34	0.27	0.30
no	0	0	∞	∞	all*	all	0.06	0.43	0.11
yes	0	0	∞	∞	all	all	0.22	0.33	0.26

*all WordNets: ca, en, es, eu, gl, it, pt

Table 3: Evaluating constrained projection

system configuration					evaluation		
ACoLi-neural, GLoVe 6B (TIAD-2019 system)							
-maxMatches	*-minScore*	*seed language*	*embeddings*	*length*	*P*	*R*	*F*
1	0.0	en	GloVe 6B	50	0.67	0.22	0.33
5	0.9	en	GloVe 6B	50	0.58	0.22	0.32
2	0.9	en	GloVe 6B	50	0.63	0.22	0.33
translation projection ('ACoLi baseline', unconstrained)							
m	*n*	κ	τ	*WordNet*	*P*	*R*	*F*
∞	∞	0.0	0	none	0.26	0.32	0.29
3	1	0.3	0	none	0.55	0.47	**0.51**
translation projection ('ACoLi baseline', constrained)							
∞	∞	0.0	0	none	0.52	0.25	0.34
3	1	0.3	0	none	0.58	0.43	**0.49**
concept projection ('ACoLi WordNet', constrained)							
∞	∞	0	0	en	0.34	0.27	0.30
3	2	0.3	0	en	0.44	0.44	0.44
ACoLi TIAD-2020 systems (unconstrained)							
ACoLi Baseline				none	0.26	0.32	0.29
ACoLi WordNet				en	0.03	0.36	0.05
OTIC (TIAD-2020 best-performing system, default and best threshold)							
configuration		*pivot language*		*-minScore*	*P*	*R*	*F*
default threshold		Catalan		0.5	0.65	0.19	0.30
best threshold		Catalan		0.2	0.59	0.21	0.31
default configuration		Spanish		0.5	0.67	0.21	0.32
best configuration		Spanish		0.0	0.64	0.23	0.33

Table 4: Comparing TIAD-2020 baseline, concept projection, translation projection and embedding projection techniques for predicting the Apertium EO-EN dictionary (best-performing configurations).

tion), the ACoLi baseline also falls behind that. However, in an extension of our TIAD system that implements *constrained projection*, where only the highest-scoring lexicalization and concept probabilities are preserved, lead to better F1 scores, and further improvements can be achieved if concept (translation) projection is limited to a low number of translation candidates (3) and further confidence thresholds are applied. The improvements bring both concept projection and translation projection approaches to the performance of original embedding projection technique, and the overall best-performing system (in our internal evaluation) is a configuration of the translation projection approach.

Our system is both simple and knowledge-poor. It does not require any multilingual data beyond bilingual dictionaries, and it can be applied (apparently with even better results) without monolingual sense inventories. Obviously, this is a natural starting point for further extensions. We extrapolate translation probabilities, concept probabilities and lexicalization probabilities only from the structure of the lexical resource(s), but empirical frequency measurements and other corpus-derived information may provide a much more accurate picture (for the effective use of a lexeme, at least, although maybe less so for its lexicographic characteristics). In particular, future directions may include a combination of neural and concept-based approaches. As such, translation inference from projected synsets may be more robust and the coverage may improve if lexicalization is not directly based on WordNet, but if the distributional similarity between target language words and synsets is used as a measurement of lexical prototypicality of a word for a concept. Such an approach requires synset embeddings that reside in the same feature space as the corresponding word embeddings, and indeed, this would be possible with techniques for inducing synset embeddings, e.g., as described by Rothe and Schütze (2017).

Another possible extension is to combine our approach with the OTIC baseline. In our internal evaluation, the OTIC baseline suffered from coverage issues in the pivot language dictionaries. It was thus outperformed by the projection-based approach as this takes the entire source and target language vocabulary provided by the Apertium dictionary graph into consideration. Future experiments may adopt OTIC for source language lexemes that do have a pivot language translations and use concept, translation or embedding projection for out-of-vocabulay elements.

6. Acknowledgements

The research of the first and third author of this paper on this topic was financially supported by the project "Linked Open Dictionaries" (LiODi, 2015-2020), funded by the German Ministry for Education and Research (BMBF) as an Independent Research Group on eHumanities. The research of the second and third author was financially supported by the Research and Innovation Action "Prêt-a-LLOD. Ready-to-use Multilingual Linked Language Data for Knowledge Services across Sectors" funded in the European Union's Horizon 2020 research and innovation programme under grant agreement No 825182.
We would like to thank the anonymous reviewers for helpful comments and feedback, and the TIAD-2020 shared task organizers and Marta Lanau Coronas for providing the code of the TIAD-2020 OTIC baseline.

7. References

Bond, F. and Foster, R. (2013). Linking and extending an open multilingual wordnet. In *Proceedings of the 51st Annual Meeting of the Association for Computational Linguistics (ACL-2013)*, pages 1352–1362.

Chiarcos, C., Fäth, C., and Abromeit, F. (2020). Annotation interoperability in the post-ISOCat era. In *Proceedings of the 12th Language Resources and Evaluation Conference (LREC 2020)*, Marseille, France. Accepted for publication.

Donandt, K. and Chiarcos, C. (2019). Translation inference through multi-lingual word embedding similarity. In J. Gracia et al., editor, *Proc. of TIAD-2019 Shared Task Translation Inference Across Dictionaries (http://ceur-ws.org/Vol-2493/) at 2nd Language Data and Knowledge (LDK) conference.*

Christiane Fellbaum, editor. (1998). *WordNet: An Electronic Lexical Database.* Language, Speech, and Communication. MIT Press, Cambridge, MA.

Pennington, J., Socher, R., and Manning, C. (2014). Glove: Global vectors for word representation. In *Proceedings of the 2014 Conference on Empirical Methods in Natural Language Processing (EMNLP)*, pages 1532–1543, Doha, Qatar, October. Association for Computational Linguistics.

Rothe, S. and Schütze, H. (2017). AutoEextend: Combining word embeddings with semantic resources. *Computational Linguistics*, 43(3):593–617.

Proceedings of the Globalex Workshop on Linked Lexicography, pages 106–110
Language Resources and Evaluation Conference (LREC 2020), Marseille, 11–16 May 2020
© European Language Resources Association (ELRA), licensed under CC-BY-NC

Graph Exploration and Cross-lingual Word Embeddings for Translation Inference Across Dictionaries

Marta Lanau-Coronas, Jorge Gracia

Aragon Institute of Engineering Research (I3A), University of Zaragoza, Spain
{mlanau, jogracia}@unizar.es

Abstract

This paper describes the participation of two different approaches in the 3rd Translation Inference Across Dictionaries (TIAD 2020) shared task. The aim of the task is to automatically generate new bilingual dictionaries from existing ones. To that end, we essayed two different types of techniques: based on graph exploration on the one hand and, on the other hand, based on cross-lingual word embeddings. The task evaluation results show that graph exploration is very effective, accomplishing relatively high precision and recall values in comparison with the other participating systems, while cross-lingual embeddings reaches high precision but smaller recall.

Keywords: Translation inference, Graph exploration, Cross-lingual word embeddings

1. Introduction

The fact that the open-source Apertium[1] bilingual dictionaries (Forcada et al., 2011) have been converted into RDF and published on the Web following Linked Data principles (Gracia et al., 2018) allows for a large variety of exploration opportunities. Nowadays, the Apertium RDF Graph[2] contains information from 22 bilingual dictionaries. However, as can be seen in Figure 1, where languages are represented as nodes and the edges symbolise the translation sets between them, not all the languages are connected to each other. In this context, the objective of the Translation Inference Across Dictionaries (TIAD) shared task[3] is to automatically generate new bilingual dictionaries based on known translations contained in this graph.

In particular, in this TIAD edicion (TIAD 2020), the participating systems were asked to generate new translations automatically among three languages, English, French, Portuguese, based on known translations contained in the Apertium RDF graph. As these languages (EN, FR, PT) are not directly connected in such a graph (see Figure 1), no translations can be obtained directly among them in this graph. Based on the available RDF data, the participants were asked to apply their methodologies to derive translations, mediated by any other language in the graph, between the pairs EN/FR, FR/PT and PT/EN. The evaluation of the results was carried out by the organisers against manually compiled pairs of K Dictionaries[4].

We have proposed two different systems for participating in the task.

1. *Cycles-OTIC*. The first one is a hybrid technique based on graph exploration. It includes translations coming from a method that explores the density of cycles in the translations graph (Villegas et al., 2016), combined with the translations obtained by the One Time Inverse

Consultation (OTIC) method, which generates translation pairs by means of an intermediate pivot language (Tanaka and Umemura, 1994).

2. *Cross-lingual embeddings*. The second proposed system has a different focus. It does not rely on the graph structure but on the distribution of embeddings across languages. To that end, we reuse the system proposed by Artetxe et al. (Artetxe et al., 2018) to build cross-lingual word embeddings trained with monolingual corpora and mapped afterwards through an intermediate language.

The remainder of this paper is organised as follows. In Section 2 we give an overview of the used techniques. Then, in Section 3 we comment the results obtained in the evaluation and, finally, in Section 4 we present some conclusions and future directions of our research.

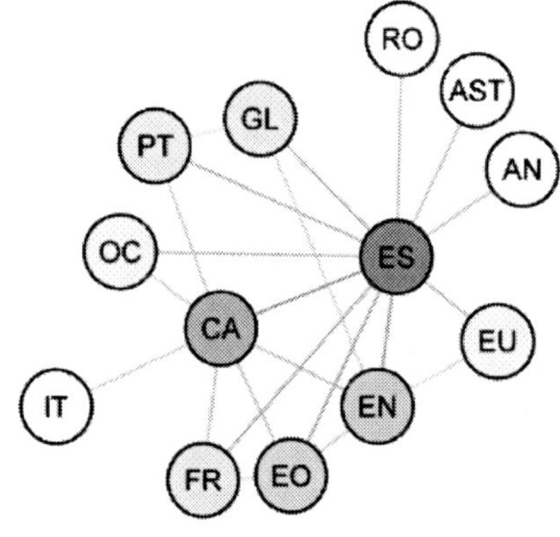

Figure 1: Apertium RDF Graph. It represents how the language pairs are connected by means of bilingual translation sets. The darker the colour, the more connections a node has. [Figure taken from https://tiad2020.unizar.es/task.html]

---

[1] https://www.apertium.org/
[2] http://linguistic.linkeddata.es/apertium/
[3] https://tiad2020.unizar.es/
[4] https://lexicala.com/resources#dictionaries

2. Systems overview

As it was stated previously, we developed two different techniques in order to automatically generate new bilingual dictionaries between the language pairs proposed in the task. Following the TIAD rules, the output data of the system was encoded in a TSV (tab separated values) file and had to contain the following information for all the translation pairs: *source and target written representation, part of speech and a confidence score.*

2.1. Cycles-OTIC system

Cycles-OTIC is a hybrid system that combines the translation pairs generated by means of the two graph-based methods described in the following paragraphs. The objective of this collaborative system is to reinforce both techniques and cover translations that can not be reached separately by any of the two methods.

Because of word polysemy, translation cannot be considered as a transitive relation. Specifically, when an intermediate language is used to generate a bilingual dictionary, the ambiguity of words in the pivot language may infer inappropriate equivalences. Avoiding those wrong translations is the main motivation of both methods.

2.1.1. Cycle-based method

The Cycle-based method was proposed by Villegas et al. (2016). The idea was using cycles to identify potential targets that may be a translation of a given word. A cycle can be considered a sequence of nodes that starts and ends in the same node, without repetitions of nodes nor edges. The confidence value of each translation is calculated by means of nodes' degree and graph density. The density is higher when higher is the number of edges in the graph, as can be seen in the Equation 1, where E represents the number of edges and V the number of vertices (nodes).

$$D = \frac{|E|}{|V| * (|V| - 1)} \qquad (1)$$

The confidence score of a potential target is assigned by the density value of the more dense cycle where the source and target words appear. This value can achieve values from 0 to 1 (from completely disconnected to fully connected graph). Table 1 (Villegas et al., 2016) shows an illustrative example of some target candidates obtained in the Apertium RDF graph when translating the English word 'forest', along with the confidence score and the more dense cycle.

2.1.2. OTIC method

The second method utilised in our system was proposed by Tanaka and Umemura (1994) and adapted by Lim et al. (2011) afterwards for the creation of multilingual lexicons. This method is known as One Time Inverse Consultation (OTIC) and its objective is to construct bilingual dictionaries through intermediate translations by a pivot language. The OTIC method, even if relatively old, has proven to be a simple but effective one and a baseline very hard to beat, as it was shown by the previous TIAD edition results (Gracia et al., 2019) and corroborated with the latest TIAD 2020 results (see Table 6).

The OTIC method works as follows. In order to avoiding ambiguities caused by polysemy, for a given word, a confidence score is assigned to each candidate translation based on the degree of overlap between the pivot translations shared by both the source and target words. The higher is the overlap, the higher is the confidence score. The computation of this value is calculated by the Equation 2, where *T1* and *T2* are the number of translations into the pivot language from the source and target words respectively, and *I* the size of the intersection between those translations.

$$score = \frac{2 * I}{T1 + T2} \qquad (2)$$

As it was mentioned before, the Apertium RDF Graph has been the source data of the experiments. In order to chose a suitable pivot language for the experiments, we explored the two possible ones: Spanish and Catalan. Table 2 shows a comparison of the size of the translation sets depending on using Spanish or Catalan as intermediate language. It can be observed that the Catalan language is quite unbalanced. For this reason, Spanish has been chosen as pivot language in our experiments[5].

2.1.3. Hybrid Cycles-OTIC method

Both methods have obtained good results in previous experiments (Villegas et al., 2016; Gracia et al., 2019). Our hypothesis is that the addition of the Cycles method should increase the coverage of the OTIC baseline, since there are possibly some translation pairs that cannot be linked through Spanish (our pivot language) but trough other languages in the graph. Additionally, we wanted to measure the benefits of adding the Cycles method in terms of precision and recall.

During development, some experiments with the Apertium RDF Graph were carried out to evaluate the performance of two possible ways of combining both methods: through the union and through the intersection of the translations results provided by both techniques. Some existing Apertium dictionaries were removed from the Apertium RDF graph and used as golden-standard during the development phase, where the explored method had to re-construct the removed Apertium dictionary. Results provided by those experiments showed that whereas the union of the translations sets from the Cycle-based and the OTIC method reached similar o even better results than the OTIC method alone, the results of the translations obtained from the intersection between both methods achieves much worse values of recall, as many correct translations reached by only one method were dismissed. Therefore we opted for the union operation when combining both systems. It was also observed that the hybrid system improved the results of the OTIC method when the pivot language has a small translation set with source and/or target languages.

Thus, the Cycles-OTIC method is simply the result of the union of the sets of translations generated by both methods individually. The translation pairs keep the confidence score obtained by the individual methods. However, when the same translation is provided by the two methods, the

---

[5]Spanish is also used as pivot language in the baseline evaluation carried out by the organisers, which uses also the same implementation: `https://gitlab.com/sid_unizar/otic`

bois-fr	0.9	[bosque-es, bosc-ca, bois-fr, arbaro-eo, forest-en]
fort-fr	0.9	[bosque-es, fort-fr, bosc-ca, arbaro-eo, forest-en]
bòsc-oc	0.833	[bosque-es, bòsc-oc, bosc-ca, forest-en]
bosque-pt	0.833	[bosque-gl, bosque-pt, bosque-es, forest-en]
floresta-pt	0.7	[fraga-gl, floresta-pt, bosque-gl, bosque-es, forest-en]
selva-es	0.619	[bosque-es, bosc-ca, arbaro-eo, fort-fr, selva-es, baso-eu, forest-en]

Table 1: 'Forest-en' best targets, its scores and cycles (Villegas et al., 2016).

	EN	FR	PT
ES	25,830	21,475	12,054
CA	33,029	6,550	7,111

Table 2: Size of the translation sets (in number of translations) for different intermediate languages (ES, CA).

score assigned is the maximum of the two values. The default threshold proposed for this combined method is 0.5.

2.2. CL-embeddings system

The second system developed makes use of cross-lingual word embeddings and a third intermediate language to generate new dictionaries. The vectors of the three languages (source, pivot and target) were all trained with monolingual corpora on Common Crawl and Wikipedia using fastTest (Grave et al., 2018). Then, they were mapped in pairs into a shared vector space through VecMap (Artetxe et al., 2018), a framework to learn cross-lingual word embedding mappings. The VecMap system allows for either a supervised or an unsupervised mode. In our case, it was supervised since we use the Apertium dictionaries as source of initial mappings between the source and intermediate monolingual embeddings, and also for the intermediate and target vectors. Given a word in the source language contained in the source vector, the algorithm gets the closest word vector in the embedding mapped. It is obtained by means of the cosine similarity metric, which can reach values from 0 to 1. The closer the vector, the higher the cosine metric. Afterwards, the same mechanism is done for getting the closest word in the target language from the one in the pivot language. Finally, the confidence score of the pair generated is computed by the product of both cosine similarity values calculated. The translation only is considered as candidate if the part of speech of source, pivot and target words are the same.

The language used as pivot between source and target were Spanish. In Table 3 can be seen the sizes of the extracts used for doing the initial mappings. These translation sets were obtained from the Apertium RDF Graph excluding those which contain spaces.

EN-ES	FR-ES	PT-ES
21610	18484	11634

Table 3: Size of the translation sets (in number of translations) used for mapping the monolingual vectors.

3. Results and Evaluation

The final evaluation of the results was carried out by the organisers against the test data[6]. These gold-standard consisted of the intersection between manually compiled pairs of K Dictionaries and the entries in Apertium dictionaries. The performance was measured in terms of precision, recall, F-measure and coverage. The official results of our systems with variable threshold are shown in Table 4 and Table 5. It can be seen that in both systems, when threshold gets higher values, precision increases while recall is reduced, as expected.

Threshold	Precision	Recall	F1	Coverage
0.0	0.64	0.47	0.54	0.76
0.1	0.64	0.47	0.54	0.76
0.2	0.64	0.47	0.54	0.76
0.3	0.64	0.47	0.54	0.76
0.4	0.64	0.47	0.54	0.76
0.5	0.65	0.47	0.54	0.75
0.6	0.67	0.45	0.54	0.73
0.7	0.73	0.38	0.49	0.63
0.8	0.74	0.36	0.48	0.60
0.9	0.77	0.31	0.44	0.53
1.0	0.77	0.31	0.44	0.53

Table 4: TIAD results for the Cycles-OTIC system with variable threshold

Threshold	Precision	Recall	F1	Coverage
0.0	0.58	0.33	0.41	0.81
0.1	0.58	0.33	0.41	0.81
0.2	0.58	0.33	0.41	0.81
0.3	0.59	0.33	0.41	0.81
0.4	0.59	0.33	0.42	0.79
0.5	0.62	0.32	0.42	0.73
0.6	0.68	0.29	0.40	0.60
0.7	0.75	0.20	0.31	0.38
0.8	0.79	0.07	0.13	0.12
0.9	0.40	0	0	0
1.0	0	0	0	0

Table 5: TIAD results for the CL-embeddings system with variable threshold

---

[6]Notice that one of the co-authors is co-organiser of TIAD. However, the test data was also treated as blind for the participating systems reported in this paper, to allow a fair comparison

System	Precision	Recall	F1	Coverage
Baseline-OTIC	0,70	0,47	0,56	0,70
Cycles-OTIC	**0,64**	**0,47**	**0,54**	**0,76**
NUIG	0,77	0,35	0,49	0,54
Multi-StrategyI+II+III+IV	0,61	0,33	0,43	0,63
Multi-StrategyI+II+III	0,62	0,33	0,43	0,63
CL-embeddings	**0,62**	**0,32**	**0,42**	**0,73**
Multi-StrategyI+II	0,65	0,30	0,40	0,59
ACOLIbaseline	0,60	0,28	0,38	0,48
Baseline-Word2Vec	0,30	0,37	0,33	0,68
Multi-StrategyI	0,63	0,22	0,32	0,44
ACOLIwordnet	0,61	0,16	0,25	0,28

Table 6: Averaged results per language pair for every system and ordered by F-measure in descending order.

A graph of the average of F-measure per threshold comparing all systems can be seen in Figure 2. The Cycles-OTIC system achieves the second position in terms of F-measure, although is beaten by the OTIC baseline. The other system, based in cross-lingual word embeddings gets the fifth position. As it is shown in Tables 4 and 5, both systems obtain high precision values, and the graph-based system obtains the highest coverage score among all the participating systems and baselines.

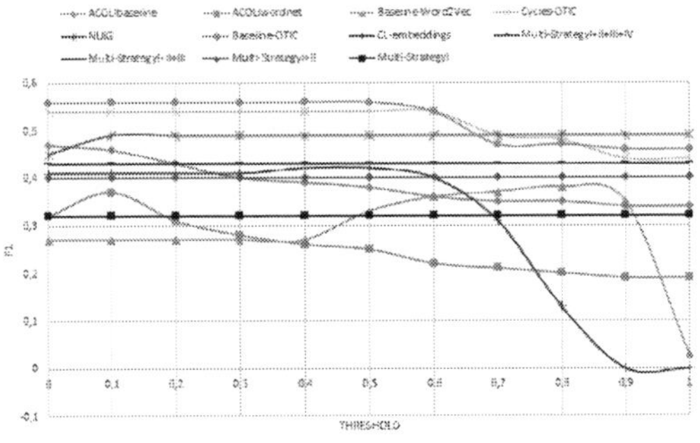

Figure 2: F1 results per different values of threshold for all systems

Discussion. The results prove our hypothesis that the addition of the Cycles method increases the coverage of the OTIC baseline. In particular from 0.70 to 0.76, being the largest value achieved in the shared task. The reason is that the Cycles method helps to discover, through alternative paths, some translation pairs that cannot be discovered through the pivot language. We see, however, that many of these extra translations are not present in the golden standard, since the value of precision drops from 0.70 to 0.64, while recall is preserved (0.47). We will perform a more careful inspection of the validation data results to better understand this effect. Out initial intuition is that the explored languages (PT, EN, FR) are already very well connected through the pivot language (SP), therefore OTIC can be very effective; while the Cycles strategy could play a more important role between other language pairs that are less directly connected in the graph.

As it can be seen in Table 6, the evaluation related to the CL-embeddings method shows that, in average, this technique has the second better value of coverage (0.73), just after the Cycles-OTIC method. The precision achieves also a high value (0.62), but regarding the recall, the value is not so high (0.32). One of the possible reasons behind this is that the embedding-based method only gives one target candidate per source entry (the one with best score). A further research considering different numbers of translations per word will be done in order to optimise recall while minimising the loss in precision.

4. Conclusions

In this paper we have described our participation in the TIAD 2020 shared task with two different techniques: one based on graph exploration and another one based on cross-lingual word embeddings. The official results provided by the organisers demonstrate that the performance of such methods for translation inference across dictionaries are good, specially in terms of precision and coverage. However none of the systems could beat the OTIC baseline in terms of F-measure, although the analysis of the results suggested us some improvements that will be carried out as future steps in this research line.

5. Acknowledgements

This work has been supported by the European Union's Horizon 2020 research and innovation programme through the projects Lynx (grant agreement No 780602) and Prêt-à-LLOD (grant agreement No 825182). It has been also partially supported by the Spanish projects TIN2016-78011-C4-3-R (AEI/FEDER, UE) and DGA/FEDER 2014-2020 "Construyendo Europa desde Aragón".

6. Bibliographical References

Artetxe, M., Labaka, G., and Agirre, E. (2018). A robust self-learning method for fully unsupervised cross-lingual mappings of word embeddings. In *Proceedings of the 56th Annual Meeting of the Association for Computational Linguistics (Volume 1: Long Papers)*, pages 789–798.

Forcada, M. L., Ginestí-Rosell, M., Nordfalk, J., O'Regan, J., Ortiz-Rojas, S., Pérez-Ortiz, J. A., Sánchez-Martínez,

F., Ramírez-Sánchez, G., and Tyers, F. M. (2011). Apertium: a free/open-source platform for rule-based machine translation. *Machine translation*, 25(2):127–144.

Gracia, J., Villegas, M., Gomez-Perez, A., and Bel, N. (2018). The apertium bilingual dictionaries on the web of data. *Semantic Web*, 9(2):231–240.

Gracia, J., Kabashi, B., Kernerman, I., Lanau-Coronas, M., and Lonke, D. (2019). Results of the Translation Inference Across Dictionaries 2019 Shared Task. In Jorge Gracia, et al., editors, *Proc. of TIAD-2019 Shared Task – Translation Inference Across Dictionaries co-located with the 2nd Language, Data and Knowledge Conference (LDK 2019)*, pages 1–12. CEUR Press.

Grave, E., Bojanowski, P., Gupta, P., Joulin, A., and Mikolov, T. (2018). Learning word vectors for 157 languages. In *Proceedings of the International Conference on Language Resources and Evaluation (LREC 2018)*.

Lim, L. T., Ranaivo-Malançon, B., and Tang, E. K. (2011). Low cost construction of a multilingual lexicon from bilingual lists. *Polibits*, (43):45–51.

Tanaka, K. and Umemura, K. (1994). Construction of a bilingual dictionary intermediated by a third language. In *Proceedings of the 15th conference on Computational linguistics-Volume 1*, pages 297–303. Association for Computational Linguistics.

Villegas, M., Melero, M., Bel, N., and Gracia, J. (2016). Leveraging rdf graphs for crossing multiple bilingual dictionaries. In *Proceedings of the Tenth International Conference on Language Resources and Evaluation (LREC'16)*, pages 868–876.

Proceedings of the Globalex Workshop on Linked Lexicography, pages 111–115
Language Resources and Evaluation Conference (LREC 2020), Marseille, 11–16 May 2020
© European Language Resources Association (ELRA), licensed under CC-BY-NC

Multi-Strategy system for translation inference across dictionaries

Lacramioara Dranca
Centro Universitario de la Defensa
Ctra. de Huesca, Zaragoza, España
licri@unizar.es

Abstract

This paper describes four different strategies proposed to the TIAD 2020 Shared Task for automatic translation inference across dictionaries. The proposed strategies are based on the analysis of Apertium RDF graph, taking advantage of characteristics such as translation using multiple paths, synonyms and similarities between lexical entries from different lexicons and cardinality of possible translations through the graph. The four strategies were trained and validated on the Apertium RDF $EN \leftrightarrow ES$ dictionary, showing promising results. Finally, the strategies, applied together, obtained an F-measure of 0.43 in the task of inferring the dictionaries proposed in the shared task, ranking thus third with respect to the other new systems presented to the TIAD 2020 Shared Task. No system presented to the shared task exceeded the baseline proposed by the TIAD organizers.

Keywords: Dictionary generation, Automatic inference translation, Graph based heuristics

1. Introduction

The TIAD (Gracia and Kabashi, 2020) shared task is aimed at exploring methods and techniques that infer translations indirectly between language pairs, based on other bilingual resources.

The organizers provide Apertium RDF (Gracia et al., 2014), a set of 22 Apertium bilingual dictionaries, published as linked data on the Web. The Apertium RDF groups the bilingual dictionaries in the same graph, interconnected through the common lexical entries of the monolingual lexicons that they share.

Although the Apertium RDF graph contains multiple connections that represent translations, not all the Apertium RDF lexicons are interconnected. The challenge of the task is to automatically infer translations between English and French lexicons, French and Portuguese lexicons, and Portuguese and English lexicons, respectively, based on the existing bilingual dictionaries from Apertium RDF. Additionally, there is also possible to make use of other freely available sources of background knowledge to improve performance, as long as no direct translation among the target language pairs is applied.

The automatically inferenced translation methods could reduce the costs of constructing bilingual dictionaries. Nevertheless, despite the advantages that the automatic translation inference across dictionaries might have, this task is still challenging (Gracia et al., 2019).

Translation inference across dictionaries based on current methods such as word embeddings (Donandt and Chiarcos, 2019; Garcia et al., 2019) still obtains lower results than more traditional heuristics (Tanaka and Umemura, 1994). Some graph traversal heuristics for this shared task have been proposed previously in (Torregrosa et al., 2019). The hypothesis of this work is that graph-based heuristics may still have potential for improving results. The aim of this work is to try to take full advantage of the potential of translation inference heuristics, based on the Apertium RDF graph, with the benefit of obtaining possibly more interpretable methods.

2. Materials and methods

The Apertium RDF (Gracia et al., 2014) is used to develop the proposed translation heuristics proposed in this paper. The Figure 1 shows the Apertium RDF graph available for the TIAD shared task. The graph contains 13 lexicons, the solid lines show the available translations, the dashed line between English (EN) and Spanish (ES) lexicons is the available translation set that is used in this work for training and validation of the translation strategies proposed in this paper. The dotted lines show the translations aimed to infer with the TIAD shared task and are used for testing the strategies.

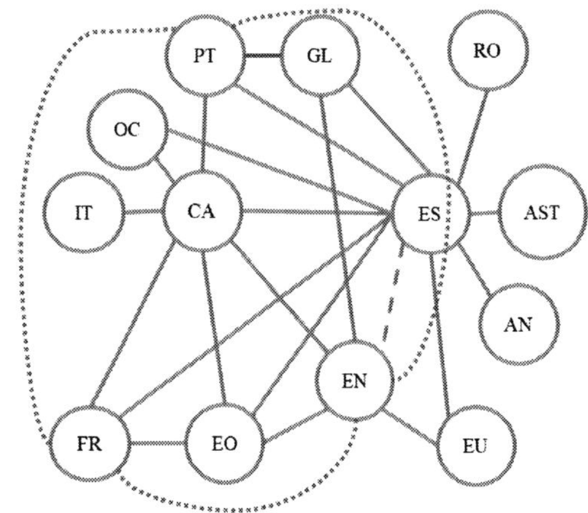

Figure 1: Apertium RDF Graph

As explained by (Saralegi et al., 2011) inferring an A-B bilingual dictionary by merging A-P and P-B dictionaries, using P as pivot lexicon, often produce wrong translations due to polysemous pivot words. To avoid this problem, four translation heuristics or strategies are proposed here, in order to infer translations from a lexicon A to a lexicon B. These strategies are presented below.

2.1. Strategy I

A natural way to address the problem, when multiple paths are available between lexicons A and B, is to validate a translation from $a \in A$ to $b \in B$ if there are multiple paths from a to b across different pivot lexicons. We consider the translation $T = a \leftrightarrow b$ as correct if:

$$b \in translation_{A \leftrightarrow P \leftrightarrow B}(a) \cap translation_{A \leftrightarrow P' \leftrightarrow B}(a) \tag{1}$$

where

$$\begin{aligned} translation_{A \leftrightarrow P \leftrightarrow B}(a) = \\ translation_{P \leftrightarrow B}(translation_{A \leftrightarrow P}(a)) \end{aligned} \tag{2}$$

The strategy requires the existence of two different paths from word a to word b, each path crossing a different pivot lexicon (P and P'), in order to consider the translation as correct. Figure 2 illustrates this strategy (solid lines show existing translations, dashed line shows a new inferred translation). Notice that a, p, b, p' form a 4-cycle graph, a heuristic already used by (Torregrosa et al., 2019).

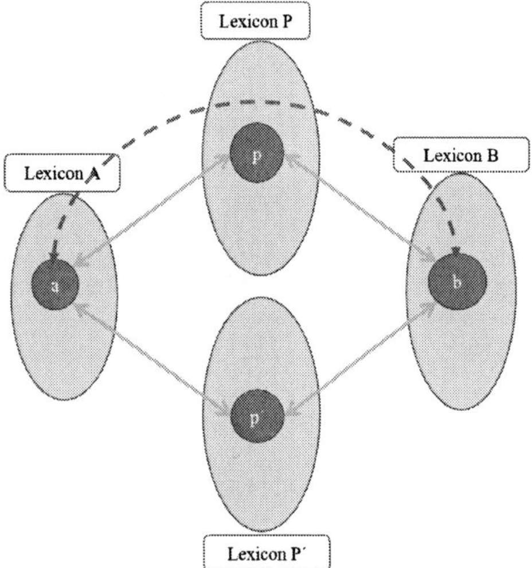

Figure 2: Translation inference across multiple paths

2.2. Strategy II

As mentioned before, the main problem of a direct translation through a pivot lexicon is polysemous words. The polysemy of pivot words implies several meanings for the same word. However, considering the available dictionaries as complete, if the cardinality of a translation through a pivot lexicon is one in both directions, then we assume that it is less likely the translation to be influenced by polysemous words in the pivot lexicon. For these situations we have considered the translation as correct, as expressed in the following equation:

$$\begin{aligned} a \in A, b \in B \\ (translation_{A \leftrightarrow P \leftrightarrow B}(a) = \{b\}) \\ \wedge (translation_{B \leftrightarrow P \leftrightarrow A}(b) = \{a\}) \\ \Rightarrow \exists T = a \leftrightarrow b \end{aligned} \tag{3}$$

2.3. Strategy III

This strategy attempts to exploit the similarities between different lexicons. A lexical similarity measure s is defined for $a \in A, b \in B$ as follows:

$$s(a,b) = \frac{2 * levenshtein(a,b)}{length(a) + length(b)} \tag{4}$$

This similarity measure is based on the levenstein distance and the leght of the compared words. Notice that for $a = b$ then $s(a,b) = 0$.

Before calculating the lexical similarity between two words, the special characters, typical of each lexicon, have been replaced by the most similar characters from the English alphabet.

For the inference of translations based on lexical similarity for $a \in A, b \in B$ we have considered three settings as follows.

The equation 5 exploits the end-to-end lexical similarity across a path with P as pivot lexicon:

$$\begin{aligned} (b \in translation_{A \leftrightarrow P \leftrightarrow B}(a)) \wedge (s(a,b) < t_1) \\ \Rightarrow \exists T = a \leftrightarrow b \end{aligned} \tag{5}$$

The equation 6 exploits the overall lexical similarity across a path with P as pivot lexicon:

$$\begin{aligned} (p \in translation_{A \leftrightarrow P}(a)) \wedge (b \in translation_{P \leftrightarrow B}(p)) \\ \wedge (s(a,p) + s(p,b) < t_2) \\ \Rightarrow \exists T = a \leftrightarrow b \end{aligned} \tag{6}$$

The equation 7 exploits the lexical similarity between translations of the same word $a \in A$ to different lexicons:

$$\begin{aligned} (b \in translation_{A \leftrightarrow P \leftrightarrow B}(a)) \\ \wedge (p' \in translation_{A \leftrightarrow P'}(a)) \\ \wedge (s(b,p') < t_3) \\ \Rightarrow \exists T = a \leftrightarrow b \end{aligned} \tag{7}$$

The three equations have a corresponding threshold that has been adjusted during training phase. In this work, t_1 and t_3 have been set to 0.17 and t_2 to 0.5.

2.4. Strategy IV

This strategy attempts to exploit the existence of synonymous words in a lexicon, words that might have the same translation to another lexicon. As with the previous strategy 2.3, three settings have been considered.

The first approach is shown in Figure 3 (solid lines show existing translations, dashed line shows new inferred translation)

The equivalent equation is shown below. For $a \in A, b \in B$,

$$\begin{aligned} \{p_k, p_l\} \in translation_{A \leftrightarrow P}(a)) \\ \wedge \{p_k, p_l\} \in translation_{B \leftrightarrow P}(b)) \\ \Rightarrow \exists T = a \leftrightarrow b \end{aligned} \tag{8}$$

where p_k anf p_l might be synonymous words in lexicon P, as reported also in (Torregrosa et al., 2019).

The second approach related to synonymous words is shown in Figure 4 (solid lines show existing translations, dashed lines show new inferred translations)

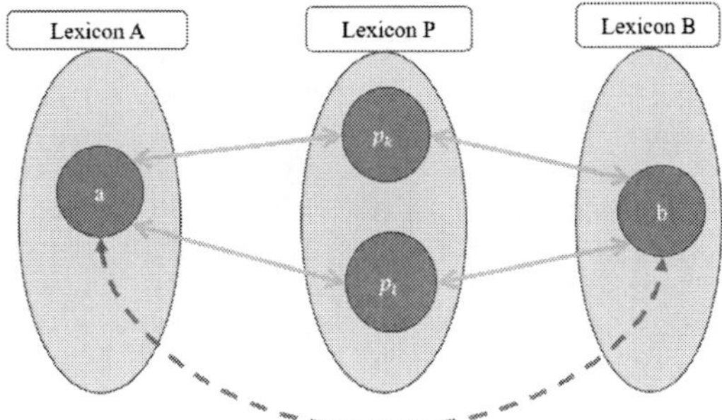

Figure 3: Synonymous strategy across one path

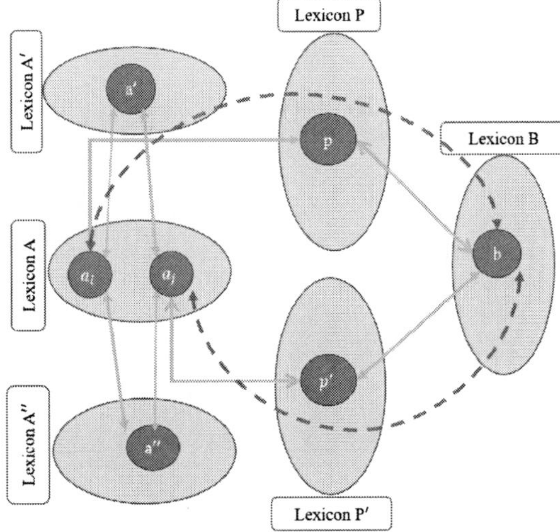

Figure 4: Synonymous strategy across two paths

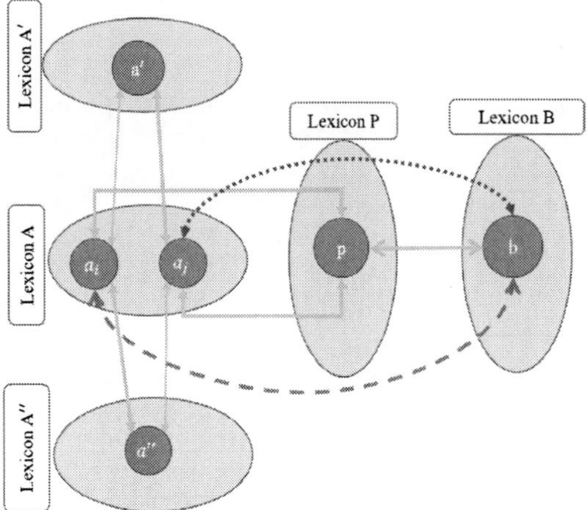

Figure 5: Synonymous strategy across one paths, with previously inferred translations

For $a_i, a_j \in A, b \in B$,

$$
\begin{aligned}
&(a_i \in translation_{A \leftrightarrow P \leftrightarrow B}(b)) \\
&\wedge (a_j \in translation_{A \leftrightarrow P \leftrightarrow B}(b)) \\
&\wedge (\exists T_1 = a_j \leftrightarrow b) \\
&\wedge (\exists a' \in A') \wedge (\exists a'' \in A'') \\
&\wedge \{a_i, a_j\} \in translation_{A' \leftrightarrow A}(a')) \\
&\wedge \{a_i, a_j\} \in translation_{A'' \leftrightarrow A}(a'')) \\
&\Rightarrow (\exists T_2 = a_i \leftrightarrow b)
\end{aligned}
\tag{10}
$$

where a_i and a_j are synonymous words in lexicon A.

3. Results and discussion

The strategies have been evaluated on the available $EN \leftrightarrow ES$ Apertium dictionary and tested by TIAD organizers on $EN \leftrightarrow FR$, $PT \leftrightarrow EN$ and $FR \leftrightarrow PT$ dictionaries. The obtained results are shown below.

3.1. Validation of $EN \leftrightarrow ES$ inferred translations

The validation results of the different translation inference strategies can be seen in Table 1. Proper nouns were not considered for training and validation tasks.

As may be noticed in Table 1, individually, the best strategy for the $EN \leftrightarrow ES$ translations case, considering its F-measure, is strategy II. However, the lexical similarity, the basis of strategy III, is close to strategy II and largely overlaps its correct translations. In the case of Strategy I, it seems important the correct selection of the paths to use, that is, the lexical pivots. Different combinations of two lexical pivots may obtain high degrees of precision (see results for strategy I'), depending on the pivot lexicons used. The path $EN \leftrightarrow EO \leftrightarrow ES$ proven lower precision for both strategies I and IV.

The combination of strategies II, III, IV, without considering Strategy I, also produces competitive results.

The equivalent equation is shown below. For $a_i, a_j \in A, b \in B$,

$$
\begin{aligned}
&(a_i \in translation_{A \leftrightarrow P \leftrightarrow B}(b)) \\
&\wedge (a_j \in translation_{A \leftrightarrow P' \leftrightarrow B}(b)) \\
&\wedge (\exists a' \in A') \wedge (\exists a'' \in A'') \\
&\wedge \{a_i, a_j\} \in translation_{A' \leftrightarrow A}(a')) \\
&\wedge \{a_i, a_j\} \in translation_{A'' \leftrightarrow A}(a'')) \\
&\Rightarrow (\exists T_1 = a_i \leftrightarrow b) \wedge (\exists T_2 = a_j \leftrightarrow b)
\end{aligned}
\tag{9}
$$

where a_i and a_j are considered as synonymous words in lexicon A.

This configuration assumes a graph cycle of $length = 7$ $words$ across 6 lexicons.

The third approach related to synonymous words is shown in Figure 5 (solid lines show existing translations, dotted line show an inferred translation in a previous step of the algorithm, dashed line shows a new inferred translation)

The equivalent equation is shown below.

Strategy	Precision	Recall	F measure
I	0.87	0.39	0.54
I'	0.94	0.29	0.44
II	0.85	0.48	0.62
III	0.88	0.46	0.60
IV'	0.81	0.15	0.25
$I + II$	0.83	0.63	0.72
$I + II + III$	0.81	0.66	**0.73**
$I + II + III + IV'$	0.80	0.67	**0.73**
$II + III$	0.83	0.59	0.69
$II + III + IV'$	0.81	0.65	0.72

Table 1: Validation results of $EN \leftrightarrow ES$ translations

I' path $EN \leftrightarrow EO \leftrightarrow ES$ has not been considered
IV' path $EN \leftrightarrow EO \leftrightarrow ES$ has not been considered

3.2. Test of TIAD inferred translations

Several systems have been presented to TIAD 2020 shared task. The average results of those systems can be seen in Table 2 (in bold letters the strategies proposed in this paper).

System	P	R	F
Baseline-OTIC	0.70	0.47	0.56
Ciclos-OTIC	0.64	0.47	0.54
NUIG	0.77	0.35	0.49
Multi-StategyI+II+III+IV	**0.61**	**0.33**	**0.43**
Multi-StategyI+II+III	**0.62**	**0.33**	**0.43**
CL-embeddings	0.62	0.32	0.42
Multi-StategyI+II	**0.65**	**0.30**	**0.40**
ACOLIbaseline	0.60	0.28	0.38
Baseline-Word2Vec	0.30	0.37	0.33
Multi-StategyI	**0.63**	**0.22**	**0.32**
ACOLIwordnet	0.61	0.16	0.25

Table 2: TIAD shared task - average systems results

P stands for Precision
R stands for Recall
F stands for F-measure

As it can be seen, the four strategies proposed in this paper, applied together, obtain a medium result, ranking third with respect to the other new systems presented to the shared task and below the Baseline-OTIC of the task. (results ordered by F-measure - F columns in Table 2). It should be noted that the OTIC method proposed as baseline by the TIAD organizers continues to be the method with the best results, despite being a traditional method (Tanaka and Umemura, 1994) that only use the Apertium RDF graph.

The results for the three dictionaries that we have inferred with the strategies presented in this work can be seen in Table 3 for $EN \rightarrow FR$ translations, in Table 4 for $PT \rightarrow EN$ translations and in Table 5 for $FR \rightarrow PT$ translations, respectively.

As may be observed, the precision of this proposal is superior to the Baseline-OTIC only in the case of the dictionary

System	P	R	F
Ciclos-OTIC	0.57	0.44	0.50
Baseline-OTIC	0.64	0.38	0.48
NUIG	0.68	0.31	0.43
CL-embeddings	0.52	0.35	0.42
Multi-StategyI+II+III+IV	**0.52**	**0.34**	**0.41**
Multi-StategyI+II+III	**0.52**	**0.34**	**0.41**
Multi-StategyI+II	**0.53**	**0.31**	**0.39**
Multi-StategyI	**0.53**	**0.28**	**0.37**
ACOLIbaseline	0.48	0.24	0.32
Baseline-Word2Vec	0.23	0.39	0.29
ACOLIwordnet	0.54	0.13	0.21

Table 3: Systems results for $EN \rightarrow FR$

System	P	R	F
Ciclos-OTIC	0.68	0.43	0.53
Baseline-OTIC	0.71	0.40	0.51
Multi-StategyI+II+III+IV	**0.74**	**0.32**	**0.45**
Multi-StategyI+II+III	**0.76**	**0.31**	**0.44**
CL-embeddings	0.80	0.28	0.41
Multi-StategyI+II	**0.8**	**0.27**	**0.4**
ACOLIbaseline	0.66	0.26	0.38
Baseline-Word2Vec	0.37	0.33	0.35
Multi-StategyI	**0.74**	**0.17**	**0.28**
ACOLIwordnet	0.67	0.16	0.25
NUIG	-	-	-

Table 4: Systems results for $PT \rightarrow EN$

System	P	R	F
Baseline-OTIC	0.74	0.54	0.62
Ciclos-OTIC	0.67	0.55	0.6
NUIG	0.84	0.40	0.54
Multi-StategyI+II+III+IV	**0.58**	**0.34**	**0.43**
Multi-StategyI+II+III	**0.59**	**0.34**	**0.43**
CL-embeddings	0.55	0.34	0.42
Multi-StategyI+II	**0.62**	**0.31**	**0.41**
ACOLIbaseline	0.63	0.27	0.38
Multi-StategyI	**0.61**	**0.21**	**0.31**
Baseline-Word2Vec	0.27	0.34	0.30
ACOLIwordnet	0.62	0.15	0.24

Table 5: Systems results for $FR \rightarrow PT$

$PT \rightarrow EN$. This may be due to the fact that the strategies developed here have been trained on the $EN \leftrightarrow ES$ dictionary and the Portuguese lexicon might have more similarities to the Spanish lexicon and the pivot lexicons used. Perhaps, having used other dictionaries for training, either as an alternative or in addition to the $EN \leftrightarrow ES$ dictionary, could have improved the results of the approach used in this work. The worst precision of this strategy is obtained for the $EN \rightarrow FR$ dictionary, that might prove that using EO lexicon as pivot was not a correct approach.

From the results obtained in the shared task, it can be seen that Strategy I is the least stable, with disparate results, depending on the dictionary to be inferred. This was also observed during the training and validation phases. This strategy is highly dependent on the pivot lexicons used (see results in Table 1). Those good results for Strategy I in the vaidation phase, as concerns the precision, have been a mirage. This may be because some of the pivot lexicons used for the shared task might be related to each other and might share polysemous cases.

Strategy II has better precision than Strategy I in the shared task and it seems a good strategy to maintain in a future work.

Regarding Strategy III, lexical similarity could be useful to improve results in dictionary inference. It improves de F-measure results in the three inferred dictionaries for the shared task, with respect to StrategyI+II. It could be a good method to improve results of other approaches. This method still has room for improvement, using, for example, other similarity measures and optimization techniques to set the thresholds of the method.

Strategy IV, based on the use of synonyms, has proven to be a valid strategy, although it improves the final results very little, at least when used in conjunction with Strategy I. In the validation phase, Strategy IV, used in conjunction with strategies II and III, has shown more significant improvements in the results with respect to the StrategyII + III configuration. Nevertheless, the second setting of Strategy IV (see Figure 4) might have similar drawbacks as Strategy I. It would have been interesting to test a Multi-StrategyII+III+IV in the TIAD shared task, as the results in the validation phase were promising.

4. Conclusion

In this paper four strategy for translation inference across dictionaries have been proposed. The strategies are based on translation using multiple paths, the use of synonyms and similarities between lexical entries from different lexicons and cardinality of possible translations through the graph. The strategies have been trained and validated on the Aperium RDF graph using the dictionary $EN \leftrightarrow ES$, showing promising results. The four proposed strategies, applied together, obtained an F-measure of 0.43 in the task of inferring the proposed dictionaries for the TIAD 2020 Shared Task, thus ranking third with respect to the new systems presented to the shared task. Among the four strategies, the strategy based on lexical similarity stands out. It is a strategy that could enhance other systems and that still has room for improvement.

5. Acknowledgements

This work has been supported by the European Union's Horizon 2020 research and innovation programme through the project Prêt-à-LLOD (grant agreement No 825182). It has been also partially supported by the Spanish National projects TIN2016-78011-C4-2-R (AEI/FEDER, UE) and DGA/FEDER 2014-2020 "Construyendo Europa desde Aragón".

6. Bibliographical References

Donandt, K. and Chiarcos, C. (2019). Translation inference through multi-lingual word embedding similarity. In *Proceedings of TIAD-2019 Shared Task – Translation Inference Across Dictionaries)*, Leipzif, Germany, May.

Garcia, M., García-Salido, M., and Alonso, M. A. (2019). Exploring cross-lingual word embeddings for the inference of bilingual dictionaries. In *Proceedings of TIAD-2019 Shared Task – Translation Inference Across Dictionaries*, Leipzif, Germany, May.

Gracia, J. and Kabashi, B. (2020). 3rd Translation Inference Across Dictionaries shared task. In conjunction with the GLOBALEX 2020 at LREC2020. Marseille, France, May. URL: `https://tiad2020.unizar.es/`.

Gracia, J., Kabashi, B., Kernerman, I., Lanau-Coronas, M., and Lonke, D. (2019). Results of the translation inference across dictionaries 2019 shared task. In *Proceedings of TIAD-2019 Shared Task – Translation Inference Across Dictionaries*, Leipzif, Germany, May.

Saralegi, X., Manterola, I., and Vicente, I. S. (2011). Analyzing methods for improving precision of pivot based bilingual dictionaries. In *Proceedings of the Conference on Empirical Methods in Natural Language Processing*, pages 846–856. Association for Computational Linguistics.

Tanaka, K. and Umemura, K. (1994). Construction of a bilingual dictionary intermediated by a third language. In *Proceedings of the 15th conference on Computational linguistics-Volume 1*, pages 297–303. Association for Computational Linguistics.

Torregrosa, D., Arcan, M., Ahmadi, S., and McCrae, J. P. (2019). Tiad 2019 shared task: Leveraging knowledge graphs with neural machine translation for automatic multilingual dictionary generation. May.

7. Language Resource References

Jorge Gracia and Esther Lozano and Julia Bosque-Gil. (2014). *Apertium RDF*. URL: `http://linguistic.linkeddata.es/apertium/`.